MODERN ALBANIA

Modern Albania

From Dictatorship to Democracy in Europe

Fred C. Abrahams

NEW YORK UNIVERSITY PRESS

New York and London

NEW YORK UNIVERSITY PRESS
New York and London
www.nyupress.org

References to Internet websites (URLs) were accurate at the time of writing. Neither the author nor New York University Press is responsible for URLs that may have expired or changed since the manuscript was prepared.

Library of Congress Cataloging-in-Publication Data
Abrahams, Fred.
Modern Albania : from dictatorship to democracy in Europe / Fred C. Abrahams.
pages cm   Includes bibliographical references and index.
ISBN 978-0-8147-0511-7 (cl : alk. paper)
1. Albania—Politics and government—1990– 2. Post-communism—Albania.
3. Democracy—Albania. I. Title.
DR978.3.A35   2015
949.6504—dc23   2014044426

New York University Press books are printed on acid-free paper, and their binding materials are chosen for strength and durability. We strive to use environmentally responsible suppliers and materials to the greatest extent possible in publishing our books.

Manufactured in the United States of America

10 9 8 7 6 5 4 3 2 1

Also available as an ebook

To my parents, Carole and David, for the roots and wings.

CONTENTS

Map of Albania

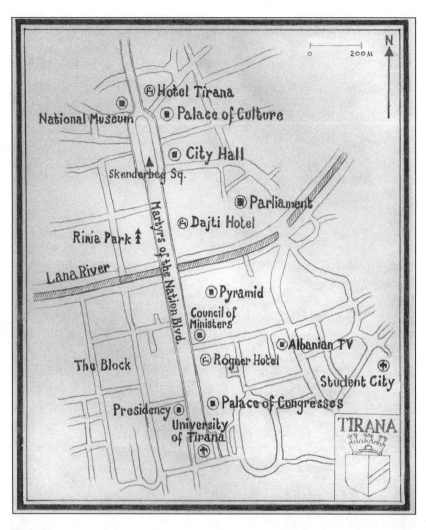

Map of Tirana

INTRODUCTION

For four decades after World War Two, tiny Albania was hermetically sealed. The Stalinist dictator, Enver Hoxha, banned religion, private property, and "decadent" music such as the Beatles'. Secret police arrested critics and border guards shot people who tried to flee. But as communism crumbled across the Eastern Bloc, the regime loosened its grip. Pressed by demonstrations and poverty, in late 1990 the communists allowed other parties to exist. In early 1992, more than two years after the fall of the Berlin Wall, a democratically elected government came to power and started to bring Albania in from the cold.

Albania made a rapid switch. It transformed from a country with sealed borders to a smuggler's dream, from the world's only officially atheist state to a playground for religions, from a land with no private cars to a jumble of belching cars, buses, and trucks. Albania flipped from a country of harsh, top-down repression to a vibrant state where most anything goes.

This book describes that dramatic jump. It tells the inside story of Albania's democratic awakening, the so-called revolution, when rigid Stalinism collapsed and wild pluralism stormed in. And it explains the effort since then to build a more just and tolerant society after decades of labor camps, thought police, and one-party rule.

The participants in this drama drive the tale: a paranoid dictator, an ambitious doctor, a scheming economist, an urban artist. Over two decades, I interviewed most of the influential Albanians in the country's political life and many of the foreigners who played a role. They describe the first student protests, the last Politburo meetings, and the struggle to build democracy after dictatorship. To supplement their accounts, I cite articles from the Albanian press and previously secret records from Albania and the United States, mostly from the State Department and CIA.

I also enjoyed a front-row seat. I first went to Albania in 1993 and worked there for one year at a media training center, watching the wobbly first steps of democracy. I then covered the country for Human

Rights Watch and saw the resilience of one-party rule, the pull of dictatorship, and in 1997 the crash of massive pyramid schemes, when defrauded people torched city halls and looted military depots. The next year, war erupted in neighboring Kosovo, culminating in NATO's air assault on Serbian and Yugoslav forces. Albania offered a staging ground and supply route for the ragtag Albanian insurgency, and later a grave site for its victims. After 2001, I observed mostly Muslim Albania serve as a devoted ally of the United States. The government detained and helped render terrorist suspects, accepted released Guantanamo prisoners, and sent troops to Afghanistan and Iraq. Albania is probably the only country outside the United States with a statue of George W. Bush.

During this time, I watched the United States and other Western democracies repeatedly make shortsighted decisions that stymied Albania's transition. For many years, the U.S. and West European governments supported an authoritarian or corrupt Albanian leader for the sake of stability in the Balkans and, later, Albania's cooperation in the "war on terror." These governments frequently backed an individual more than the country's institutions; for this, Albania is today paying a significant price.

Through it all, I had the opportunity to mingle with Albania's elite. I watched former political prisoners join the government and government ministers go to jail. I saw foreigners who loved Albania get declared persona non grata while swindlers won business contracts and the highest state praise. I have been called a Communist, a CIA agent, pro-Albanian, anti-Albanian, pro-Greek, anti-Greek, pro-Serb, anti-Serb, and by one journalist, "a whimsical boy with an earring and short pants." But above all, I have been privileged to peer behind the curtain of a society that is for many outsiders opaque.

The book has limitations. First, it focuses on the capital, Tirana, and the boulevard that forms its spine. Second, it deals primarily with men, who dominate Albania's public life. Third, it mostly explores Albania's relationship with the United States, with less attention on other countries. With these in mind, I hope the book helps dispel myths, spark debate, and shed light on a tiny country in Europe going through a remarkable time.

Fred Abrahams

New York City

Prologue

On the Boulevard

The dry, rocky mountains of Montenegro drew near as the plane decended from the north. The high peaks of Albania rose to the left, flashing their fangs to the sky. The jagged teeth settled into deep valleys and dense forests that held the highlanders I had read about and would soon meet for myself.

The mountains got shorter and rounder as the plane slid south. The gray rock ran down the country's eastern length like a spine. Albania is a small country, a saying goes, but it would grow ten times if it were ironed flat. On the western side, the ridges melted into barren hills and farm land, which slid in brown and gray to the Adriatic Sea. Albania is like an amphitheater, I thought, with high seats in the mountains offering views of the coastal plain and greenish sea. Except for the soft water, the country looked harsh. It resembled a fortress or massive crag, and this geography, I learned, has shaped the peoples' lives. Oft invaded and overrun, Albanians honor guests but view outsiders with a leery eye.

The fields looked choppy and parched. Gray flecks dotted the land like acne on a teenage face: the concrete military bunkers built during communism on almost every farm, field, and mountain to repel invasion and, more important, to instill fear of outside attack. The pillboxes proved difficult to destroy and for years served as food stands and sometimes as homes for the poor.

The plane circled and the capital Tirana lay to the west, nestled at the base of Mount Dajti like runoff from the hills. It basked in a golden, dusty light. Like so many things in Albania, even the light seemed old.

The passengers stirred. Most on the charter flight from New York were Albanians from the United States who were visiting their homeland for the first time in almost fifty years, or for the first time ever. They knew Albania from stories and songs and faded photos torn at the sides.

Many had left family behind when they fled for a better life. The landing gear descended and they jumped in excitement for their bags.

The plane landed with a bump, and then a startling tick and tack, as if the tires were flat. The runway had hexagonal, concrete slabs rather than asphalt. Cows grazed under plane wings as soldiers with faded green uniforms huddled in the shade looking bored. They were boys, but with weathered skin and tired eyes. From the plane we walked down a wide path flanked by palm trees and patches of burnt grass. The air felt dry and hot. Rinas Airport stood before us, the tower missing windows and tilting to one side. A tractor rumbled by with our luggage in tow.

In the parking lot I found a frantic scene of dust and tears. Families separated for decades were hugging tightly and kissing each other on the cheeks, with boxes of televisions, clothes, and toys piled high. Young boys tugged at my sleeve: "Bon giorno!" "Taxi?" and "Hello!"

It was July 1993, one year and a bit since Albania's first free elections after four decades of isolation and dictatorship, and the country was awaking, rubbing its eyes. To the world it was that crumpled bill in the back pocket that you forgot was there.

Tirana was chaotic and hot. A single traffic light hung in the center of the city, and it did not work. Private cars, illegal three years earlier, raced through the streets, dodging horse carts and blasting kitschy musical horns. Most were third-hand clunkers from Germany; they say Albania is where a Mercedes goes to die. Books by Stalin, Lenin, Marx, and the Albanian dictator Enver Hoxha littered the streets. Vendors used pages from Hoxha's more than one hundred books to wrap goat cheese and chunks of bloody meat.

I had come after one year of graduate school with two friends to start a student newspaper at the University of Tirana, which had been called Enver Hoxha University two years before. We rented an apartment with a crumbling balcony overlooking the Lana River, a murky stream that dribbled from Mount Dajti through the city on a concrete track. Goats grazed on its grassy banks. More than anything, I remember the smell: grilled meat, cigarettes, sweat, garbage, and the kerosene people used for their camping-style stoves. But the nights were clear and clean.

In some ways Tirana was like the Eastern Europe I knew from having worked in East Germany and Czechoslovakia before graduate school, gray and frayed. But it had a Mediterranean twist, with a hot sun and meandering pace. And it was poorer than any place in Europe's East, with few phones, dirt roads, and people living on aid. But mostly it was like entering a forgotten world, a frozen space. Albania had been so cut off from the world, isolated from the "imperialist West" and "revisionist East," that it slipped out of touch.

Thankfully we had a friend. Gazi Haxhia was the first Albanian to attend Columbia University's school of international affairs, where my friends and I had just finished the year. The son of a tailor, Gazi had studied English and worked as a guide for the state-run tourist agency, collecting tips from foreigners to finance a trip to Greece in 1991, when the borders opened, and then the United States. Gazi had the enthusiasm of a kid, extroverted and ambitious, and was eager to build something for himself and his family. That first night, he took us to a café with white plastic chairs in front of the university's Academy of Arts, where students had until recently been prohibited from studying Cubism and Impressionism. We took our first *xhiro*, the evening promenade down the boulevard, where friends and families ambled arm in arm, chatting, watching, and being watched. The Martyrs of the Nation Boulevard, built by the Italians in the early 1930s, was closed every evening for the pedestrian flow, but post-communist traffic demands soon put that practice to rest.

We sauntered down the boulevard past the president's office and the Palace of Congresses, a modern convention hall that looked like a spaceship, where the communist party had assembled each year. The Council of Ministers followed, where the prime minister sat, and then the dominant feature on the wide road—the former Enver Hoxha Museum, by then renamed the International Cultural Center. Designed by Hoxha's daughter and her husband after the dictator's death in 1985, the building is a colossal pyramid of white marble and glass, once topped by a large, red star. During communism, government guides toured visitors through the artifacts of Hoxha's life: polished shoes, party speeches, and the mended pajamas that the "people's son" had worn to bed. Children gaped at the massive statue of the omnipotent "Uncle Enver" that dominated the main hall. No one expected that by my arrival in 1993 the pyramid would house a U.S. government library and a Voice of America antenna would replace the red star. Inside sat Albania's first human rights group and the office of George Soros's Open Society Foundation,

which was funding our student newspaper. Outside, children slid gleefully down the marble slopes, oblivious to how they would have been
punished for such an indiscretion a few years before.

To the boulevard's west lay the forbidden "Block"—the previously se-
questered area of villas where Politburo members and other ruling elite
had lived. By 1993, families were strolling down the tree-lined streets,
still half expecting someone to order them out. Over time, the Block became the most expensive real estate in Tirana, home to fancy apartment
buildings and ritzy cafés named Rio and Fame. For a while, Hoxha's villa
housed a fast-food restaurant with golden arches called McMarriot.

Further north, the boulevard bridged the trickling Lana River and
reached the Hotel Dajti, built by Italians during their occupation of
Albania in 1941. The hotel lobby had soft chairs, dirty carpets, and a
Vienna-style café, which for years remained a quiet place to escape Tirana's frenetic din. Across the street lay Rinia Park (Youth Park), a patchy
green quad with crisscrossing paths and an abandoned restaurant that
Albanians called Taiwan because construction finished after Hoxha had
severed Albania's ties with China in 1978. North of the park, we passed
pedestals where the statues of Stalin and Lenin had stood, facing each
other across the boulevard. Lenin's hand had pointed towards Hotel
Dajti and Stalin's had rested on his chest. "Joseph, do you want coffee
at the Dajti?" Albanians had joked that Lenin asked. "No thanks," Stalin
replied, with hand to heart in respect. Now the crumbling pedestals held
only rusted bolts, and someone had spray painted "Pink Floyd" across
Lenin's base.

Next came the Ministry of Interior and Tirana's city hall, designed
by Mussolini's architects. The pastel-colored façades were chipped and
cracked. Then the boulevard spilled into Skanderbeg Square, a stretch of
concrete surrounded by the national museum, national bank, and Palace of Culture. In the middle stood the bold statue of Albania's national
hero, Gjergj Kastrioti, aka Skanderbeg, who led the Albanian resistance
against Ottoman Turks in the fifteenth century. His efforts failed, as the
Turkish-built Et'hem Bey mosque next to the statue affirms. Albania
remained part of the Ottoman Empire for 434 years, becoming the last
Balkan state to gain its independence in 1912.

On a platform in front of the national museum lay the base of Hoxha's
statue, which an angry crowd had toppled two and a half years before.

Above the museum entrance, workers chiseled away at a colorful Social-ist Realist mosaic of marching peasants and Partisan fighters, trying to remove the yellow communist star from the red Albanian flag. Albania was marching towards democracy, trying to erase its past.

From the start, I felt excited to be a special guest. Albanians welcomed all foreigners with Balkan hospitality and the giddiness of people emerg-ing from a fifty-year sleep. But they embraced Americans in particular as the victors of the Cold War. They did not carry my car from the air-port as they had tried with Secretary of State James Baker two years before, but they treated me with curiosity and respect. Some thought me a CIA spy, and to them that was perfectly fine.

My first conversation with an Albanian stranger took place at the Dajti Hotel. While I was escaping the heat in a plush lobby chair, a man asked in English if I could help him establish contact with Guinness. "The beer?" I asked. "No," he said. "The book of world records." He had broken the record for the longest stretch juggling a soccer ball: 18 kilo-meters, 106 meters.

The list of characters quickly grew. I met Spartak Ngjela, who had spent twelve years as a political prisoner for "agitation and propaganda against the state." The quick-witted lawyer would later become justice minister in one of Albania's most difficult times, after massive pyramid schemes collapsed in 1997. "What is more important in art—color or the line?" he asked when we first met, his finger raised for emphasis before extending his hand. "The line," I ventured cautiously. "Good," he said, with a sigh of relief, and gave a firm shake.

In a tin-and-glass kiosk on the boulevard I spent a night drinking with a husky young man named Azem Hajdari, who explained how he had led Tirana's students against the communist regime in late 1990, his charm growing with each story and drink. Eight years later, gunmen as-sassinated Hajdari in Tirana, sparking a violent protest and attempted coup. His role in the student movement, I later learned, was controver-sial, as was his alleged involvement in organized crime.

In contrast, I befriended Fatos Lubonja, the son of a senior commu-nist, who had spent seventeen years in prisons and labor camps for po-litical crimes. Two years after his release, Lubonja was still living in an occupied kindergarten classroom. On a low school desk he showed me the jewelry he had made in prison: finely polished stones sanded over time from peach pits. From a small wooden box he pulled the novel he had secretly written in prison and copied onto cigarette paper with a pencil sharp enough to draw blood. More than most, Lubonja had the right to detest communists and support the new Democratic Party in power, but he was among the first to criticize the new leaders for using old methods. When he spoke, I took note that something was amiss.

* * *

The head of the journalism department at Tirana University welcomed me and my two friends with a handshake and smile, not caring if we liked color or the line. Rudolf Marku was a member of parliament for the Democratic Party, which had defeated the communists in elections sixteen months earlier. "This is my office," he said, waving his hand through a simple room with a few wooden desks, some books, and a rotary phone. "Call America anytime." At the university he provided a small room to house two donated computers and a classroom for us to teach a newspaper-writing class twice a week. "This is the swimming pool where they will learn to swim," he said.

Marku belonged to the generation of Albania's middle-aged "intellectuals"—writers, teachers, professors, and artists—whom the communist party had brought to Tirana in the 1970s and 1980s from their provincial towns. Many of them paid the price for living in the capital by becoming spies. Whether Marku had succumbed I did not know, but his loyalty to the new leader was soon clear.

The students had zeal. They did not know how to type, let alone use a computer, but they ached to make up for lost time. They came from all over Albania, some of them the children of the politically persecuted, who had earned privileges after years of abuse. One came to school late with scraggly hair and dirty nails because he had spent the summer working illegally in Greece, trekking home through the mountains. Others came from neighboring Kosovo and Macedonia, parts of the former Yugoslavia where ethnic Albanians lived. For years these Albanians had viewed Albania as a paradise, soaking up the propaganda of Enver Hoxha's radio and TV. But in Tirana they were seeing a university with broken windows, rickety desks, and servile deans.

As the newspaper's name, the students chose *Reporteri* (The Reporter), which they considered a new concept in a place where the

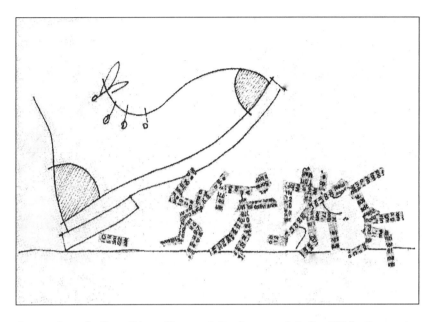

Cartoon from the first edition of *Reporteri*, October 1993. © Redina Tili for *Reporteri*

communist media had served as loudspeaker for the party. "Our aim is to present the news as we see it, not as we feel it, imagine or wish it to be," the students wrote in the first issue. "Our responsibility is to provide objective and balanced information free of political or ideological taint."[1]

The paper caused a scandal right away. Albania's new, democratically elected president was pushing a press law with vague terms and high fines that many journalists feared would muzzle the media. A student wrote a front-page article that quoted those in favor of and against the law. In an editorial, the students said the law threatened free speech. Next to the piece ran a cartoon by a talented art student: contorted figures cut from newsprint getting trampled by a boot.

The paper appeared on a Thursday, and the students bicycled it, tied with a red ribbon, to the city's newspapers, party offices, and embassies. On Monday morning, I stopped for coffee on my way to the university and an older journalism student looked surprised. "Why aren't you at the department?" he asked. "Something is going on." I biked to the university to find Rudolf Marku changing the padlock on the computer room. The newspaper was closed, he said, and we had to leave. The swimming pool was dry.

The reasons Marku and the deans gave were contradictory and confused. Although we had taught the newspaper class for weeks, as graduate students we were no longer considered qualified to teach. The donated computers were not for the newspaper, and the students should use them for other work. The article on the press law should not have been above another story on AIDS and youth. Marku called us communists. The deans threatened the students with expulsion.

Angry and confused, we went to the recently opened U.S. embassy for help. Ambassador Bill Ryerson, a grandfatherly figure with glasses and balding head, listened politely. He offered to confirm our credentials as graduate students so we might teach, and he did so with a red wax stamp on the transcripts that Columbia faxed from New York. As we were leaving the embassy, Ryerson's deputy called us into a room and growled about the deans' obnoxious behavior. He suggested we "stay calm" until things got sorted out.

We ignored his advice and issued a statement about the closure that got published in the vocal opposition press. The deans responded by kicking us out of the university; the once-friendly guard blocked our entrance at the door. A vice-dean named Aurel Plasari wrote a scathing article in the newspaper *Zëri i Rinisë* (Voice of the Youth), the former organ of the communist youth. "I would have preferred skinning a dead dog to explaining university regulations to foreigners who consider Albania to be a Zululand," he wrote.[2] The newspaper of an opposition party fired back. On a full page, the paper published embarrassing poems by another dean, including one called "I Loved You Communism."[3] Naïvely, we had stepped into a storm.

In fact, I learned later, *Reporteri*'s closure had nothing to do with us or the deans. It stemmed from a conflict Albania's president was having with the Soros Foundation—funder of our project—and in particular with the foundation's fiery director. At the time, I thought two stubborn men were locking horns. But I soon saw that the foundation director was boldly criticizing the president's increasingly authoritarian ways—perhaps the first foreigner to scratch the veneer. The new leader disliked dissent.

By then Albania was in my blood. My friends Stacy Sullivan and Marianne Sullivan (no relation) and I deferred school for one year and the Soros Foundation hired us to work at its new media center in Tirana, where *Reporteri* published again, albeit on softer issues. At the same time, Albania's president was turning me into a human rights activist. I gathered information on the press law, which passed, and other media restrictions, and I sent updates to human rights groups abroad. The topics expanded to include harassment of the opposition, the abuse of secret police files, and beatings by police. The president was being touted abroad as a champion of democracy, but I watched how he used remnants of the dictatorship to enforce control. I knew change would take time, but this leader had a vindictive and nasty edge, as if he could not tolerate anyone else having success. Albanian friends were telling me how they lost their jobs for failing to support the new ruling party. They feared speaking out. After decades of harsh repression, fear lay like an ember in the Albanian gut, and the president knew how to stoke the flame.

The harassment and arrests of critics continued during the year, but a parade made me realize how far Albania had to go. On March 22, 1994, the Democratic Party celebrated the second anniversary of its historic election win over the communists. A festive procession marched down the boulevard, led by boys in white shirts and pants waving colored flags, a style I recognized from communist-era films. I could imagine Enver Hoxha waving from the rostrum. Clanky helicopters swooped overhead as the crowd flowed by the artificial lake on the edge of town to a sports complex. Soldiers performed military exercises for politicians from the new ruling clan to music from Voice of America radio. A line of Democratic Party leaders stood on the stage, condemning communism, praising democracy, and guaranteeing prosperity. My Albanian was not good at the time, but I understood when one of the men punctuated his speech with the phrase "Rrofte Partia Demokiratike!" ("Long live the Democratic Party!"). Up until two years before, speakers had only said "Rrofte Partia," and everyone knew what that meant.

"It's exactly the same as the old days," a teenage girl next to me said. "Only the music has changed."

Of course it was not the same, and throughout the year, I saw Albanians rejoice in their newfound freedom. They traveled abroad for the first time, marveling at world art, as well as highways, highrises, and escalators. They formed clubs and opened shops. Newspapers told stories long censored or ignored. *Eros* and *Playboy* hit the streets with blurry black-and-white photos of topless foreign women.

Churches and mosques sprouted across the land, mostly with foreign funds. After years of enforced aethiesm, some mosques posted instructions on how to pray. Evangelists, Hare Krishnas, and Moonies battled for the Albanian soul. White-shirted Mormons trolled the dusty streets and L. Ron Hubbard's *Dianetics* appeared in kiosks that sold books.

Of the roughly three million people in Albania, about 70 percent were Muslim, 20 percent Orthodox Christian, and 10 percent Catholic—Europe's only Muslim-majority state. But young people of all faiths proudly wore crosses around their necks as a symbol of what they previously could not do and a desire to join the West. When I asked a young Muslim man why he was active in an Evangelical group he said he enjoyed the novel pleasure of talking about God. The chance to practice English was also nice. A friend called Albanians "sex, drug, and rock and roll Muslims." They liked to drink, smoke, and enjoy good pork.

I found it difficult to tell if I was in the East or West. Local music had an oriental flair, but pop icons came from Hollywood and Italian TV. At a wedding in the north, revelers fired pistols in the air while the DJ played that year's biggest hit, "All That She Wants," by the Swedish band Ace of Base. Albanians drank gritty Turkish coffee but their most famous personality was Mother Teresa, an Albanian born in Macedonia. The national hero Skanderbeg, his statue in Tirana's main square, had defended Christian Europe from an Ottoman encroach.

Economically Albania was moving fast, and my barometer was our Columbia friend Gazi. When we first arrived, his family used water from an outside spigot and cooked on a kerosene burner that sat on the ground. Over time, they installed a sink and stove. Across the country, families bought color televisions and satellite dishes to catch the outside world. Bathrooms got tiles, water heaters, and porcelain toilets to cover open pits.

But the economic gap was shockingly clear when I visited Macedonia, a few hours to the East. The trees looked greener. The streets were cleaner. Shops had glamorous items such as packaged meat. A trip south to Greece revealed a wider divide. Crossing back into Albania one literally stepped from asphalt into mud.

Most troubling was the chaotic development, without planning or care. Rinia Park on the boulevard, once a serene green square, grew kiosk cafés with plastic chairs. They soon had awnings, patios, and walls. By 1995, the park was consumed, as were the banks of the Lana River, smothered by cafés and shops, their garbage tossed into the fetid water. Behind the Palace of Culture yawned a massive hole with mud and rock. Nobody knew why it had been dug in 1991. The most common explanation was a hotel that never got built; most people called it the Sheraton Hole. It remained a giant urinal in the center for more than ten years. At the pleasant beach near Durres on the Adriatic Sea, twenty miles west of Tirana, visitors threw watermelon rinds onto the sand. One day I watched a car speeding on the hard sand strike and kill a boy playing soccer with his friends. After years of forced order and control, Albanians viscerally rejected the common good. Democracy meant the right to break rules.

* * *

My American friends and I spent much of our time in Tirana's cafés—there were few in those days, but their number was growing fast. They mostly had names from abroad, such as Nuremberg, Napoli, Munich, America, Berlusconi, and Amy Carter, a kiosk on the boulevard so named because Jimmy Carter had stopped there during a visit in 1993. In those cafés, work and politics took place. To find a person I never went to an office but to the café where he or she was known to sit. "Ku pi kafe?"—"Where does he drink coffee?"—I learned to ask.

Gradually I learned to converse in Albanian. Albanians have a cadence, a rhythm fueled by cigarette smoke and olive oil. The way they speak, the way they engage, is ceremonious, lyrical. There are introductions, then coffee, then allusions, and only then the point, if a point is ever made. Often it is communicated with a squint of the eye or a tilt of the head. Whole conversations transpire with the twitch of a face. If in some cultures one must read between the lines, in Albania one must read between the words. After years of invasive monitoring, they learned to speak in subtle twists.

The newspapers were even more complex. The apparent topic of an article—"President to Visit Germany"—was usually a pretext for swipes at the president's adversary of the day. The cafés would bubble with debate, and I could not understand why a visit to Germany provoked such fervent talk until I learned that the article revealed someone's code name from the communist-era secret police, such as Lapsi (the pen), Elektron (the electron), or Tavolina e punës (the desk). Other writings ranged from language and literature to politics in the Balkans, the war in Yugoslavia. I was amazed that people so isolated could know so much about Ezra Pound, James Joyce, and Sigmund Freud—far more than I. The night guard at the restaurant we frequented spoke English, Russian, and Italian. Languages were a refuge, an escape from dictatorship, he said.

Mostly, however, I was struck by the stories of brutality and survival under the previous regime, and almost every Albanian had a tale to tell. Critics were thrown into prisons and their families into work camps. One man was arrested because he complained that a shop had no cheese—in Hoxha's paradise the shop always had cheese. Another man was imprisoned for singing the Beatles' "Here Comes the Sun." One artist nailed his paintings together and hid them in the attic because they violated the party's interpretation of acceptable art. He was betrayed by a family member and spent years in jail. The Association of Former Political Prisoners said the regime had imprisoned 34,135 people for political reasons over four decades, and sent 59,009 others to labor camps. After bogus trials, 5,487 people were sentenced to death.

Listening to these stories, I recalled a lecture by a Czech dissident at my university the previous year. The greatest hurdle the former communist countries face is to overcome fear, he had said. At the time I missed the point. I had never experienced fear as part of my everyday life. Fear had never dictated what I said or with whom I spoke. But in the cafés of Tirana I was beginning to understand what it meant to live in an oppressive regime, where families were torn apart to maintain control, and top officials were petrified of stepping out of line. I was seeing how fear warped the way people acted and thought. To understand Albania, I realized, I had to look back at the source of that terror: the fierce Stalinist system and, above all, the man who dominated the country for more than forty years.

PART I

Out of the Dark

The Leader's Demise, 1985–1990

1

Hoxha's Heart

Enver Hoxha's doctors enjoyed their work. The dictator treated them well, and they had access to modern medical gear. They felt honored to care for the country's elite.

The most coveted task was night duty in Hoxha's large but unglamorous villa in Tirana's forbidden "Block," just west of Martyrs of the Nation Boulevard. After checking on Hoxha, the doctors slipped into the large library, full of banned books, mostly in French, which Hoxha spoke well. Translations of Shakespeare, Nietzsche, and Dostoyevsky lined the shelves, as did writings by Lenin, Machiavelli, and Joseph Fouché, Napoleon's minister of police, and novels by Agatha Christie and John le Carré.

One night towards the end of Hoxha's life, the cardiologist Ylli Popa checked on his patient and retired to the library for a late-night read. He chose a book about Lavrenty Beria, Stalin's chief of secret police. To Popa's surprise, Hoxha had underlined a passage with a red pen. It told of the infamous "Doctors' plot" and the arrest of prominent physicians for allegedly conspiring to kill Soviet leaders. Trembling, the diminutive and soft-spoken cardiologist quickly returned the book to its place on the shelf.

The story, which Popa lived to tell, hints at Hoxha's complex life. On the one hand, the leader was a cultured man who studied in France, wore dapper suits, knew history, and enjoyed literature. On the other hand, he was a paranoid and brutal dictator with a ravenous appetite for power who eliminated opponents real and perceived. He created enemies, distrusted friends, and ruled Albania with a mix of cruelty and charm.

* * *

Born in 1908 into a middle-class family in the southern town of Gjirokaster, Hoxha studied at the prestigious French lycée in another southern town, Korça, and won a government scholarship to attend the University of Montpellier. He returned to Albania in 1936 without a degree and taught French in his former Korça school—a cheerful and mild-mannered man, one of his pupils recalled. He became active in a local communist group, although Albania had no communist party at the time and, as an agricultural society, not much of a working class.

Nazi Germany occupied Czechoslovakia in 1938. The next year, Mussolini invaded Albania and easily deposed its ruler, Ahmed Zog, a former prime minister and president who had declared himself king. Zog fled with his wife and two-day-old son, Leka, whom I watched try to retake the throne fifty-eight years later.

Under Italian rule, Hoxha lost his teaching job. He moved to Tirana—at the time with less than twenty thousand people—and opened a tobacco shop, which became the secret meeting place of the budding communist movement. The Yugoslav communist leader Josip Broz Tito offered help, and under his tutelage the Albanian Communist Party was founded in November 1941. Enver Hoxha, then thirty-three years old, became secretary general. He held the position for the next forty-four years.

During World War Two, Hoxha played a major role in the communist resistance with his close friend Mehmet Shehu, the Partisan military commander. The Partisans fought the Italians alongside other groups, notably the followers of King Zog, known as Legaliteti (Legality), and an anti-royalist nationalist movement called Balli Kombëtar (National Front). As in other Balkan countries, the resistance fractured along political and regional lines.

Italy capitulated in 1943 and Germany occupied Albania, installing a puppet regime with help from the nationalist Balli Kombëtar. In return, Hitler expanded Albania's borders around Kosovo, the predominantly ethnic Albanian–inhabited region in Yugoslavia, and North Epirus, the area of northern Greece where many ethnic Albanians live. But by 1944 the Partisans were pushing north towards Tirana with help from the British. In October they formed a provisional government with Hoxha as prime minister. One month later, the Germans withdrew from Albania, and the Partisans marched triumphantly into Tirana under cover of Allied planes. Communist propaganda boasted that Partisan bravery had liberated Albania after a heroic fight. The history books conveniently ignored support from the Yugoslavs and hardware from the

British and Americans, let alone Hitler's decision to leave Albania. Instead, Hoxha crafted the image of a hardened guerilla fighter from the hills. The resistance and liberation myth, with stoic poems, movies, and songs, became the unifying theme that permeated post-war life.

Albania in 1945 was rural, poor, and devastated by war. The provisional government, with Hoxha at its head, began to nationalize industry, transportation, and land. Elections for a legislature in December 1945 had candidates only from the communist Democratic Front. The new assembly declared Albania a "People's Republic" and appointed Hoxha prime minister, foreign minister, defense minister, and the army's commander in chief.

From the start, Hoxha showed political skill and ruthless determination. The influential Central Committee member Sofokli Lazri, in the upper echelons of power throughout Hoxha's rule, explained it to me matter-of-factly: "Hoxha had an incredible sense of smell for protecting his position." Special tribunals tried "war criminals"—mostly supporters of King Zog and Balli Kombëtar—and sentenced hundreds of people to death. A targeted campaign hit the Catholic clergy in the north, whom Hoxha labeled Vatican spies.

Relations with the West soured. Britain and the United States disliked the lack of free elections and, more importantly, the country's pro-Russian drift. In 1945, diplomats from both countries left. In spring 1946, Albania fired on two British ships in the Corfu channel. Five months later, two British destroyers struck mines while sailing near Corfu, killing forty-three men. Albania refused to pay compensation, and the U.K. withheld more than 2.5 tons of Albania's gold, which it had confiscated from Germany. The gold remained a point of contention between Albania and the U.K. until 1992.

For support Hoxha relied on Tito. Yugoslav experts advised the government and brought food to ward off starvation. Yugoslav investments rebuilt the agricultural sector and some light industry. In return, Albania did not contest Yugoslav claims on Kosovo. Yugoslavia became the first state to recognize the Albanian government. In 1948, the Albanian parliament, under pressure from Tito, voted to merge Albania and Yugoslavia's economies and militaries.

At the same time, divisions emerged in Albania over the extent of Yugoslav control. Some argued for even closer ties, but others feared that Tito would annex the small and vulnerable state. Hoxha remained neutral in the debate, but then made a decisive move. When Tito severed ties with the Soviet Union in 1948, Hoxha labeled the Yugoslav leader a corrupt, revisionist communist who had betrayed Marxist ideals. He gave Yugoslav advisors forty-eight hours to leave.

Hoxha seized the chance to eliminate his rivals, purging Albanian officials with real or suspected ties to Yugoslavia. He had fourteen of thirty-one members of the Communist Party's Central Committee executed, as well as thirty-two of 109 deputies in parliament. The reign of terror had begun.

In need of a new benefactor, Hoxha turned to Stalin. Soviet advisors replaced the Yugoslavs, and the USSR offered a steady flow of aid. The Soviets built a submarine base on the island of Sazan off Albania's southern coast, giving them a strategic post on the Adriatic Sea. At the first Albanian Communist Party congress in November 1948, on Stalin's advice, delegates changed the party's name to the Albanian Party of Labor. Soviet aid helped Hoxha improve the electrical grid, education, and health care. Illiteracy and infant mortality declined. Still, the country remained an agricultural backwater, neglected and remote.

Stalin died in 1953 and Soviet leaders tried to disperse the power that he had amassed. Hoxha mirrored the move towards "collective leadership" by handing the foreign affairs and defense ministries to loyal aides. In 1954 he passed the prime minister's post to Mehmet Shehu, his loyal comrade who had led the Partisans' military campaign during the war. Hoxha remained the all-powerful head of the Party of Labor, the undisputed head of state.

Two years later, after the Soviet leader Nikita Khrushchev denounced Stalin's cult of personality, the Albanian Party of Labor held a conference in Tirana, and delegates asked sensitive questions about developments to the east: Do Albanian party leaders enjoy special privileges? Are people punished illegally here? Is there a cult of personality in Albania? Hoxha rushed to Tirana and burst into the hall on the second day. The 580 delegates took to their feet and rhythmically clapped.

"I hear the meeting has become electrified," one of the party delegates remembered Hoxha said.

At first Hoxha allowed the critics to speak. Then he struck. He insisted that the party was democratic, that no cult of personality existed, and that outside powers were trying to destabilize Albania. He defended Stalin and attacked the dissenters, some of whom stood to renounce their words. He expelled the critics from the party, forcing the most vocal out of Tirana or into prison.

Dissent in the party had been crushed, and along with it any hope of challenging Hoxha from within. Until that point, the party had tolerated some idealistic members. After 1956, the party drew opportunists and pragmatists who were looking to advance.

To the public, Hoxha was a caring and gentle man, always dignified and well dressed. His shoes and hats came from abroad. An Albanian tailor made his double-breasted suits with imported cloth. At home he ate with his wife, Nexhmije, a devout communist and the only person he fully trusted, and their three children—two sons and a daughter. They rarely had guests. One of his cooks told me that his biggest challenge was preparing three healthy meals a day because Hoxha suffered from diabetes. No taster checked his food. Hoxha smoked Chinese cigarettes but rarely drank, and his only sport was billiards in the Politburo Club.

Unlike Albanian politicians today, Hoxha studied and prepared. In remote districts he cited production figures and the region's fables and epic songs. Building on a clan-based and patriarchal society in a poor country, he played the loving but strict father of a people in need. He was called the "Leader" and, by many Albanians, "Uncle Enver."

Five bodyguards protected Hoxha around the clock, but the absolute control kept him safe. "He walked in the Block and we had no guards on the roofs because the people loved him," his chief bodyguard for many years, Sulo Gradeci, told me. Gradeci said there was never an attempt on Hoxha's life.

The secret police, or Sigurimi (Security), enforced control. An estimated one in four Albanians worked for the ever-listening agency, usually as informants. Neighbors spied on neighbors, husbands on wives, and pupils on teachers. Friends testified in court against their oldest mates. Unlike Eastern European countries that allowed a degree of dissent, Hoxha tolerated virtually none. The slightest word against the party could bring prison or worse. Whole families were banished to internal exile, where they worked remote fields, checking in twice a day with police. Children born into such conditions were marked for life.

The people nearest to Hoxha felt most at risk, former Politburo and Central Committee members said, because he repeatedly purged and executed long-time comrades and friends. Over time, the Politburo became a gaggle of obedient sycophants—villagers from the provinces who were indebted to Hoxha for their rise.

To his staff, Hoxha was polite. He did not interrupt people when they spoke, and he entertained dissenting views on technical matters from those bold enough to speak. But he ran meetings with authority. He came to the podium first, followed by members of the Politburo. Central Committee members tried to sit in the back, like schoolchildren who had not done their homework. When angry with a person, Hoxha pretended to mispronounce his or her name.

"You, Hamdi, why aren't you taking notes?" he asked a Central Committee director in the 1980s, Hamit Beqja.

"Comrade Enver, I am Hamit," Beqja replied.

"No!" Hoxha boomed. "You are Hamdi!"

Hoxha read the international press and closely followed international affairs. He knew world leaders by name and cited their speeches. He used advisors but conducted analysis himself, and he crafted much of Albania's foreign policy. Among his special talents was utilizing shifts in global politics to his advantage at home, as he did after the Stalin-Tito rift. During his rule, Albania severed ties with all of its patrons—Yugoslavia, the Soviet Union, and China in succession. He used each break to justify a domestic purge, eliminating those with doubtful devotion to his despotic rule.

When relations between the Soviet Union and China soured in 1960, Hoxha sided with the Chinese. Moscow responded by cutting aid and supporting pro-Soviet elements within the Party of Labor. Hoxha ordered a group of Moscow sympathizers, labeled "pro-Soviet revisionists," arrested and shot.

China came to the rescue with large-scale aid, which helped build a hydroelectric plant in the north and the Enver Hoxha Metallurgical Plant, known as the "Steel of the Party," in the central town of Elbasan. Hoxha introduced reform based on Mao's Cultural Revolution, sending bureaucrats and government officials to work the rural fields. He revised the education system to filter outside ideas. Independent-minded writers and artists lost their jobs or went to jail.

In 1967 Hoxha banned religion, as if he were jealous that someone had faith in a force higher than him. He ordered the destruction of mosques, churches, and cloisters and their conversion into sports halls or warehouses. The Catholic cathedral in Shkoder became a basketball arena with "Glory Marxism-Leninism" inscribed on the court in large red letters. Albania was never a religious country, but Hoxha officially declared it the world's first atheist state. Albanians buried sacred relics or hid them in their homes, where they stayed until freedom of religion returned in 1990.

After the Soviet invasion of Czechoslovakia in 1968, Hoxha withdrew from the Warsaw Pact, although Albania had not attended a meeting for years. The Ministry of Defense began a colossal project to build an estimated seven hundred thousand concrete, steel-reinforced bunkers. The military put the concrete mushrooms along the coast and borders, on mountain tops, farms, and even city streets. Arrow tips were mounted atop fence posts to thwart parachutists. Too expensive to remove, the bunkers dotted the country years after communism's fall. Lovers visited them for trysts and poor families used them as homes. Farmers who got back nationalized property spoke of how many bunkers they had received.

Engineers who worked on the bunker project told me they developed different designs, with protection from Russian tank shells most in mind. An engineer, topographer, and infantry specialist planned the bunkers' strategic placement, putting goats and dogs inside for weapon tests. At the time, the government boasted the bunkers could withstand four nuclear blasts. That claim was shattered in 1999, during the Kosovo war, when NATO jets attacking Yugoslav forces mistakenly bombed and destroyed bunkers on the Albanian side. Albanian soldiers positioned nearby ran from their posts. "Damn Enver," a person who saw the bombing told me they yelled. "He said these things were safe!"

The beginning of the 1970s saw a degree of cultural liberalization, inspired by Italian television, as young people tried to dress and dance like their contemporaries across the Adriatic Sea. Tirana women wore makeup and men grew sideburns. That came to a crashing halt after the eleventh Albanian song festival in December 1972, which offended the regime with its Western flair. Hoxha railed against corrupting "foreign influences" and young artists paid the price. A well-known singer was imprisoned and a popular songwriter was banished to the north. The head of state TV, Todi Lubonja, was blamed for the transgression. He and his son, Fatos Lubonja, were jailed until the regime fell. Other moderate voices in the media and culture fields were purged, as were many in the military. It was necessary, Hoxha said in 1974, to "cleanse the army with an iron broom."

At the same time, Hoxha's relations with China worsened after U.S. president Nixon visited Beijing in 1972, and China cut economic and military ties six years later. Albanians hoped for a new path, either back to the Soviet Union or perhaps towards the West. They got neither. Proud and stubborn, Hoxha embarked on a path of self-reliance, declaring Albania the only true socialist state in the world. "Better to eat grass than betray our principles," a saying went.

Albania was a determined soldier surrounded by fiends, and Hoxha developed a linguistic flair to enforce the point. The Greeks to the south were "monarchofascists" and Russians were "socio-imperialists," as in socialist imperialists. The Yugoslavs were "Titoists," after Josip Broz Tito, former patron of the Albanian Communist Party.

The isolation thrust Albania into a corner. The already meager industrial production slowed. Lines grew for butter, meat, and cheese. Hoxha needed a patron to provide military and economic aid, so he cautiously approached the more palatable Western states, such as Canada, Spain, and Germany, writing the policy paper himself.

Hoxha suffered his first heart attack in 1973. A secret medical team of at least six doctors tended to his every need. They placed modern equipment in his home and brought medicine, mostly from France, which Sigurimi agents purchased in random pharmacies to avoid any poisoning attempt. By 1980, his diabetes required insulin shots twice per day. Hoxha's kidneys were failing and his vision was bad. At party congresses he sat at the podium symbolically turning the pages of his speeches as loudspeakers broadcast prerecorded words to the crowd.

In 1981, Hoxha summoned strength for one last purge to eliminate his partner from World War Two and heir to the throne, Prime Minister Mehmet Shehu. The trigger was the engagement of Shehu's son to a woman from Tirana who had an anti-communist relative in the United States. Under pressure, Shehu agreed to cancel the engagement but Hoxha convened the Politburo to debate the affair. Politburo members attacked Shehu for his treachery and forced him to engage in self-criticism. Hoxha did not speak. The next morning, Radio Tirana announced that Shehu had committed suicide. Apparently sensing his impending demise—and perhaps hoping to spare his family—Shehu shot himself. Some say he was shot.

The party denounced Shehu as a foreign spy and police arrested his wife and three sons. One son killed himself the next year by wiring his iron bed to a light plug. Shehu's wife died in prison six years after that. In 2001, the family found Shehu's remains in an unmarked grave: bones, a skull, some clothes, a watch, and a pair of shoes.

Some believe Hoxha eliminated Shehu, either by murder or by driving him to suicide, because of differences over policy. But former senior party officials told me a serious policy dispute was impossible given Shehu's subservient relationship for decades under the Leader. Although a powerful force, Shehu never challenged Hoxha's rule. Even the U.S. government, which struggled for information on Albania, considered Hoxha "*primus inter pares*" in the regime. "Although information on the inner workings of the Albanian leadership has always been extremely difficult to obtain, few reports have ever alleged that Shehu had serious difficulties with [Hoxha] or challenged his authority," one U.S. intelligence report said.[1]

According to Albanian leaders from that time, the most likely explanation for Shehu's death is the megalomania of the man he served. By 1981, Hoxha was gravely ill. His logical successor was Shehu, the second most powerful man in Albania, and considerably stronger than numbers three and four. But Hoxha craved power even on his deathbed, and wanted history to hold him high. He needed a successor who was ideologically agreeable and would not overshadow the Leader. As omnipotent as Hoxha was for forty years, the determined war hero Shehu, notoriously calculating and stern, could minimize Hoxha's aura of invincibility.

"Enver wanted a smooth transition where his name would stay on top," Central Committee member Sofokli Lazri said. Another Central Committee member, the writer Dritëro Agolli, agreed that Shehu was eliminated to protect Enver's legacy. "If Kapo had been alive, he would have been eliminated too," he said, referring to Hysni Kapo, the third most powerful leader, who died of natural causes in 1979.

Enver Hoxha with arms around Central Committee Secretary Hysni Kapo (L) and
Prime Minister Mehmet Shehu (R), with Central Committee Secretary Ramiz Alia at
far right, May 1, 1979. © Gani Xhengo

Hoxha's choice as successor was a mild-mannered and obedient party
official from Shkoder named Ramiz Alia, who did his job, avoided trouble, and slowly climbed the party ranks. Alia enjoyed Hoxha's trust but,
most importantly, he was not a forceful character to outshine the star.

"It was better that power went to his pupil instead of his friend," Lazri
said, comparing Alia and Shehu.

By 1982, two doctors were monitoring Hoxha full-time, but Hoxha
hated seeing them at his home. "He did not tell us everything about his
health and we were nervous he would not complain," one of Hoxha's
doctors said. "He did not want to give the impression he was sick."[2]

On February 17, 1984, the doctors heard the alarm and rushed to Hoxha's room. They found him slumped unconscious half on the bed, his
wife Nexhmije by his side. They attached him to monitors in the room
and managed to resuscitate him.

Hoxha had suffered a stroke and it caused one side of his face to sag.
He became weak in the right hand and leg and Nexhmije pushed him in

a wheelchair with a floral pattern on the seat. Doctors stayed with him day and night, close enough to administer care within one minute.

The morning exam on April 9, 1985, went better than on previous days. Hoxha went for a stroll in the garden with Nexhmije, leaning on a walker for support. Around 10:00 a.m. Nexhmije rang the alarm from the bedroom. The doctors rushed in, giving Hoxha oxygen and electric shocks to restart his heart. They succeeded, and the signs looked good at first. But his kidneys had deteriorated beyond repair. Doctors kept his heart beating for two days, but they knew he had no chance. Just after midnight on April 11, a second heart attack struck the fatal blow.

* * *

The loudspeaker sprang to life in the cold cell at 5:00 a.m. The prisoners rose from mattresses on the floor and shuddered in the mountain air. Prison life had a plodding routine—roll call, breakfast, political class, work—but this day seemed different. Instead of news from the state-run radio, a funeral song filled the air.

Some of the men in Burrel prison had committed common crimes: theft, assault, or worse. But many of the 250 men were there for crimes of the mind: they had dared to question the dominant role of the Leader. They had written poems, listened to Western music, complained of poor food, or tried to escape on foot or by raft, or their relatives had committed these treasonous acts and Hoxha was making the family pay. In the prison's center stood a special wing for former communist leaders, men who had fallen from Hoxha's good grace, swept away with the iron broom.

Trapped behind bars in the barren mountains of northern Albania, the prisoners were keenly aware of the slightest change in routine. They could read every sign, and the message on this brisk morning was flashing bright: Albania's omnipotent leader was dead. Excited and nervous, the prisoners discussed the breaking news. They debated the impact on Albania, the choice of a successor, and their chances of release. Would the monarchists or nationalists come to power? Would Albania open to the world? The guards outside had no idea.

Around noon, Radio Tirana released the news: "Comrades, communists, workers, cooperativists, intellectuals, women, and the youth of Albania, veterans of the war and compatriots," the announcer said in a grave tone. "Today, the 11th of April, 1985, at two hours fifteen, the heart of the beloved and glorious leader of the party and our people, Comrade Enver Hoxha, first secretary of the Central Committee of the Party of Labor of Albania, chairman of the General Council of the Democratic Front of Albania, commander in chief of our armed forces, ceased to beat."[3]

The construction suggested that Hoxha was not dead, only his heart had stopped.

The prisoners erupted in joy. They shrieked and jumped like free men. Some days later they paid the price for their exultations with beatings and a twenty-day lockdown, but repercussions entered no one's mind on that cold day.

Outside of the prisons, all Albania mourned. Even those who despised the regime felt a sense of loss. Hoxha was the guardian of a patriarchal land—the man who had shepherded Albanians from the destruction of World War Two, steered them between the hostile East and West, and built a society with electricity and schools in the furthest hills. His indoctrination had seeped into every crack of life, a cult of personality so complete that his death was traumatic even to those who had suffered from persecution. "Daddy, will the Germans invade Albania?" a young girl nervously asked her parents. Hoxha was so important to Albania, so central to its identity, his name engraved in mountains, that Albanians found it difficult to imagine he would ever die.

Thousands of mourners stood in long lines winding down Tirana's boulevard to view the body as it lay in state. They cried and held their right fists to their heads in the communist salute as they passed his open casket ringed by flowers, a large portrait of Hoxha looming behind.

A few days later, the funeral procession snaked down the boulevard under high, gray clouds. Mourners lined the street dozens deep as the coffin, atop a cannon and draped in the red-and-black Albanian flag, made its way to Skanderbeg Square. In a light rain, Politburo members led a procession to the Cemetery of the Martyrs on the outskirts of town, where they carried the coffin and watched it descend into a marble crypt. Hoxha's wife and party leaders sprinkled dirt from his hometown and stroked the golden letters of his name.

In the rocky and desolate Spaç labor camp, political prisoners watched the ceremony from wooden benches in the television room. No

Mourners wait in line to view Enver Hoxha's body in Tirana on April 15, 1985. © ATA

one dared smile or cheer. Would Hoxha's death mean their liberation or execution? Some of the prisoners had written a telegram of condolence to Hoxha's widow.

"Stand and honor this great man!" a man barked from the back of the room. The prisoners spun around expecting to see a guard. But it was the political prisoner Allem, who had lost his mind in 1980 after being shot in a failed escape.

2

Fences Fall

A balding head and soft face gave Hoxha's successor, Ramiz Alia, a gentle look. His speech and manners were calm and measured, not the attributes of a forceful man. But dark eyes and a sly smile betrayed a clever and ambitious operator with a skill for working his way up the communist elite. A young Partisan during World War Two, Alia survived forty years of purges and sweeps.

In some ways, Hoxha's attempt to protect his legacy might have aided Albania. True to form, Alia was a less dogmatic character who dealt with changes in Eastern Europe and Albania as a politician trying to survive, rather than as a hawk defending his nest. In the end, grasping the inevitable, he initiated some reform. Most significantly, Alia was not a brutal man. On the contrary, he took steps to avoid spilling blood. "I was not like Enver Hoxha," he told me in 2002 when reflecting on his rule. "I did not use the fist."

Alia's first major project was to honor his teacher and guide. Hoxha statues rose in Tirana and other towns. In the center of the capital came the colossal white marble pyramid to house the Enver Hoxha Museum.

As statues rose, the economy sank. The government rationed meat, cheese, coffee, butter, and oil, and the quality of those goods got worse. Shoppers stood in lines from 5:00 a.m., and often went home empty-handed. The only vegetable readily available was leeks, and it became a symbol of Albania's despair. Collectivized to the extreme, the economy had exhausted its possibilities, like a human body burning muscle and fat to survive.

Eager to tease Albania from the Soviet sphere, the West was ready to provide aid after Hoxha's death, but Alia declined. Central Committee members criticized him later, but few if any of them advised such radical moves at the time. In retrospect, it is unrealistic to expect that a leader weaned on the party and handpicked by the dictator would assert himself with such bold moves as Western aid.

In 1985 the party allowed some discussion of economic reform: how to improve the system. In January 1986, authorities cut prison sentences by a quarter, and released a few political prisoners who were serving their final year. But the Party of Labor's Ninth Congress in November 1986 kept change in check. The slogan of the meeting, chosen by Alia, was the "Congress of Continuity." The next year, the government allowed farmers to own two sheep, but they had to be the same sex. The reform could not propagate.

With the economy failing, Alia cautiously resumed the policy that Hoxha had started and approached some Western European states, in particular Germany, which had diplomatic relations with all the other states in Eastern Europe. In 1987 Germany agreed to give fifty million marks in development aid in return for diplomatic relations. France soon gave credit for hydroelectric plants and Italy provided a modest amount of aid.

Inside Albania the party loosened its grip. Homemade devices called "tin cans" converted televisions from VHF to UHF, letting viewers watch the forbidden Italian RAI 2 and Yugoslav 2. Snide remarks and critical huffs against the regime increased, although thousands of political prisoners remained behind bars. Unheard of during Hoxha, political jokes emerged. Cannibals were cooking two Politburo members over a fire, one joke went. The cannibals had to remove them from the fire because, while roasting, they ate the potatoes.

Albanians scanned for signs of change. They analyzed the leaders' glances on TV, the firmness of handshakes, and the seating at meetings. They believed that every Reagan-Gorbachev summit addressed their fate. Hope for emancipation assumed mystical forms. Northern Albanians near the coast talked about "the monster of Lezhë," an underwater beast that lived in Lezhë Bay. The creature was later discovered to be a trapped whale, but its presence assumed surreal and magical tones that hinted at change.

At the same time, Alia needed to show he had control, both for the public and party conservatives who feared change. In December 1986, he signed a regulation that allowed the internment of people who are "socially dangerous" because they opposed the "rules of socialist coexistence." The double message, slight opening and new controls, became a pattern over the next four years.

By 1988, the party had open debates about inefficiency and reform. In factories, schools, hospitals, and the university, party members spoke about increasing productivity, modernizing education, and improving social services. That year the party also published a fawning eulogy to Hoxha, entitled "Our Enver," ostensibly penned by Alia himself.

In February 1988, Albania attended a conference of foreign affairs ministers from Balkan states in Belgrade—the first multilateral meeting that communist Albania had attended outside the United Nations. "The delegations were surprised to see us," recalled Muhamet Kapllani, deputy foreign minister at the time. That July, party censors allowed a new book that caused a stir. The detective novel *Knives* by Neshat Tozaj was not openly provocative but its plot—concerning a bungled investigation by the Sigurimi—hinted at the failures of the security apparatus. One month later, Albania received its first distinguished foreign guest, an ethnic Albanian born in Macedonia named Gonxhe Bojaxhiu, better known as Mother Teresa. The government presented her trip as a "private visit" to some family graves, which were renovated before she arrived. At the cemetery she paid homage to Hoxha, the state press said.

At Enver Hoxha University in Tirana, students became more defiant, wearing "imperialist" jeans and leather jackets. Art students made T-shirts with images of the band U2 or from the cartoon *Tom and Jerry*. Radio Tirana began to play the previously banned music of ABBA and the Beatles.

Consistent with the pattern, the party balanced openness with control. The state media attacked democratic movements in the Soviet Union and Eastern Europe, which were quickly gaining pace. Party leaders denounced Gorbachev's *perestroika* and *glasnost* as revisionist. Hungary and Poland, they said, were veering off course. In September 1989, Hungary opened its border with Austria, allowing thousands of East Germans to flee, the first major flow from the East.

As these dramatic events took place, Ramiz Alia addressed the Party of Labor's Central Committee on September 25, and denounced Gorbachev as a traitor and counter-revolutionary. "Vigilance should be sharp; the political level of the masses raised; the rates of economic development progressive; the competence of defense high; and diplomatic activity skillful," Alia said in response to the historic changes across the Soviet bloc. "All this should be inspired and led by the Party."[1]

* * *

After weeks of demonstrations, the most poignant symbol of the Cold War crumbled. On November 9, 1989, East German authorities opened the Berlin Wall and jubilant Germans attacked it with chisels and sledge-hammers. Publicly, the Albanian government pretended it was not true. An article in the party organ *Zëri i Popullit* (Voice of the People), headquartered on Stalin Boulevard, mentioned the resignation of the East German government and Politburo but provided no details on the extent of change.[2] For three days, as peddlers in Berlin sold chunks of the wall, the Albanian media kept Germany out of the news, as if the regime hoped the story would disappear.

Behind the scenes, party leaders engaged in nervous debates. "The Berlin Wall fell and people wondered whether our fence could resist the winds of change," then deputy foreign minister Muhamet Kapllani told me. The older and more conservative forces, mostly World War Two veterans, believed that Albania could withstand the changes in Eastern Europe. Younger officials tended to appreciate the inevitability of *glasnost* coming to Albania. Alia sided with those who predicted change, but believed he and the party could manage the shift. "After the Berlin Wall fell, it was clear that the process would include Albania," he told me. The question was what changes and at what speed.

The government remained silent as Czechoslovakia's regime toppled in late November. After ignoring anti-government demonstrations in Prague for one week, *Zëri i Popullit* said that "ultra-revisionists" there wanted to "restore capitalist order."[3] But the government could not block other reports from leaking in. The Albanian program of the Voice of America had become a daily routine for Albanians since 1988; everyone was at home with their ear pressed to a radio for news in Albanian about communism's dying days. By mid-December, events forced Alia to respond. "There are foreigners who ask: 'Will there be a similar process in Albania as that which is happening in Eastern Europe?'" he said in a speech. "We answer flatly and categorically: No, there will not."[4]

Two weeks later, events proved Alia wrong. In Romania, furious crowds forced the long-time dictator Nicolae Ceaușescu and his wife to flee the capital. They were captured and, on Christmas Day 1989, hastily tried by a military court, convicted, and executed by firing squad.

The Albanian government downplayed the executions, running re-dacted versions of Romania's dramatic news on *Zëri i Popullit*'s back page. Party functionaries hit the streets to argue that Ceauşescu's mur-der had no effect on Albania. But Albanians from factory workers to Politburo members understood the implications of Ceauşescu's death. The fall of the Berlin Wall had been a sign, but Germany was far away. Romania, with Ceauşescu's feared regime, was closer to Albania geo-graphically and politically. If the Romanian leader had met a violent death, what might happen in Tirana?

Years later, many Albanians still recall Ceauşescu's death as the key impetus for the communists' defeat. They saw that a repressive system could fall. Also, Albania stood as the lone communist state in the East. Seven hundred thousand bunkers and legions of Sigurimi spies could not stop the inevitable course.

Some former party leaders told me years later that they never feared a bloody uprising because the party had extensive control. "Ceauşescu's death had no impact because Albania was not in the Warsaw Pact," said Sofokli Lazri, Alia's chief foreign policy advisor at the time. "Albania was not part of the dominos." But most former officials said the Romanian events rattled Albania's elite. As then deputy foreign minister Kapllani explained, "They were thinking: this could happen to us."

Alia said he understood Romania's importance, but he denied having been afraid. "With his [Ceauşescu's] murder, we saw the aggressiveness of the new forces that were attacking the socialist order," he told me. "It was clear for us that the collapse of socialism would include all of Eastern Europe, including Albania. There was no fear. It stressed our conviction that changes were coming."

Frightened or not, Alia knew he had to adapt, if for no other reason than the collapse of the Eastern European market. The more insightful party leaders around him realized the need for reform. But even they, with Sigurimi informants on every corner, underestimated the extent of people's rage.

* * *

The northern city of Shkoder rejoiced at Nicolae Ceauşescu's end. The city had an anti-Hoxha slant. The Leader had come from Gjirokaster in the south, and he discriminated against Albanians from the north.

Plus, Shkoder is largely Catholic, and the Sigurimi treated the clergy as Vatican spies. Cafés in town grew thick with rumor and cigarette smoke. Radical graffiti appeared on walls: *Poshtë Komunizmi!* (Down with Communism!), *Poshtë Partia!* (Down with the Party!). Word spread that a demonstration would take place on January 11, the day the communist Albanian republic had been established, to topple the bust of Stalin that stood in a square.

On the eleventh, a small group gathered around the bust. Curious onlookers watched from the periphery with a contingent of police and secret police. Small in number and surrounded by Sigurimi, the crowd dispersed.

A group of Shkoder men agreed to try again on January 14. The Sigurimi arrested the key organizers the night before but people still drifted to the square, hoping for a crowd to hide their faces and lose the fear. They had no such luck. Fewer than one hundred people shuffled around Stalin's bust. Snipers and Sigurimi agents watched from the windows of the Hotel Rozafa and the post office roof. Security forces hid in ambulances. Around midday the hesitant crowd encircled its prey. Two policemen in civilian clothes moved to arrest one of the men but he fought back as the police threw him into a van. Factory workers hurled ball bearings at the police. Two brothers who had spent time in a psychiatric hospital scaled the Stalin bust. "Go Vllaznia!" somebody yelled, meaning "Brotherhood" (and also the soccer team of Shkoder), and the crowd joined the brothers' assault. The police and Sigurimi attacked with stun guns and dispersed the crowd. Stalin still stood, but Shkoder had made its point.

That night the police arrested more than four hundred people. Most were released, but eleven men were sentenced to prison terms up to twelve years. The Stalin-scaling brothers were returned to a psychiatric ward.

"The day came to say what people didn't dare to say for a long time," said Tomë Sheldija, an elderly organizer of the demonstration, when reflecting years later on that day. "Here are the seeds of this fucked-up transition."

* * *

Two weeks after Shkoder, Tirana groaned. Nobody I spoke with knows how the idea arose, like a folk song with an unknown composer, but it apparently started at the Kinostudio, the state-run film enterprise on the outskirts of Tirana. At the end of January, people began walking around Tirana whispering "28–18, 28–18" to those they passed. January 28, it meant, at 6:00 p.m. Everyone knew the police had arrested the demonstrators in Shkoder, so they intended to walk silently along Martyrs of the Nation Boulevard to see how many people emerged.

The Sigurimi learned of the plan and the party ordered its members to walk the boulevard that day. When people saw apparachiks and party chiefs strolling, they understood their moment was gone, and the silent demonstration dispersed. Three days later, the Sigurimi detained some of the suspected organizers, but eventually let them go.

In early February, the party's Central Committee held its ninth plenum. On economic policy, the party admitted mistakes. "Nothing can justify the shortages of vegetables, milk and even meat in the market of any city," the plenum report said.[5] The party agreed to let farmers sell their own vegetables and some livestock. At the same time, the title of Alia's speech showed commitment to the course: "The Deepening of the Revolutionization of the Life of the Party and the Country—A Permanent Duty." The answer to "bourgeois propaganda" and "counter-revolutionary processes," Alia said, was for party members to intensify their discipline and determination. Trade unions, women's organizations, and youth groups must revive their work, he implored, so that "the word of the party reaches the masses more quickly."[6] If the party worked harder and communicated better, the logic went, the system could be saved.

The effort failed. Party activists who visited factories and universities got rebuffed by workers and students with questions and complaints. "Why can't our artists meet artists outside Albania?" one student asked a party representative who was visiting the Acadamy of Arts. "Why must we paint in the Socialist Realist style?" asked another. "And why can't I see my uncle in Canada?" Speaking in a large lecture hall with sloping seats, the visitor said that socialism did not follow a straight, climbing path but rather an upward spiral. "I understand what you mean," a student from the top row replied, looking down on the speaker. "But from my perspective it looks like a vicious circle."

* * *

In the central Albanian town of Kavaja, some young men decided to take another step. On a February night, Çezar Petja and Gezim Çelhyka broke into a local school and used coffee-colored metal paint to cover a classroom for Marxism-Leninism lessons with anti-government slogans:

"Down with the Dictatorship"

"Enver-Hitler"

"Nexhmije the Whore"

Gezim, who had studied painting, wrote with his left hand so the police could not recognize his script. The next morning the saboteurs left Kavaja at 6:00 a.m.

The slogans caused a scandal in town. The police investigated, detaining and beating suspects, but Çezar and Gezim remained hidden and safe. When tempers cooled, they returned and formed a small group with a third friend, Xhevat Ylviu, to provoke the regime and to show it was time for change.

Conspiring in a boiler room, the young men wrote anti-government leaflets, again using their left hands. They made copies with a home-made contraption that used acid, a box, and a lamp. Among a host of anti-communist slogans, they boldly announced: "In the 80th minute the stadium will fill with blood!" In a few days, the Kavaja soccer team was scheduled to play a home game against Partizani from Tirana, the team of the Ministry of Defense. Kavaja should ride the energy, the young men thought, and push the regime to react.

A secret report from the interior minister to Ramiz Alia and the prime minister quoted the leaflet's provocative text:

> We call all those who are convinced that our communist propaganda is from head to toe a deception. . . . Let's gather together with our unified, energetic voices at the match on March 25 "Partizani"–"Besa" and at the 80th minute of the game let's raise our fingers while yelling loudly and without break: "Freedom, Democracy" . . . let's wash the stadium's stairs with our blood.[7]

Nervous and excited fans filled the stadium on March 25, as well as members of the Sigurimi and police, Xhevat Ylviu recalled for me years later. At the eightieth minute, a spectator pulled one of Enver Hoxha's books from his coat. He cocked his arm but remembered that the book's first page had his name written in pen. He ripped out the page and hurled the book onto the field. A policeman scurried between the players and scooped it up, Ylviu said. When he saw Hoxha's name on the red cover, he thrust it under his jacket and ran off the field. The Sigurimi converged on the stands and grabbed two men, while the agitated crowd lobbed rocks at the police.

Minister of the Interior Simon Stefani's report to Alia matched Ylviu's account. "During the course of the game there was no calm, but a police officer caught a youth from Kavaja who was yelling, 'Come on boys, ready for revolution,' and some other indentified people who shouted, 'Democracy—Democracy,'" the report said. After the match, a group of about two hundred young men threw stones at the police, Stefani reported. "A television camera was used to learn and indentify who they were."

That night and the next day, the police summoned dozens of Kavaja residents for handwriting tests and beatings. Undeterred, the three friends went around town to announce a demonstration for the next day.

On March 26, around 7:00 p.m., a group gathered in the center of Kavaja and walked to the communist party headquarters and police station. When the police saw the crowd approaching, they retreated inside. One policeman tried to leave and got pelted with rocks.

"At that moment, the sky grew dark with stones," Ylviu said.

The protesters marched to the main square, where they shouted anti-government slogans as the police watched. Again the secret police report matched Ylviu's account:

> Around 7 p.m. on this date [March 26] a large crowd of people was seem coming in the direction of the police, mostly young men, who were chanting: "Free our friends; freedom, democracy; Long live Ramiz Alia; Down with the dynasty; Down with dictatorship; Down with the people's power" and afterwards they began to attack with stones, which broke some windows of the building.[8]

The interior minister gave Alia his blunt analysis. "It's a fact that the masses' opinion of some employees, especially the police, is not good," he wrote. "This perhaps has been incited, used as propaganda, and abused by the class enemies." Stefani said that Kavaja had about two thousand unemployed young men in 1989 and shortages of meat, eggs, and milk, as well as electricity cuts. "With the exception of a palace of culture and cinema, there are no other recreational or entertainment places for youth, not to mention the slow pace of apartment construction," he reported. Under such conditions, the minister predicted that "similar situations will be repeated." At the same time, he warned that "the hand of foreign agencies" might also be behind the protests in Kavaja, Tirana, and Shkoder.

* * *

Party plenums usually occurred twice per year, but after six weeks the Central Committee convened plenum number ten. The party improved physical conditions in the prisons and released political prisoners who had served more than twenty-five years. A family of five named Popa that had claimed asylum in the Italian embassy five years before was allowed to leave the country.

On May 1, Alia gave a speech to workers in Korça that stressed Albania's independence and a theme that permeated the government's propaganda for the rest of the year. "Socialism for us means to be free, independent, and not swallowed by others," he said. Other roads threaten "the freedom and independence of the country."[9]

The position stemmed from Hoxha, who had stoked fear by warning of external threats. Alia admitted this twelve years later, when I asked if Albania had really faced existential threats. Perils from abroad existed, he said, but they were "not in the dimensions in which we described them."

Despite the threats, Alia reached out to the world. In New York two Albanian diplomats met secretly with U.S. officials at the United Nations to discuss reestablishing diplomatic ties. In May the government opened telephone lines to the West, allowing Albanians to speak directly with relatives abroad for the first time since World War Two. To Albanians' surprise, the new telephone book included a list of international codes. That month parliament legalized private practice for lawyers and reopened the Ministry of Justice, which was closed in 1968. It removed internment and expulsion as punishments, and reduced the illegal crossing of Albania's borders from a counter-revolutionary act to a criminal offense. Parliament also redefined the notorious Article 55 of the penal code—"Agitation and Propaganda against the State"—which the state had used for years to imprison and execute critics. An amendment abolished the death penalty for "anti-socialist agitation and propaganda" and narrowed the definition to acts aimed at "overthrowing the state and social order as defined in the constitution."[10] Criminalization of religious propaganda was removed.

In explaining the changes to Article 55, Deputy Prime Minster Manush Myftiu implied its previous abuse. "The definition of the crime agitation and propaganda is very broad and can be interpreted in different subjective ways," he told parliament. "[This] can bring undesirable consequences, as different people can be convicted as enemies, even though they are not."[11]

On June 12, parliament legalized the issuance of passports, which for decades were given only to the drivers of state-owned companies and the party elite. Travelers had gotten a passport from the Interior Ministry, an oversized red book that drew smirks from foreign border guards, and returned it when they came home. Now every citizen could get a document to leave the prison state.

The next day, thousands of Catholics gathered at the mountainside remains of the Church of St. Anthony in the northern town of Laç to commemorate St. Anthony's feast. The Sigurimi stepped aside and watched.

As Alia introduced reform, taboo topics slowly appeared in the state-run press. Party newspapers and magazines began to publish previously forbidden writers like Kafka, Joyce, and Camus. The U.S. government's Voice of America played a crucial role, especially after Albania's government opened telephone lines with the United States. The Albanian-language program interviewed economists, doctors, and academics who cautiously gave alternative views. When the show aired at 6:00 p.m., nary a soul walked the streets.

On March 21, 1990, the newspaper of the party's youth organization, *Zëri i Rinisë*, published a controversial interview with Albania's most famous writer, Ismail Kadare, whose work was widely read in Albania and abroad. The goal was to publish "a delicate interview," Kadare told me, in order to "emancipate Albanian society." Kadare called for the rehabilitation of forbidden Albanian writers like Faik Konica and Gjergj Fishta, and for Stalin's bust to be removed from in front of the Academy of Science.[12] Five days after the interview ran, a mysterious explosion in front of the academy granted Kadare his wish.

On April 28 and 29, *Zëri i Popullit* ran a lengthy piece by Ylli Popa, the cardiologist who had served Enver Hoxha and found the book in his library with the underlined section on the Doctors' Plot. Entitled "In Search of Lost Time," the article quoted "Comrade Ramiz" and called for reform in the arts, education, science, and culture. "New things cannot be attained using old attitudes," Popa wrote. The success of reform "will only be assured if people are free to say what they think."[13]

Popa said he received threatening phone calls after the article from provincial party officials, but the leadership kept mum. "Alia wanted things to change but he didn't want to do it himself," Popa told me in 2000 from his office at the Academy of Sciences, where he was president. "I understood he wanted some change."

Ramiz Alia denied that he had instructed Popa or other writers of that time to present progressive ideas. But a senior Alia aide who dealt with media at the time said Popa's article was strategically planned to sensitize the public and to set a tone before the arrival of United Nations secretary-general Javier Pérez de Cuéllar, who was due to visit Albania in early May. "We wanted to create a certain atmosphere before the visit and not let him create that atmosphere," the former aide said.

Whoever wrote the article, the process revealed a guiding dynamic of Albania's transition, which repeated itself over the next two years. Alia wanted reform, but only enough for him to maintain control, either for the welfare of the country (as he claimed) or to preserve power (as his opponents claimed). The best people to promote careful change, Alia thought, were the state-sanctioned intellectuals such as Kadare and Popa who had influence in society and relations with the ruling elite. Alia believed he could keep them close. Much more dangerous to the regime were the Stalin statue climbers in Shkoder and the book throwers in Kavaja, who had nothing to lose.

Over time, the newspapers *Bashkimi* (Union), *Drita* (Light), and *Zëri i Rinisë* took bold positions on freedom of thought and religion. On May 20, 1990, another cardiologist gave an outspoken interview in *Drita*, criticizing "every pseudo-patriotic supporter of isolation."[14] Quoting Alia, the doctor called for more freedom of thought and expression. He followed this in September with an article in *Bashkimi* that supported Alia, called for further democratization, and urged support for the Albanians of Kosovo.[15] The author was Dr. Sali Berisha, forty-five years old, a respected cardiologist, professor, and communist party member. No one imagined he would soon take Ramiz Alia's place.

3

The System Shakes

Bujar Alikaj was a jovial street guy, a thirty-year-old bus driver from the Kombinati neighborhood of Tirana—the workers' area named for the textile mill Kombinati Stalin. Throughout Albania, Bujar's generation of young men, most of them unemployed, all of them gazing west, was making the regime nervous. They had rioted in Kavaja and were restless in other towns. They were not overtly political but they wanted the system to change. They saw how a clique of elites was carousing in the Block at their expense.

Bujar had known he wanted to leave Albania since 1979, when he started teaching himself English from books. He considered crossing the border illegally but the shoot-to-kill order posed too great a risk. The only way, he thought, was to enter one of the embassies in Tirana, as the Popa family had done in 1985. Others had the same idea and, in the spring of 1990, a few tried to enter some Western embassies in Tirana's diplomatic quarter. According to a secret report by the interior minister that June, the danger of people entering the embassies was "very acute."[1] The police increased their patrols.

Bujar's neighbor worked as a cook at the Greek embassy. In mid-June she brought Bujar a letter from a Greek official named Leonid, who was known around Tirana. "Meet me at Rinia Park on Friday at 9:20 p.m.," Bujar recalled the letter said. No contemplation was required and Bujar went to the park in the center of Tirana that evening, as people were enjoying their evening stroll. Leonid told Bujar that he should try to enter the Greek embassy. He guaranteed that, if Bujar made it, the Greek government would grant him asylum. If Bujar was interested, Leonid said, he should meet another person in a couple of days to discuss the plan.

A few days later, Bujar went at the assigned time to the bathroom in the restaurant in Rinia Park, where he saw an overweight Greek man. They washed their hands in the sinks and spoke in Albanian. "I'm interested in you," Bujar remembered the Greek man said. "What is your name? What languages do you know? I give you a promise of asylum if you make a try." Bujar readily agreed.

On June 20, Bujar made his move. The bus he drove was called an accordion—two wagons connected by a rubber bridge. At 7:00 a.m., he parked on Durres Street, around the corner from the embassy. He strolled for twenty minutes to case the scene; an embassy car blocked the gate. He returned to the accordion, released the latch on the roof escape, and started the engine. A friend of Bujar's locked the door from the outside as Bujar hit the gas. He sped up Durres Street, turned right, drove one block, and swung right again, aiming straight for the embassy, which was surrounded by a fence. Another car, a Romanian Aro, unexpectedly appeared and Bujar steered abruptly to squeeze by. The bus slid between the Aro and the car at the embassy gate, knocking them out of the way and slamming against the fence. Bujar jumped out of his seat, climbed through the hatch onto the roof, and jumped the fence into the yard. He was in.

Three days later, around 9:45 p.m., a truck with six people burst into the Italian embassy. Around midnight, Deputy Foreign Minister Muhamet Kapllani summoned the Italian ambassador to explain. The storming of the embassy was a criminal and terrorist act, Kapllani told the ambassador, according to an Albanian government report on the meeting.[2] "We cannot understand how you can give shelter in the embassy to such people when we know that Italian public opinion and the Italian government itself have condemned terrorist acts."

"These people seem to be normal, although the way they entered was not normal," the Italian ambassador replied, according to the report. "But it seems that they are pushed by these motivations I mentioned before, so by the desire to go abroad."

The next day, twelve people stormed the Turkish embassy. Four people entered the Cuban embassy but the Cubans threw them back.

Watching all this, the senior diplomat at the West German embassy got upset. "I was deeply troubled," said Werner Daum, the German chargé d'affaires and de facto ambassador. "I couldn't accept that people wouldn't seek safety with the Germans." Without orders from Bonn, he opened his front gate, turned on the embassy lights, and ordered the security home. That night between fifty and seventy people walked in. "I didn't do it for humanitarian reasons to help the people," Daum said. "I did it because I knew a massive exodus would make the regime collapse."

The exodus swelled. According to a secret Albanian government report, on July 2 six people entered the Italian embassy with a Tatra truck, breaking the fence and surrounding wall, and thirty-four people entered the German compound with a Skoda truck. Two hours later, another truck slammed into the Greeks. "After this action other people entered in the Greek, Polish, Czech, German etc," the report said.[3] At some embassies, officials helped people climb the fence.

At times the police opened fire. At the West German embassy, someone shot a seventeen-year-old man in the stomach. That night a policeman entered the German compound holding a pistol, but he fled when a security officer knocked the gun from his hand. "The pistol (which has fired one bullet) will be returned together with seven bullets," the German embassy informed the Albanian Foreign Ministry in a letter of complaint.[4]

Rumor spread of mass killing, but the police mostly held their fire. For several days they even withdrew from the area around Embassy Street, returning on July 9 after the exodus had mostly stopped. Even if ordered to shoot, low morale would have likely prevented the security forces from opening fire. Many of the police and soldiers wanted to leave too.

Interviewed more than a decade later, Politburo members and Sigurimi agents who had served in 1990 told me they had gathered information about foreign support for subversive plots, pointing the finger at Germany, Italy, France, Yugoslavia, and Greece.

"This looked like something spontaneous. But for sure there were hands behind it," Alia claimed. "But not from our state. There could have been from others. From the foreign embassies."[5] Ramiz Alia's chief foreign policy advisor, Sofokli Lazri, was less diplomatic. "July 2 was an experiment of Berlin," he said. "It was like the embassies of Czechoslovakia in East Germany. It was not spontaneous."

Werner Daum rejected this as "pure nonsense." He said the Greeks did encourage people to enter their embassy, mostly ethnic Greeks, and others followed when the crisis began, but it was a sudden response without coordination. "The leadership did not understand how much Albanians wanted change," he said.

By week's end, about five thousand Albanians had crowded the embassies. The German compound housed 3,199 people, who slept in the garden and used a hand-dug latrine. A woman gave birth to a baby girl she named Germana. Eight hundred and seventy people slept in the Italian embassy, and about five hundred stayed with the French.

The Albanian government denied requests from Bonn, Rome, and Paris to provide food and tents. Either take them out of the country or give them to the police, the government said. Instead, the authorities cut off the embassies' water and Sigurimi agents infiltrated the crowds to learn why people had left.

"The reason was the lack of trust in the rules in force," one person told an agent who had slipped into the German embassy, according to a Sigurimi report. The person explained: "I have had a great desire to go abroad, and I was glad to hear the speeches and plenums of the party on providing passports to the people. Meeting after meeting and no answer at all. Decrees after decrees and we are always at the same point."[6]

"The reason is to be dressed like the people of my age abroad (blue jeans or other clothes like this) and to have a scooter," another person told an agent. "I have never thought to have these things without working, but I don't know how to buy a scooter in Albania or the clothes."[7]

The state media lambasted the asylum seekers as "hooligans" and "ex-convicts." *Zëri i Popullit* ran letters sent to Ramiz Alia from workers around the country that condemned the treasonous act of desertion.

On July 8, a United Nations envoy arrived for talks and the government announced it would allow the people to leave the country. Alia realized that they were not going to return home, even with a promise of immunity, so it was better to let them go. Two days later, the plane of the new Czechoslovak president Václav Havel picked up fifty-one Albanians who were in his country's embassy. "Long live Havel," they yelled upon landing in Prague.[8] At 4:00 a.m. on July 12, the authorities herded the remaining people onto buses and drove them in a convoy to Durres. The group was terrified they would be executed, Bujar Alikaj recalled. Villagers lined the road to wave good-bye. The passengers threw their watches and money out the bus windows, as if they wanted to leave it all behind.

In Durres, five ferries waited at a dock. The Albanians walked past a line of police and Sigurimi with video cameras. On board, foreign journalists swarmed, wanting to know why the people had fled.

* * *

The embassy stormers changed the game. The crisis in Albania became an open topic for debate with two camps: those demanding the new versus those defending the old. In favor of the former was the realization that the security forces had been unwilling or unable to stop the crowds.

Ramiz Alia moved in both directions. On July 8 some party hardliners had resigned or been dismissed from the Central Committee. One week later, the government increased salaries. At the same time, the party organized a large demonstration in Tirana that attacked the asylum seekers as traitors and vagabonds.

To stem discord, Alia proposed a new concept called "pluralism of thought." This was not political pluralism—a direct challenge to the Party of Labor—but the fostering of debate to improve the system.

"It's like speaking seven languages, all of them Albanian," an inmate in Spaç labor camp remarked at the time.

To spread the idea, the party organized meetings around the country with workers, artists, and students. Sometimes the strategy worked, especially in meetings with those who had benefited from the regime. But some meetings devolved into open attacks. Living in their villas, Alia and the party had drifted out of touch with people's needs. While still afraid, Albanians were beginning to speak.

On August 11, 1990, Alia invited a group of Tirana intellectuals, most of them party members, to the Palace of Congresses for a meeting, the topic of which the participants did not know. The guests took their seats and Alia said he had invited them for an exchange of views. Did anyone want to go first, Alia asked. If not, he reassured the group, he could begin. "You go first," the audience said at once, according to two participants and a transcript of the meeting published by the party. Alia launched into an attack on the counter-revolutionary forces that were trying to destabilize Albania:

> First, support for the enemy's activity is a conglomerate of disorientated people, who are dreaming to have a paradise existence, like in the advertisements on TV screens. Among this category are some unemployed people, some immature youth, some idle individuals, even some former prisoners, some adventurists and so on. Such a contingent does not have any declared or conscious program against the Party and the power . . . but its opossition to the Party line and activity, even if unconscious, is

dangerous. It produces gossip and disinformation. From this strata comes the main contingent of those who entered the embassies; these were the protagonists of the events that took place in Tirana, Kavaja, Shkodra and elsewhere.[9]

With this introduction setting the tone, Alia opened the floor. "Nothing is excessive in this meeting," he said. "We are among ourselves at home, as they say, and we can discuss without reservation."

The conversation that ensued remains a point of contention among Tirana elites. Alia told me he wanted the intellectuals to help him rebut the party's conservative wing. "I opened the way, I gave them something to talk about," he said. "But they could not do it." According to one of Alia's advisors at the time, Minister of Education Skënder Gjinushi, the meeting was to take the pulse. "If there had been a stronger demand for political pluralism, [Alia] would have moved faster," Gjinushi said. Participants in the meeting counter that Alia was aggressive and intimidating. Still, the transcript shows that some people demanded quicker reform, an end to police abuse, and more freedom of expression.

Six weeks later, the famous writer Ismail Kadare shocked the country by announcing that he and his family would not return from a trip in France. The request for asylum by the country's cultural icon sparked fierce debate. Some Albanians felt betrayed that Kadare had abandoned ship. Others felt proud that he had stood against the regime. Many wondered if Kadare, long promoted by Hoxha, would still be studied in schools.

The defection hurt Alia, especially because Tirana was preparing to host a conference of Balkan foreign ministers in October, the first high-level international meeting ever in the country. "With this ugly act, which heavily offends the patriotic conscience of our people and citizens, [Kadare] abandons the people in the fatherland and puts himself in the service of the enemies of Albania," declared *Zëri i Popullit*.[10] Kadare defended his decision as a response to broken promises. "Because there is no possibility of legal opposition in Albania, I have chosen this course, which I never wished to take and which I will not recommend to others," he wrote.[11] Ten years later, back in his Tirana apartment, Kadare told me that his defection was intended to "stimulate the democratization of Albania." He wanted to "unmask the hypocrisy of the regime's reforms."

* * *

While Kadare left, foreigners increasingly got in. On May 11, Albanians had lined the road from the airport to see Secretary-General de Cuéllar. About a dozen foreign reporters, including two from the United States, covered his trip, getting interviews with Albanians in the secrecy of their homes. In meetings with Alia and others, de Cuéllar pressed the government on human rights. He visited Burrel prison, but the authorities had transferred the prisoners to a work camp before he arrived. The government said it was considering whether to reopen houses of worship, de Cuéllar announced when he left.[12]

The next day, Alia held his first-ever press conference before the foreign press. "The process of development in Albania will never stop," he said, appearing calm and in control. "Albania will follow the way of freedom, independence and socialism."[13]

Later that month, the Democratic U.S. congressman Tom Lantos and a former Republican congressman named Joe DioGuardi, who ran an organization called the Albanian American Civic League, arrived in Tirana as government guests. "If you didn't know he was the head of a communist state, you'd be impressed with the guy," DioGuardi told me about Alia. During their meeting, Alia asked Lantos and DioGuardi to deliver a message to the U.S. president: Albania was interested to reestablish diplomatic relations. After the meeting, the Americans dropped by the grounds of the former U.S. embassy in Tirana, which the Italians had been renting since 1953. Anticipating a resumption of diplomatic ties, the State Department and CIA had asked them to take a look.

On August 19, 1990, a delegation from the U.S. Helsinki Commission, a congressional body that monitors human rights in Europe, arrived in Tirana. The meeting with Alia was polite, one of the delegates recalled. The president seemed relaxed, eager to present his views, although he rejected a request to visit political prisoners. Alia had also forbidden the head of the Voice of America's Albanian program, Elez Biberaj, to join the delegation as a translator. If Biberaj is on the plane, the delegation had been told, you cannot come in.

On August 20, the delegation hosted a reception at the Dajti Hotel with members of the government and individuals close to the party, based on a list drafted by Biberaj. Hoxha's widow, Nexhmije, was invited but refused to attend. That evening, three commission staff members strolled along the boulevard. Albanians steered clear, but when the foreigners stopped before an invalid selling photos of Hoxha, a curious crowd quickly gathered. One of the staffers picked up a photo, which he had promised to bring home for a friend. By buying this memento, he wondered, would the onlookers think he was a sympathetic tourist helping an invalid or a seasoned diplomat sending a message? He bought the photo.

Back in Washington, the State Department and CIA asked about the trip. Without a presence on the ground, they were desperate for news, photographs, and impressions. As intelligence reports from the 1980s reveal, reliable information on Albania was difficult to obtain.

That September, Alia and his foreign policy advisor, Sofokli Lazri, traveled to New York for the opening of the U.N. General Assembly. In a U.N. hallway, they met President George Bush, and the leaders talked for two minutes, Lazri said. At the General Assembly, Alia repeated that Albania was a special case. "The mere exaltation of democracy and human rights cannot be the magic key to the solution of the major, indeed we would say the dramatic, problems of those countries," he said, referring to Eastern and Central Europe.[14]

After getting permission to leave New York, Alia visited Boston, where he met the Albanian American community, including a dinner at the Albanian-owned restaurant Pier 4. Anti-communist demonstrators protested in boats outside. Eating seafood, Alia told the crowd that the changes in Albania were "not an imitation of the events in Eastern Europe."[15]

Thus far, he was right. Despite widespread discontent, protesters had not taken to the streets en masse. Intellectuals were not demanding political pluralism. Perhaps Albanians lacked a leader to galvanize a movement. Or maybe they were cowed by fear after decades of prisons and executions. Until then, the changes in Albania had mostly come from above. It was a strategy employed by regimes around the world, Sofokli Lazri told me ten years after the events. The government undertook just enough reform to avoid an explosion, like the safety valve on a pressure cooker.

But this strategy carried risks. It required accurate information, constant calibration, and careful control. Albania now stood as Europe's last communist state. Try as he might, Alia could not stop the inevitable pressures from within and abroad.

PART II

Blinded by Light

The Democratic Movement, 1990–1992

4

Student City

The student quarter of Tirana, called Student City, sits atop a low hill in the southeast of the capital. In 1990, the squat beige-and-gray dormitories surrounded an open area consisting of concrete and trampled grass. The communist elite controlled most aspects of Albania's political shift, but that autumn the students took charge of that drab hilltop and rattled the regime.

Ramiz Alia and the party leadership grasped the regime's precarious state. They postponed the start of classes for two weeks, claiming that some university buildings needed repair. When classes began, party functionaries condemned "the vagabonds" who had stormed the embassies in July. They urged students to respect the law and work together towards what Alia called "the democratization of the life of the country."

The students rejected the vague appeal. Many of them came from other cities, including Shkoder and Kavaja. They had seen the first protests in those cities and brought that energy to Tirana. They had watched the revolutions in Hungary, Czechoslovakia, and Romania, and had hoped Alia would follow through on his promises of change. Instead, every move was mixed. The government issued passports, but soldiers shot those attempting to flee. Taboo topics appeared in the media, but Alia slandered those who wanted to leave.

In mid-October, some students refused to eat the deplorable food at the cafeteria. Two days later, someone posted a handwritten appeal: "The food is bad! Do you agree?" It was a minor protest for most universities, but a significant step in a place so closed and afraid. In November some of the faculties wrote letters to Alia and the government, asking for reform. The communist youth organization from the mechanical engineering faculty requested a meeting with Prime Minister Adil Çarçani and complained about physical conditions at the university. "You can't make a new coat with old cloth," the letter said.

"The idea was not to go against but to be different," one of the letter's co-authors, Pandeli Majko, explained to me in 2005 from his office as minister of defense.

As winter neared, the students' anger grew. The university and Student City had broken windows, no heat, sporadic water, and electricity cuts, made worse that year by a drought. When the lights went out at night, voices sprang from the dormitories: "Freedom!" "We want democracy!" Students banged on the heating pipes. Music students answered with a chorus of horns.

* * *

On December 8, around midday, Prime Minister Çarçani, together with the ministers of education and construction, came to Student City unannounced while the students sat in class, allegedly to inspect the renovated buildings. "We had to be careful that conditions were not a reason for revolt," then minister of education Skënder Gjinushi said. About four hundred students gathered in a hall to meet the prime minister. They spoke respectfully to Çarçani but asked for better conditions. When the three officials left, they understood that, in Gjinushi's words, "something was burning."

That night around 8:00 p.m., the lights went out—again. A small group of mostly engineering students gathered at the transformer in Student City to protest. They chanted and sang an old patriotic song, "Eja mblidhuni këtu, këtu . . ."—"Come and gather here, here . . ."

Years later, it remains unclear why the lights went out. Some former students say they died from excessive demand, as happened many nights. Others say students threw a cable or metal coil into the transformer, eager to blow the lights and draw a crowd. Maybe foreign governments encouraged some students to sabotage the lights and start a revolt, as they had pushed people to enter the embassies five months before. Yet others believe the Albanian government had a hand, sending agents to provoke a crowd that it could then control.

A reconstruction of events suggests that all these theories have their place. Without doubt, the students were ready to move; some of them were demanding political change. It is also likely that Western governments encouraged the students to revolt. While none of the former student leaders I interviewed gave details, and they all denied having contact themselves, many admitted that various secret services were active in Albania during those days. In addition, the Albanian government may have placed trusted students among the group to help steer events. And many of these plots melted and merged over time. Power corrupted honest students. Government plants turned against their masters. People aligned and realigned themselves in a chaotic and fast-changing scene.

Regardless of the blackout's cause, about one hundred chanting students drifted towards the open space in the center of Student City. Other dormitories had lights, and the group called on supporters to extinguish them in solidarity. "Every light out was a great joy," said one of the student leaders, Arben Lika, as he walked me down the route taken that night, recalling the event with pride.

The students walked past Building 14 and there, standing on a low concrete bench, was a husky young man with wavy brown hair and a shiny black leather jacket, asking for the crowd's attention. He supported the students' protest and exhorted them to march. "I have two children," the man yelled. "But I swear I am with you!"

The man was Azem Hajdari, a twenty-seven-year-old philosophy student from Tropoja in the far north, who would soon become the most powerful student leader and eventually the head of Albania's first opposition party. A courageous hero to his fans, a thuggish spy to his detractors, he played an important and controversial role in Albanian politics until his murder in 1998.

Gaining momentum, Hajdari and the protesters continued downhill. They veered towards the women's dormitories, where they called to friends and girlfriends, urging them to join. Some came outside and joined the crowd.

At the same time, Central Committee member Piro Kondi telephoned Minister of Education Gjinushi. "There's chaos up there," Kondi said. Gjinushi called the university rector, and the two men drove to Student City, arriving as the students were heading into town. They saw Kondi addressing the students with a megaphone, telling them to go back uphill. "The students did not like the lights," Gjinushi recalled. "They feared the Sigurimi was filming."

On Budi Street below Student City, a cordon of police lay in wait, commanded personally by Interior Minister Hekuran Isai. The minister ordered the protesters to turn around but the students demanded to see

Ramiz Alia. Isai left to consult and returned with surprising news. "Get fifteen people and go to the university," he said. Alia was ready to talk. The students suspected a trap, but they chose a delegation and walked to the university's main building. "If we don't come back then we've been arrested," Hajdari said before heading off.

Tirana party chief Xhelil Gjoni, a stern man with a reputation for strict views, entered the lecture hall first and sat up front to the right. "So boys, what do you want?" he asked. The students refused to speak until Alia arrived. He soon did, walking straight to the podium. "You're young, good-looking boys," he said with a tired smile. "Why do you wake an old man like me?" He asked their names, home towns, and areas of study.

The students complained that the prime minister had fooled them by coming to Student City while they sat in class. They protested about conditions in Student City: the blackouts and terrible food. They faltered and got confused, but who would not when facing two of Albania's most powerful men in the middle of the night?

When I interviewed Alia, he remembered the night well.

"They told me they had economic concerns," he said. "I asked them, or better said, I told them: 'Listen, the problem you have, why do you have the [communist] youth organization? Discuss it with them.' A few of them said, 'We don't trust that organization. We want to create our own independent organization.' After my intervention, they presented this issue. It was clear that it was a political rather than economic problem."

Alia agreed that he would meet the students again to discuss their complaints, but only if they calmed the crowd in Student City and returned to class. He promised they would not be harmed.

The delegation returned to Budi Street after 1:00 a.m. to relay the news. As they were talking, a police officer suddenly screamed.

"Pistol! They took my pistol!" he yelled.

Before the students could react, the police attacked with batons. They threw three students into a van and badly wounded one girl. Rumor quickly spread that she had died.

"It was terrible," the former student leader Arben Lika recalled twelve years later, as he stood on the spot of the beating, next to a restaurant called Made in Italy. "[Minister of the Interior] Isai was there. He said, 'Beat the hell out of them.'"

Hekeran Isai declined to be interviewed for this book but Alia remembered the incident.

"After the meeting with me, I went home and I didn't know what happened," he said. "The next day, I learned there had been an incident between the students and the police. Allegedly it was a banal incident—an officer said the students had grabbed his gun and the police attacked to get it back, and they beat three or four students with batons. That is what they told me."

Alia's senior advisor Sofokli Lazri was equally dismissive but more honest about the government's intent. "It was just a light message," he told me with a wave of the hand.

* * *

It rained the morning of December 9, a makeup day of class, and students from Tirana came to Student City cold and wet. They saw students' muddy pants and shoes hanging from the balconies, some stained with blood from the previous night. No one had died and the three arrested students were released, but the police showed they would use force. For the students, the violence galvanized the cause. Change would not come from above, they realized. Alia could not be trusted.

A group of twenty students met on the first floor of the cafeteria and formed an organizing committee. They agreed to stage a protest in a public space to catch the attention of Tirana. At 9:00 a.m., two of them met the head of the communist youth organization, Lisen Bashkurti, on Bashkurti's request. He said the students had left Alia without sleep. He proposed they form a group, named as they wish, to become part of the communist youth. The students refused.

By 10:00 a.m., thousands of students had gathered at Student City's central space. The organizing committee announced a demonstration in front of the main university offices. The eager crowd marched, armed with hormones and high hopes.

The riot police blocked most of the roads from Student City and funneled the crowd down the larger Elbasan Street. A few blocks away, in front of the High School for Arts and next to the Museum of Marxism-Leninism, the riot police closed the road with shields and batons. A few thousand students pushed up against the police. Bashkurti tried to speak with the students from behind police lines. The Sigurimi filmed from the nearby roofs. The chants grew louder: "We want Albania like all Europe!" "All Tirana is with us!"

By 2:00 p.m., the cold, rain, and fear had whittled the crowd to a few hundred. But the Sunday soccer match in the nearby stadium started at 2:30 p.m. The Ministry of Defense's team, Partizani, was playing Dinamo from the Ministry of Internal Affairs. Fearful of the dangerous cocktail of students and football fans, the government decided the protest should end. The students in the front row heard the order on the police radio: "Disperse them with force!" The students bolted through a field next to the Italian embassy, muddy from the day's rain. They sprinted and jumped into apartment buildings, hidden by sympathetic residents. School books and shoes littered the sloppy field.

For the first time, the government acknowledged that the police had clashed with protesters. A brief report by the state news agency said that some students, angry over a power failure in Student City, had "tried to make use of this dissatisfaction for political goals." Under these circumstances, the report said, "the forces of order were compelled to intervene in order to disperse them."[1]

That evening rumors and confusion reigned: Alia is cracking down, the student Azem Hajdari has been killed, Alia is changing his mind, Hajdari is alive. At the same time, divisions began to emerge among the students. Some wanted to push for political pluralism, taking their protest to the Tirana streets. Others feared a confrontation and wanted to focus on economic complaints within the comfort of Student City.

* * *

As the students regrouped in Student City, two middle-aged men from Tropoja decided to pay them a visit. One of them was a writer, Besnik Mustafaj. The other was a well-known cardiologist named Sali Berisha, who had written critical articles over the past year and spoken at the intellectuals' meeting with Alia that summer. Berisha had just returned from a World Health Organization meeting in Italy and, with Mustafaj, had watched the police disperse the students with force.

The students were upset, Berisha and Mustafaj recalled. They worried about their friends who had been beaten and detained, and they asked the doctor and writer for help. According to Berisha and Mustafaj, the two men offered to visit the Tirana party headquarters on the students' behalf.[2]

The influential Tirana party head Xhelil Gjoni was in the building at the time. When he heard the two men had come, he summoned them to his office, both Mustafaj and Gjoni told me. He then called Ramiz Alia to say he was sitting with the writer and doctor. "Let me speak with Sali," Alia replied. After a brief conversation, Alia asked Berisha to visit him at once. Gjoni's car took Berisha and Mustafaj to Alia's residence in the forbidden Block, and Berisha met Alia alone for about fifteen minutes while Mustafaj waited outside.

"One night before, when I was with the students, I asked where they were from," Alia recalled for me twelve years later. "Two or three of them said from Tropoja—Azem and the others whose names I don't remember. I thought, because Sali is from Tropoja, it would be reasonable for this guy to transmit to the students a couple of words."

Alia presented his version of the conversation that night. "I told him that, when I had met the students the night before, we agreed that they would go to class and that I would come at 5:00 p.m.," Alia said. "I did not go, but the students are to blame because they did not keep their word." Alia said he told Berisha that he was willing to meet the students, but only if they returned to class. "Tell them this in my name," he said. "And when you're done, come back."

Berisha refused to be interviewed for this book but he has spoken briefly about the meeting in interviews. He said he challenged Alia about beating the students but agreed to deliver his message.[3] "Ramiz wanted to convince the students that they should go meet him," Berisha said.[4]

From Alia's perspective, Berisha was a trusted messenger. He had been head of the party for Tirana Hospital and was trusted enough to let study in France and attend a workshop in Italy. An ambitious and accomplished cardiologist, he had cared for a senior Politburo member, Hysni Kapo, and came close to joining Enver Hoxha's medical team. At the same time, Berisha was known for his critical views expressed in interviews and articles, in which he had praised Alia but called for reform. He was the middle man Alia could use.

The students were debating their options when Berisha and Mustafaj returned. After being blocked and beaten that morning, some of them wanted to storm Skanderbeg Square. Berisha and Mustafaj argued against leaving Student City because it might provoke a confrontation. With violence, they said, Alia could reassert control.

Mustafaj introduced Berisha to the student Azem Hajdari, who had exhorted students from the concrete bench in Student City the night before, and whom Mustafaj knew from their common Tropoja home. It was the first time Berisha and Hajdari met. They would play a complicated game with one another for the next eight years. The three men retreated to the cafeteria basement for a quiet talk in an alcove, Mustafaj recalled, where Berisha asked Hajdari about the students' demands. We want better living conditions, Hajdari replied. "You don't start this by putting sugar in your tea," Berisha replied. "You should demand pluralism." The students should not leave Student City, Berisha urged, but put political pluralism atop the list.

Berisha remembered the meeting too. "I went with Besnik to a nearby café where I met Azem for the first time," he told an Albanian interviewer. "I was very glad. I told Azem to tell me the list of demands. I said put it aside, one is fundamental and essential: pluralism."[5]

Why Berisha told Hajdari to demand pluralism remains a matter of debate. Berisha supporters present the doctor as a democrat who craved to topple the regime. Critics claim Berisha was serving Alia, who wanted the students to push for change that the party could control. The most likely scenario is that Berisha played both cards. As the skilled politician he would soon become, he stayed close to each side.

When the three men rejoined the students, they found them agitated and confused. A few hundred people had slipped out of Student City to protest in Skanderbeg Square. Hajdari tried to convince those remaining that it was better to stay. The crowd booed and called him a traitor, while Berisha and Mustafaj watched from a corner in shock.

"You betrayed us!" someone yelled at Hajdari, pointing at Berisha and Mustafaj. "Those two were sent by Ramiz Alia to deceive us."[6]

"We will all die together and we will not permit anyone to trick us," Hajdari asserted. "I will be the first to die."[7]

Gradually Hajdari calmed the crowd. "This was one of the most delicate moments when everything was at risk of being destroyed," Mustafaj later wrote.[8]

According to Alia, Berisha returned to him after midnight. "You cannot understand those people," Alia claimed Berisha said. "I did not get anywhere with them. If one said one thing, another said something else.

If you agreed with one, another disagreed. I told them what you said, but they said they have no trust."

Berisha maintained that he did not see Alia again that night. "Here he's lying," Berisha said. "Because I stayed very late with the students and afterwards I went straight home."[9]

* * *

The next day, December 10, more students filled Student City's open space, which would soon be called Democracy Square. Professors and professionals joined the crowd. Factory workers who earned five hundred leks per month—about sixty U.S. dollars—threatened to strike. Someone brought a sound system and the square resounded with music and chants. The students named an organizing committee with many of the people who had been active the previous two days: Azem Hajdari and Arben Lika, as well as Tefalin Malshyti, Mimoza Ferraj, and Shinasi Rama, who had slipped out of Student City the previous night with a small group to protest in Skanderbeg Square. With the exception of Ferraj, the only woman, all of the committee members came from the north. In part this reflected the southern leanings of the Party of Labor; Enver Hoxha had largely drawn political elites from his native south. It also revealed the personalities of those involved. The brave and hard-headed highlanders from the north demanded to speak their minds.

The students prepared a list of nine demands for Ramiz Alia, including political pluralism, punishment for the police who had beaten students, and a meeting with Alia. "We are supporters of the democratic reforms undertaken by President Ramiz Alia, and we are for their acceleration," point number one began, revealing the cautious approach. "This was and is the goal of our peaceful demonstration."[10]

That afternoon, Alia sent two officials to negotiate with the organizing committee: Minister of Education Gjinushi, the wily politician with thick, dark eyebrows, and Lisen Bashkurti, head of the communist youth. With them came Sali Berisha. Three other men from northern Albania took part in the discussions in the director's office at Student City: Berisha's friend Besnik Mustafaj, editor of the communist youth newspaper Remzi Lani, and a writer named Preç Zogaj.

The meeting was chaotic and tense, six of the participants separately recalled, as the crowd chanted outside. The students demanded that Alia come to Student City for negotiations. Gjinushi insisted that Alia could not negotiate while students were on the street—any discussion had to be with a small group in a quiet place. Berisha and others suggested the students form a delegation to meet Alia. The students agreed but with a symbolic condition: the delegation must meet Alia as president of the republic and not as first secretary of the Party of Labor. Gjinushi found that acceptable but said the students must return to class before the meeting. The students refused, fearing they would lose momentum and legitimacy if the protest stopped.

Gjinushi left to confer with Alia, believing his boss would refuse to meet while the protest continued. To his surprise, Alia agreed. The meeting was set for the next evening at the presidential palace, called the Palace of the Brigades.

* * *

December 11 marked day four of the Student City revolt. Students, professors, and workers took the microphone to demand political pluralism, economic reform, "Freedom and Democracy!" Students from other universities and citizens of Tirana came in solidarity. The state media barely mentioned the news. *Zëri i Popullit* ran a three-paragraph story on the bottom of the front page that said the situation in Student City was "irregular" and the students had requested a meeting with President Alia.

Throughout the morning, university faculties conducted Albania's first free election in more than fifty years. With secret votes they chose delegates from each faculty to meet Alia, mostly students but some young professors too. While the crowd chanted in Student City, forty-five elected representatives assembled in the television room of Building 15. The delegation was too big so fifteen people volunteered to resign.

At the same time, unbeknownst to the students, Ramiz Alia had convened a meeting of the Central Committee. There he presented three options to address the crisis and made his preference clear. First was to continue dialogue with the students. Second was to use force. "Naturally this can also be done, but actions cause reactions," Alia said. "We could disperse them today by force and tomorrow there'd be twice as many as we had dispersed."[11] Third was to close the university, but this would not

STUDENT CITY | 61

stop the protests, he said. Then Alia posed the central question of the moment: "Should we accept their demand for the creation of organizations, which without doubt is a direct step to the pluralism of parties?"

A few hardline members of the Central Committee opposed the idea. But with a show of hands, the party leadership voted to allow independent political organizations, effectively ending the Party of Labor's five-decade grip on power. Of the more than hundred members of the committee, two voted against.[12] Hoxha's widow, Nexhmije, voted in favor.

"If we had not done it, there would have been blood up to the Central Committee," then Central Committee member Dritëro Agolli told me.

The crafty Alia was snatching victory from the students. They had started the protest, but he would take credit for allowing reform; he would dictate the pace of change. As Gjinushi later explained: "Once the Central Committee had decided, the [students'] meeting with Alia was in vain."

* * *

The government sent a white bus with red stripes to Student City around 5:50 p.m. The students feared arrest so the government officials Gjinushi and Bashkurti climbed aboard as a guarantee. "When we saw them smiling we knew everything was okay," one student said. Word had already spread about the Central Committee's momentous decision, but the details were unclear.

Students surrounded the bus, slapping its sides. From inside, one saw faces full of hope pressed against the glass. The crowd in Student City had swelled to eighty thousand people. It was rainy and muddy but no one cared.

At the Palace of the Brigades the delegation entered an elegant room with a red oriental carpet, white curtains, and beige velvet drapes. Three rows of chairs were arranged at a slight curve across from a low wooden table with a glass top and two microphones. The students and professors sat and Alia arrived a few minutes later, escorted by Gjinushi and Bashkurti. The *Zëri i Rinisë* editor Remzi Lani took a seat in the back. The students stood and applauded as Alia shook hands with those in the front. He then sat at the low table with Gjinushi on his left and Bashkurti on his right. Two television cameras, one static and one roaming, recorded the event.

Party head Ramiz Alia, flanked by Lisen Bashkurti (L) and Skënder Gjinushi (R), tells students and young professors on December 11, 1990, that pluralism has been legalized. © ATA

"Shall I talk a little, and after that you can speak," Alia said calmly, according to the recording.

Reading from handwritten notes on small pieces of paper, he presented that day's decision by the Central Committee. The committee had reached a number of decisions about the next party congress, the party platform, and some dismissals from the Politburo, he said. It had also recommended that the Council of Ministers change the government. Then came the real news.

"The plenum expressed its opinion that it is for the good of the further democratization of life in the country and pluralism to have the creation of independent political organizations in accordance with the laws in effect," Alia said.

The students and professors applauded cautiously, not knowing what to make of the radical news. Alia then explained for fifteen minutes in a gentle but determined tone.

"Everything should be solved with calm and understanding," he intoned. "The road to democracy is not a boulevard. . . . It demands respect for friends and respect for the law. Otherwise it opens the possibility for anarchy, which is dangerous for everyone."

The cunning Alia had played it well. Sensing the irreversible pressure from Student City, he had preempted the students. At the same time, his message was mixed. He had allowed the creation of "independent political organizations in accordance with the laws," but had not specified what kinds of organizations were permitted and under what laws. According to the constitution, the Party of Labor was the "sole leading political force of the state and society."

The delegation had difficulty articulating its views. Two of the students present went on to become prime ministers but on that day they and the others displayed understandable confusion and restraint. Mostly addressing Alia as "Comrade Ramiz" instead of "President Alia," they asked for clarification of the committee's decision.

"What about our party of youth?" the drama professor Arben Imami asked.

"It is not forbidden," Alia said. "No law forbids parties."

"Can we form a party?" the student Shinasi Rama pursued in a scratchy voice, broken from shouts in the square.

"Yes, with this law it's finished," Alia answered. "Send your program to the Ministry of Justice."

"What shall we say to the thousands of people waiting for us in Student City?" an incredulous student inquired. "Do you call this pluralism or not? Is it true or not?"

"The decision of the Central Committee for this case will be applied." Alia said. "The constitution and laws do not forbid the application of what we have said here. We even allow the pluralism of parties."

"Can we call it a party?" an engineering professor asked.

"Yes, call it what you want," Alia said. "But respect the law and do not act against the interest of the people."

The students broke into applause.

* * *

Back at Student City, the crowd continued to swell. The students from the Alia meeting were engulfed by a swarm of faces and hands. An Albanian flag without the communist star fluttered over the crowd. The delegation played an audio recording of the meeting over the sound system. Some in the crowd complained that the delegation had been too soft.

The next day, *Zëri i Popullit* announced the news on its front page, with a photo of Alia meeting the students. The lead article reported the Central Committee's historic decision to allow "independent political organizations in conformity with the laws." The article below said the students had requested the "development of political pluralism and the formation of a party of students and young intellectuals."[13] The large subheads made Alia's views, and fears, abundantly clear:

"The Road to Democracy Is Not a Boulevard"

"Order, Tolerance and Culture Are Needed"

"If You Don't Respect This, It Opens the Door for Anarchy"

5

A Democratic Party

Student City rejoiced. The last communist party of Eastern Europe had succumbed. Students, professors, and workers hugged, sang, and cheered. They also began to plan. The students wanted to form a party of students and young intellectuals, as they had told Alia, but some professors and Tirana intellectuals proposed an organization with broader scope. While jubilant crowds cheered in Student City, a small group discussed what they called a "real party"—a party that went beyond the confines of student life.

The people involved gave different versions of the discussions and debates, but all agreed that approximately twenty people made their way to Student City's Building 18, where they packed a small room and spilled into the hall. The first task was to find a name. Someone proposed "Democratic League," but this was similar to another party in the region, the Democratic League of Kosovo. Another person suggested "Democratic Front," but the word "front" reeked of communism. "Democratic Union" sounded odd in Albanian and "Democratic Movement" was rejected because they wanted to form a party.

"Partia Demokrate" (Party of Democrats), someone proposed. This was how Albanians called the Democratic Party in the United States, others complained. The government would accuse them of being U.S. puppets. "Then Partia Demokratike" (Democratic Party), someone threw forth. It sounded like the communist's Democratic Front ("Fronti Demokratike"), but some argued that mirroring an existing organization would be more palatable to the conservative public. The Democratic Party of Albania was born.

Down the hill from Student City, a thirty-five-year-old economics professor named Gramoz Pashko lived in a large house with a rare desktop computer. His father had served for a while as chief prosecutor under Hoxha, but most students and professors respected Pashko for his education and moderate views, even if he was a Party of Labor member.

Pashko started drafting a party statute that night and invited others to come the following day.

At 7:30 the next morning, the student Azem Hajdari and drama professor Arben Imami left Student City, stopped for a breakfast of kebabs, and arrived at Pashko's home. Other men soon arrived, many of them meeting for the first time. Pashko's brother-in-law Genc Ruli came, as did the philosophy professor Eduard Selami, the drama professor Edmond Budina, and Dr. Sali Berisha. An acquaintance of Pashko's unknown to the others also joined, the mild-mannered archeologist Aleksandër Meksi, who would become Albania's first post-communist prime minister. Around 10:30, Pashko called Reuters in Vienna to announce that a group of students, intellectuals, and workers would present Albania's first opposition party later that day.

"I'm very happy that we are able to show to the world that we are able to move to a democratic system without violence," Pashko told the journalist. He praised Ramiz Alia's decision to allow plurlalism as a victory over party conservatives. "We are for Alia," he said.[1]

Working in Pashko's office and living room, the men drafted eleven points that stressed political pluralism, human rights, rule of law, free market reform, and the territorial integrity of Albania. A sympathetic official from the Foreign Ministry provided language on human rights. To present the party at Student City, the group agreed that Hajdari would go first, reading an introduction that acknowledged Alia. Imami, the thirty-two-year-old drama professor, would follow with the eleven points of the basic program. The introduction was prepared on a typewriter from Pashko's neighbor, the program scribbled by hand.

The police surrounded Student City and the still-unborn opposition feared losing the only copy of its program. Hajdari, Imami, and Aleksandër Meksi took a back route behind the dorms to avoid the police. When they arrived, a massive crowd was cheering and pushing for better views. The three men squeezed their way to a makeshift stage and Hajdari prepared to speak. Before he could begin, Sali Berisha approached and asked to address the crowd, Imami recalled. Imami and Hajdari agreed that Berisha could speak after the introduction.

Hajdari took the microphone and, to great applause, announced the formation of the Democratic Party. According to audio and video recordings of the event, he spoke these words with a cherry-red face:

"Long Live Democratic Albania"—the Democratic Party announcement in Student
City on December 12, 1990. © Gani Xhengo. Fourth from left (light suit): Azem
Hajdari. Sixth from left (trench coat): Eduard Selami. Seventh from left: Sali Berisha.
Eleventh from left (brown suit): Shinasi Rama. Twelfth from left (trench coat):
Aleksandër Meksi. Thirteenth from left: Arben Imami. Two women, not visible, were
among the group: Mimoza Zaloshnja and Mimoza Ferraj.

> To contribute concretely to the deepening of democracy in Albania and
> to realize the dreams and desires of the students, the intellectuals, the em-
> ployees of scientific organizations, the centers of productive work in the
> cities and villages, in continuity with the democratic reforms undertaken
> by President of the Presidium of the National Assembly, Comrade Ramiz
> Alia, we seek the creation of the Democratic Party, as an independent
> political organization!

The crowd responded with a loud cheer and chants of "*Liri,
Demokraci!*"—"Freedom, Democracy!"

As agreed, Imami gave the microphone to Berisha. According to
the two recordings of the rally, Berisha called for further reform and
political pluralism, as well as the rights of Albanians in Kosovo. Although he would later condemn the communist government in the

Sali Berisha at the Democratic Party announcement in Student City on December 12, 1990, with Azem Hajdari (L) and Gramoz Pashko (R). © Gani Xhengo

harshest terms and throw Ramiz Alia in jail, he praised the party head.

"Amidst all this, our great gratitude definitely goes first of all to the president, Comrade Ramiz Alia," Berisha said. "Who with great wisdom, with wisdom and courage, the courage with which he led the great units of our army in the liberation battle, he led our country in the new battle for the democratization of Albania."[2]

The crowd whistled loudly, the Albanian equivalent of boos.

"As a friend, as a friend, as I wish and hope to remain of the Democratic Party, I want to wish you always more and more success in your work for the prosperity of Albania, the prosperity of Albania, and for the good of our nation," Berisha said.

Arben Imami took the microphone to read the party's program, also endorsing Alia. "We call on you to support the politics of the head of the people's assembly for democracy and pluralism in Albania," he implored.

Not surprisingly, Alia responded well. He was relieved that trusted individuals, many of them still party members, had taken the lead. The next day, *Zëri i Popullit* reported on the party founding in positive terms.

"The people present cheered for democracy, for Comrade Ramiz Alia, and for political dialogue," the paper said.[3]

* * *

Right away the Democratic Party faced a test. In Shkoder, Kavaja, Durres, and Elbasan angry young men clashed with police. In Shkoder, protesters demolished the sign for Enver Hoxha Street. They broke into a bookstore and burned Hoxha's books. An explosion failed to destroy Hoxha's bust, but a crowd pulled it down as the police watched.

The state television and newspapers reported on the "hooliganism" and "vandalistic acts." *Zëri i Popullit* ran photos of destroyed buildings in Durres with the caption: "Earthquake? No. Destruction of the Dark Forces."

The Democratic Party (DP) condemned the vandalism. A statement referred to Alia and said that "democracy can never be achieved by infringing on the rules."[4] *Zëri i Popullit* published the DP statement on its front page.

Some DP members disliked the conciliatory approach, even if they disagreed with violence. The student leaders in particular rejected the party's deferential attitude. While violence should not be encouraged, they said, the communists must be confronted.

The key party founders, such as Gramoz Pashko, Sali Berisha, and Aleksandër Meksi, considered it irresponsible and dangerous to challenge Alia directly. The Party of Labor had deep roots, especially in rural areas, and rapid change could provoke loyal supporters to react. Alia needed help against the party's conservative wing, they said. The DP leaders were also nervous about being labeled troublemakers and saboteurs, which they feared Alia could use to undermine the party.

The different views did not split the group because party members wanted to maintain a common front. But the debate over radical action versus conciliation grew sharper by the day.

* * *

The DP based itself in two rooms on the first floor of Building 15 in Student City. The friends Arben Imami and Azem Hajdari slept in the office for two weeks. Students and founding members fanned out across Tirana to recruit relatives, colleagues, and friends for the three hundred signatures required by law to register a party. Aleksandër Meksi signed first, followed by Berisha, Hajdari, and Gramoz Pashko. The outspoken student Shinasi Rama was supposed to sign fourth. Symbolically, he put his name in the thirteenth spot, sensing he had no place in the group. Three weeks later, Rama became the first person to leave the DP, arguing that it had betrayed the movement's ideals.

Twelve years later, from his apartment in New York, the heavier but still outspoken Rama argued that Pashko and Berisha had done Alia's dirty work by setting up a controllable opposition force. He later wrote about Alia's "master plan," by which the president incited the students "to rise and plead to Alia for some kind of pluralism," followed by legalization of an opposition with loyalists in top slots. "The easy transformation would transmutate the Communists into capitalists but the power would stay in the family and in the caste," he wrote.[5]

Ramiz Alia and other ex-officials deny having had a master plan. The situation was too chaotic and unpredictable, they said. "Our old strategies had run their course, and for new steps there was no model," said Sofokli Lazri, Alia's influential advisor. At the same time, Lazri, who died in 2002, told me that Alia and the party leadership attempted what he called a "transfer of influence," which, he explained with a smirk, was the use of one's power to support another.

While it remains unclear how much Alia implemented a "transfer of influence" through a coordinated scheme, and a master plan in those hectic days seems unlikely, he was clearly relieved that known entitites had taken charge of the opposition, and that they were not the traditional anti-communist forces he feared, the nationalists or monarchists, nor wild protesters from the street. On the contrary, the DP was led by intellectuals with ties to the regime. They could be trusted.

* * *

Getting three hundred signatures to register the DP proved difficult. Eighty thousand people had cheered the party's formation, but few were willing to put their name on paper. The process took four days, and required the signatures of 103 students. Even more difficult was choosing the party's leadership. In an open, improvised vote on December 13 at the cinema in Student City, the group established a "Founding

Commission" with twenty-two members, including seven students and one woman.

The first meeting of the Founding Commission took place just after the vote. Arben Imami, Azem Hajdari, and Sali Berisha sat up front, and the twenty-nine-year-old philosophy professor Eduard Selami served as secretary, the position he would hold for the next four years. The commission formed committees to organize in the districts, elaborate the political platform, and coordinate media relations, foreign contacts, and finance. Azem Hajdari was unanimously chosen provisional chair.

Aleksandër Meksi and Genc Ruli took charge of completing the party statute, and they used the Party of Labor statute as a guide. "Where they said yes, we said no," Ruli recalled. A person in Switzerland faxed the statute of the Kosovo Green Party as an example, but only half the fax came through.

On December 15, Gramoz Pashko, Azem Hajdari, and Genc Ruli submitted the party statute and three hundred signatures to the minister of justice. Two days later, the DP held its first press conference. One hundred journalists and spectators, including a few members of the foreign press, sat on chairs in neat rows as Preç Zogaj, a member of the media committee, and party spokesman Genc Pollo, a young historian who spoke English, German, and Italian, addressed the crowd. As they spoke, a journalist from the state radio and television burst into the room and handed Zogaj a note.

"Stop, there is important news . . . the Democratic Party is legalized!" Zogaj said with delight.

The crowd burst into applause and then cheers of "Freedom, Democracy!" DP activists hugged each other in joy, and a number of them cried. It was the closest they would ever be, and it did not last long.

* * *

Alia moved quickly and set parliamentary elections for February 10, 1991, denying DP requests to postpone the date. The opposition lacked experience and funds, and it scrambled to mount a campaign. Tirana and other cities supported the DP, but the rural population feared land reform and the still active secret police. The charismatic leaders, such as Pashko, Berisha, Imami, and Hajdari, traveled the country to spread the word and break the fear.

On December 23, the DP held its first major rally as a legal party. Tens of thousands of people packed Student City's Democracy Square. The party founders stood on a low stage in front of a large sign that read "Long Live Democracy," most of them wearing white trench coats, the trendy uniform of the new political class. Aleksandër Meksi read a telegram from the largest Albanian party in Kosovo, the Democratic League of Kosovo (LDK), signaling a relationship between the two parties that played a role in the politics to come. Two weeks later, the DP published the country's first opposition newspaper, *Rilindja Demokratike* (Democratic Rebirth). Tirana's best young journalists, most of them students, worked day and night on coffee and adrenaline from a small office with a table, a chair, and a typewriter. For the first time in almost fifty years Albanians had an alternative to the organs of the communist party and its satellite groups. "You can't imagine our pleasure when seeing the first opposition paper in Albania," said Blendi Fevziu, one of the paper's young journalists, who went on to become a TV personality. The paper sold officially for one lek but dog-eared copies fetched ten times that by day's end.

Consistent with the DP's cautious approach, the newspaper respected Alia and focused its criticism on the bureaucracy. "*Rilindja Demokratike* was careful," the paper's first chief editor, Frrok Çupi, told me. "We did not attack communists, even Hoxha. He was an Albanian god and, if we messed that up, we could have lost everything."

A particularly sensitive issue was the fate of political prisoners—roughly one thousand remained behind bars. As an anti-communist opposition, the DP should have demanded their release, but some party leaders argued that freeing the prisoners would provoke conservative elements in the regime. Their unspoken fear was that neither the government nor the opposition had influence over these long-marginzalized and persecuted people. Some came from respected families with strong anti-communist credentials; they brought a moral credibility that the compromised DP leaders lacked.

In the end, the DP called for the release of all political prisoners and accepted them in the party. But Pashko, Berisha, and others downplayed their plight, avoiding talk of rehabilitation and compensation. *Rilindja Demokratike* rarely published the tragic accounts of arrests, deportations, and executions. On this point, the democrats and communists agreed: neither wanted to face the horrid past.

* * *

As elections neared, the Democratic Party struggled to build its structures. The party was a front of disparate groups, from monarchists to disaffected communists. It included idealists, opportunists, and adventurists. The fight for power lurked behind every meeting and move.

As a compromise between the students and others, the Founding Commission had chosen the rambunctious Azem Hajdari as temporary chairman, but he caused repeated scandals with his erratic behavior. At the same time, the party's two most charismatic leaders, Gramoz Pashko and Sali Berisha, were clashing for control.

The DP leadership understood that the unruly Hajdari had to go, but Founding Commission members feared that the election of Berisha or Pashko would split the party. As an alternative, they proposed the quiet but active archeologist Aleksandër Meksi, a short, balding man with glasses and mustache. At a Founding Commission meeting on February 11, Meksi won a majority of the vote to become the DP head.

Hajdari and Arben Imami stormed out of the meeting, saying they would leave the party. The atmosphere turned sullen, as if the group had betrayed two friends. But Preç Zogaj and Sali Berisha proposed an idea. The Founding Commission did not have a mandate to represent the party because it had been selected unofficially in the early, chaotic days, they said. Instead, the party's first National Convention, a larger and more representative body, should reelect the commission, which would then choose its chair. Meksi accepted the proposal to step down and the other commission members agreed.

The DP held its National Convention on February 13, 1991. Heads of the newly formed branches came to Tirana, about one hundred people, many of them meeting each other for the first time. DP Secretary Eduard Selami opened the meeting, followed by reports from Berisha and Genc Ruli. Hajdari spoke too, attacking those who sought his overthrow and accusing party leaders of staging a coup. The convention nevertheless moved to elect the new Founding Commission, which was renamed a Steering Committee. The Steering Committee then elected its chair.

Selami introduced the candidates and told the delegates to select nineteen people from a list of twenty-seven by checking the names of those they did not want. In the end, the convention reelected most members of the original Founding Commission. Pashko had one vote against and Berisha had two. Hajdari had forty-two votes against and was the last one voted in. Six new people came on board.

The newly elected Steering Committee met the next day at the DP office on Kavaja Street to select its chair. Four men stood for the job: Gramoz Pashko, Sali Berisha, Aleksandër Meksi, and Azem Hajdari. The Steering Committee voted on small ballots with the four names written by hand and slid them across the table one by one. The results were: Berisha 9, Meksi 5, Pashko 4, Hajdari 1.

Berisha had the most votes but lacked an absolute majority. Some said a run-off was needed, but most committee members, including those who would soon become Berisha's fiercest critics, argued against a second round. The chairman is temporary and symbolic, they said. The run-off was avoided and Berisha became chairman of the party, the position he in essence held for the next two decades.

Years later, some DP founders told me they regretted bending the rules. But the time was chaotic, they said, with people running on enthusiasm and good will. They also thought it was crucial to maintain a common front against the Party of Labor. To expose internal fights would have eroded morale. Another reason was inexperience. At that point, they thought, what harm could be done by annulling Meksi's elections or avoiding a second round. Berisha was a highly charismatic leader with clear ideas and foreign language skills. They did not know at the time that his tireless megalomania, what one former medical colleague called a "diabolical energy," would tear the movement apart.

* * *

The DP drifted further from the students, and the younger generation's frustration grew. Student leaders wanted to confront the regime, but the DP was meeting regularly with Ramiz Alia to consult. Former political prisoners also complained. When DP leaders came to Shkoder to set up the local party branch, the Catholic priest and former prisoner Simon Jubani told them bluntly: "We forgive you for being communists, but now get in line."

Pashko and Berisha countered that Albania needed a serious party. Like Alia, they argued that Albania's lack of democratic traditions demanded respect. It was irresponsible and counterproductive to move too fast.

The moderate-radical paradigm did not always explain the behavior of those involved. While two basic camps emerged, the individuals in those camps shifted their positions depending on the circumstances. Perhaps more than anything, the driving factor was not ideology or strategy, but the power struggles within the group. The Democratic Party was not Solidarity in Poland or Charter 77 in Czechoslovakia, which had confronted communism on principle. The party founders were not dissidents who had challanged power at personal expense.

In retrospect, it is predictable that people like Berisha and Pashko rose to the top. These men spoke foreign languages and understood economics and international politics better than the others. They embodied the paradox throughout the former Soviet bloc that those equipped to govern in the new system were those who had benefited from the old.

By February 1991, the students' patience had worn thin. The euphoria of pluralism had dissolved in the Democratic Party's watery approach to the state. Berisha, Pashko, and the others were too complacent, some students said, and it was time to push.

On February 5, the electricity died at the Institute of Agriculture on the edge of Tirana, and a group of students demanded that the dean resign. The dean refused and the students declared a strike until living conditions improved. When morning broke, the protest grew, with students joining from Enver Hoxha University. By midday, another crowd had gathered in Student City. As speakers took the mike, the list of demands grew: if living conditions for students did not improve, the government must resign.

The next day, the students in Student City formed a committee, which sent a public letter to the prime minister elaborating on the agricultural students' demands.[6] After demanding better heat, paved roads, and a disco in Student City, the students called for "freeing the school from ideology." Then came the most delicate ask: to remove the name Enver Hoxha from the school and call it the University of Tirana. If the government did not meet these demands, the letter said, then it should resign.

The call to remove Hoxha's name was strategic and charged. The students meant to strike at the symbolic heart of the regime. They wanted to convey a message, especially to the rural areas, that communism had died.

The government rejected the students' demands. Ramiz Alia had personally presided over the university's naming ceremony in 1985, dramatically pulling aside a curtain to reveal "Enver Hoxha University" engraved on the wall. Removing the name would insult Albania's past and its citizens, he said. To the students' dismay, the Democratic Party leaders agreed. They feared provoking the regime and its conservative wing. The party had promised Alia that it would participate in the first elections later that month peacefully and with respect for the law. They also thought a strike would take crucial time away from the electoral campaign.

"We thought if we create problems then we'll have trouble for breaking the rules," Gramoz Pashko explained to me in 2001 from his living room where the DP founders had drafted the party platform eleven years before. "Symbolically their actions were good, but it may have diminished our support because it gave the impression that change will come with chaos and anarchy."

In the end, the DP could neither stop nor oppose the students, so it walked a middle line by proposing a referendum to remove Hoxha's name. "The Democratic Party believes that stability cannot be attained by closing our ears, objecting to or denying the request of the students to remove the name of Enver Hoxha from the University of Tirana," a carefully worded statement said. "Fulfillment of the students' request through a referendum of the students and staff of the university does not affect the figure of Enver Hoxha as the leader of the Party of Labor of Albania."[7]

Student City's street theater grew larger by the day. The students used a metal microphone connected to speakers stacked on a wooden table to amplify their calls for pluralism and reform, often interrupted by raucous rounds of "Freedom, Democracy" or, more pointedly, "Down with Enver!" They told jokes and mocked the regime. The art student Blendi Gonxhe played master of ceremonies, sarcastically reading poetic tributes to Enver in front of a hand-painted sign that said "Give Peace a Chance."

Students enjoy speeches at an anti-government demonstration in Student City, February 1991. © Gani Xhengo

"The crowd was like a laundry," Gonxhe recalled ten years later in his Tirana City Hall office, where he was working as deputy mayor. "They came to clean themselves."

Students took the mike to express their frustrations and dreams. "During spring break, the students in Western Europe go skiing in the Alps," a student from Tropoja said, as a friend held the microphone to his lips, according to a video from that day. "But the Albanian students ask for a meeting with the prime minister."

"We have eight political parties and all of them are compromised by the communist party," proclaimed Shinasi Rama, referring to the other parties, such as the Republicans and Social Democrats, which had sprung to life after the DP. "It's a fictitious pluralism."

The newly established Independent Trade Union would declare a general strike if the students' demands went unmet, a representative announced. A spokesman from Enver Hoxha Factory showed a petition with two thousand names calling for their workplace to be renamed the Tractor Factory. The student and DP official Azem Hajdari also came, wearing his fashionable white trench coat. "Dear brothers and sisters,"

Anti-government demonstration in Student City's Democracy Square, February 1991.
© Gani Xhengo

he said, according to the video. "Thank you for allowing us to go around in cars."

Government officials came too, like Minister of Education Gjinushi, who tried to focus the crowd on economic demands but was repeatedly interrupted by shouts: "Remove the name! Remove the name!" He met the strike committee and offered them better physical conditions if they dropped their demand to change the name. But the name change represented the movement's heart.

For eighteen days, both sides refused to budge. The student protest grew larger and the government stressed that the name and work of Enver Hoxha "belongs to the whole people."[8] Reflecting on the students' strike years later, Ramiz Alia said that it worried him a lot. "They were young people who did not know what they were doing," he said. "Their demands would incite conflict." Hoxha was sacrosanct and party bosses in the provinces were already complaining that the party leadership had lost control. Word of a nebulous organization called the "Volunteers of Enver," ready to defend the system, had reached Tirana.

Unfazed, on Friday, February 15, the students took another step. A thick, wet snow fell on Student City, dotting the crowd's black umbrellas with heavy flakes. Blendi Gonxhe announced that the government must remove Hoxha's name by noon on Monday or the students would begin a hunger strike. The government did not bend, so on Monday at 11:30 a.m., hundreds of students lined up outside the cultural center in Student City. Seven hundred and twenty-three people signed their names to the strikers' list, kissed the Albanian flag (without the communist star), and stepped inside the center, among them a handful of professors. Guards turned away many more due to lack of space. They locked the door and one student kept the key with him in the attic, where the organizers had hidden some rusting knives, machetes, and hand guns from World War Two, more for symbolism than practical use.

"Parents, brothers and sisters," a defiant declaration from the students' organizing committee said. "With determination and without pain we tell you that we won't return as before to our family homes. We won't even return in the evening. Maybe you will miss us for days and we are confident that this absence will make you proud."[9]

The first hours were fun. The strikers lounged on the floor, smoked cigarettes, played cards, and danced to ABBA and the Dire Straits. Some wore bandannas on their heads, like kamikaze pilots. On the wall someone wrote in red letters: "Enver = Hitler + Stalin + Al Kapone + Pol Pot." The students shared a sense of purpose and solidarity. Then the police sealed off Student City.

"The first hours were enthusiastic, euphoric you might say," recalled Edvin Shvarc, one of the students in the hunger strike. "But when they sealed it off, there was a grave silence."

* * *

That night the DP Steering Committee met to discuss the crisis. They decided to see President Alia, as they had done a number of times over the past two months, and selected four people for the task: Sali Berisha, Azem Hajdari, Eduard Selami, and Preç Zogaj. Alia agreed to meet right away.

The delegation found the unflappable Alia in a nervous state, Selami and Zogaj separately recalled. He was a control freak and got upset when things slipped out of control. As they entered the president's office, he was speaking loudly on the phone with his back to the door, threatening to declare a state of emergency. "I won't let Albania slide into chaos," he shouted into the phone. The DP members were shocked, thinking Alia was giving orders to the military.

Alia hung up the phone, turned to his visitors, and shook their hands. They sat and noticed that another man was already in the room: Sabri Godo, head of the small Republican Party, which was created after the DP, many think at Alia's behest. Alia turned to Godo and asked whether he had a hand in the student strike.

"No," Godo said.

"And you?" Alia asked the DP reps.

"Yes, we do," Azem Hajdari replied.

Then you should go to the students and deal with them yourselves, Alia said. Otherwise you will be responsible for the consequences. He asked the DP to use its influence with the students to get them out of the strike and to have them drop their demand for a change of the university name. Only parliament could change the name, he insisted. The students and professors should hold a referendum, as the DP had proposed, and parliament would comply.

The DP visitors said a referendum did not meet the students' demands, and that they could not convince the students to stop the strike. At this point, the men were surprised to see Education Minister Gjinushi enter the office through a discreet door in the corner that, they learned after coming to power one year later, leads to the hall and a presidential bathroom. Had Alia's advisor been there all along?

As a compromise, the crafty Gjinushi proposed that the government "reorganize" the university into four parts and, as part of that reorganization, officially change the name. The DP members agreed to present the students with his idea.

Around 2:00 a.m., the DP delegation went to the striking students, who were sleeping, resting on blankets, or playing cards. Their answer to Gjinushi's proposal was an adamant "No!" The government must declare the name Enver Hoxha removed, they demanded. "Don't use the students to make any compromise that will help you win the election," a student said as the DP leaders walked out.[10]

For two days, the students survived on water and cigarettes, though some accepted the food and drink that sympathizers slipped in. "No Tirana parent would let their child go hungry," Gonxhe said. Outside thousands of people gathered to show their support. Workers from Tirana and miners from the mountains gave speeches. People walked more than thirty miles from Kavaja. On the third day, a student in the strike had an epileptic fit and a medical team carried him out on a stretcher, although some former students told me they staged his seizure to mobilize support. Already angry and nervous, the crowd began to chant. An actress named Rajmonda Bulku took the microphone and urged women in the crowd to march. "Let's go in front of the television, mothers and sisters," she said, according to a video of that day. "Let's gather and make a protest march in solidarity with our friends or children, with our brothers and sisters."

Women in the crowd began to move.

"The crowd was terribly tense," Bulku recalled in an interview she gave on the tenth anniversary of the strike. "They were waiting moment to moment for something to happen. . . . The crowd wanted you to say something to move them."[11]

The women marched and the men followed. The trickle turned to a stream and soon an angry river flowed from Student City down Elbasan Street, past the High School of Arts, where the police had blocked the students on December 9. Green police trucks with hoses and water tanks blasted the marchers with water, forcing them past the state radio and television building, behind the Hoxha museum in the pyramid, and onto the boulevard. Riot police and water cannons waited there to defend the sacred Block where the political leadership lived and to divert the crowd down the boulevard to Skanderbeg Square.

The police action was a physical manifestation of Alia's political strategy since 1989. Albanians' desire for change had swelled like a wave, and no wall could withstand that force. Rather than build a useless defense, Alia channeled the flow into areas that could be managed and controlled.

Security forces waited in the square. Thousands of protesters milled about, some throwing rocks, thinking of Tiananmen Square, while looking at the thirty-foot-high bronze statue of Enver Hoxha, taller still atop his granite pedestal, standing like a lightning rod in a storm.

A crowd surged, was repelled by the police, and surged again, gaining confidence as its numbers grew. Proud and determined, Hoxha

Toppling the Enver Hoxha statue in Skanderbeg Square on February 20, 1991. © Gani Xhengo

looked out over the square wearing a suit and long coat, with his left hand behind his back and right hand at his side. The crowd pushed. A boy climbed Hoxha's coat and hooked a metal cable around the dictator's thumb. Men pulled from the left, while others pushed from the right, and the Leader's body began to tilt from side to side. Just after 2:00 p.m., it separated from its base and came crashing down, predictably, to Hoxha's left.

* * *

As riotous crowds stomped on Hoxha's head, the Central Committee held an urgent meeting. Alia's secretary walked into the room and handed the president a note.

"I am informed that the monument of Hoxha has been pulled down," Alia somberly told the committee.

The room fell silent. Someone proposed getting guns, but Alia said that nothing would be solved that way. "Sometimes it is not the mind or brain that is working but emotions," Alia recalled. "This can lead to fatal mistakes."

Hoxha's widow, Nexhmije, began to cry and left the meeting without a word. The Central Committee took a break, and Alia consulted with the interior minister on what to do next.

* * *

Up at Student City, Blendi Gonxhe got a phone call around 2:00 p.m.

"E hoqem qelbësirën!" he shouted—"We got rid of that filth!"

Drunk from victory, the crowd in Skanderbeg Square tied the cable around Hoxha's neck and dragged the hollow statue off with a truck. People rode the body up the boulevard like a bronco until it broke in two. People spit on the pieces, and one man took a piss.

The truck brought the statue's remains to the striking students, where revelers tried to hoist Hoxha's head into the cultural center. A bus dragged body pieces to the DP headquarters on Kavaja Street. Some of the DP leaders slipped away, for fear of being held responsible.

That evening, state television broadcast footage of the toppled monument at 6:00 and 8:00. The government issued a statement that Hoxha's name would be removed from the university as part of the institution's reorganization. The students, some of them hungry but all of them exhausted, filtered home. That night, Alia gave a speech on television saying the university had been divided into four parts, and the name "Enver Hoxha" had been removed.

"Irritated crowds, without any sense of logic, committed acts of vandalism," Alia said, looking somber and reading notes from a brown leather chair. "They succeeded to topple the founder of our state, Enver Hoxha. Now it is perfectly clear that the anti-democratic forces have a well-developed strategy. They want the destruction of Albania."[12]

The government resigned and Alia announced an eight-member Presidential Council. The next day, mobs toppled Hoxha's monuments in Korça and Gjirokaster, the former leader's home town. In the Tirana pyramid, the Enver Hoxha Museum closed.

6

Vote for the Future

Albania's first day without Enver Hoxha had bright sun. Tirana residents strolled outside, gawking at the empty pedestal in Skanderbeg Square. But the monument's fall sent tremors from Shkoder to Gjirokaster. As the students had intended, their actions pierced the regime.

The government warned against anarchy and accused the Democratic Party of inciting the attack. The Central Committee called on citizens to restore order. "No honest and patriotic person should stand by with arms crossed," a statement said. "They should organize on the basis of neighborhood, quarter, street, shift, enterprise or institution in order that, together with the communists, they can face these situations and stop the activity of dark forces."[1]

Around 9:00 a.m., Interior Minister Isai informed Alia that a group of Sigurimi officers was protesting, furious that the party had allowed a mob to topple Albania's guiding light. They demanded that the party head explain. Alia took the protest seriously and went to the Interior Ministry.

"I told them that it could not be done differently, otherwise it would have been a massacre, butchery," Alia told me. "Not only would this have caused damage to human life, but it would have even been a disservice to Enver Hoxha himself. Everyone would say that, even dead as a monument, he caused death."

While Alia addressed the Sigurimi, gunshots echoed in the center of Tirana near the president's office. Rumor quickly spread that hardliners or the Volunteers of Enver had kidnapped or killed Alia. An angry crowd gathered at the bridge over the Lana River on the boulevard between Skanderbeg Square and the president's office. A phalanx of special police backed by the National Guard blocked the way. Two tanks closed the boulevard, and at least five more deployed on other parts of the street. The crowd pushed up against the special police, demanding to

Neritan Ceka, with megaphone, tries to calm a crowd that feared a pro-Hoxha coup on February 21, 1990. © Gani Xhengo

know what had happened. Who is holding Alia? Is he dead? Is Nexhmije staging a coup?

A group of students and Tirana youth tried to calm the crowd. DP activists urged people to disperse. The police commander promised that Alia was alive and well. A guard had fired a warning shot in the air because he thought someone on a motorcycle was trying to enter the block, he said. A white-haired DP leader, archaeologist Neritan Ceka, climbed atop a car to address the crowd. "Nothing has happened. There is no coup!" he assured them with a white-and-green megaphone in hand. "If we continue forward, the police have orders to shoot." The crowd grew quiet but they wanted proof Alia was alive, so the police let two DP activists through their lines to check. Alia's bodyguard escorted them on foot to Alia's office, where they confirmed his good health.

"I was at the Ministry of the Interior at that moment when a big demonstration came to the Lana Bridge," Alia explained about that day. "People had the idea that I had been arrested by the Sigurimi. I was obliged to go to the president's office to await a delegation that was sent to check on me."

The two men returned to the bridge with news of Alia's well-being and the crowd retreated to Skanderbeg Square, where people vented their rage on the giant red slogan atop the Palace of Culture: "Praise to the Albanian Party of Labor." The letters lay on the square like alphabet soup as enraged citizens smashed them with pieces of wood.

* * *

The fall of Hoxha's monument cracked open the prison state. More than five thousand people trekked across the mountains into Greece. In March, rumor spread that the Italians were giving visas. Hordes of desperate dreamers crammed buses, trucks, and horse carts to reach Durres and other coastal towns for a golden pass. The rumor proved false, so thousands of people commandeered boats of all sizes, from skiffs to barges, arms high on masts, legs over the sides. Shovels served as oars. On a tugboat from Vlora, a woman gave birth to a baby girl, which she named Italia. A fishing boat with forty Albanian soldiers docked at Otranto on Italy's heel, where they tossed their weapons overboard and asked for asylum. The Italians formed a blockade but ferries and freighters broke through.

The Albanian government called the exodus a "national dementia" and denied DP claims that it had spread the visa rumor to drain the country of opposition support. After urgent pleas from Italy, Alia deployed soldiers in the ports and restricted access to Durres. By then an estimated twenty thousand Albanians, mostly young men in faded slacks and tattered sweaters, had stormed Italy, especially the southern town of Brindisi. The Italians housed people in schools, hotels, and campgrounds, but many slept on the docks. A lucky few slipped past the police and over fences into town. The Italians moved people to better facilities and gave them until the end of July to find work or get deported, unless they could establish a refugee claim. About six thousand people went back over the coming weeks, realizing that Italy was not as portrayed on television. The Italian government promised Albania $9 million if Tirana blocked the outward flow. As the American ambassador to Italy explained, "The Italians in effect paid the Albanian government to keep their people home."[2]

* * *

Albanians storm boats in Durres after rumors that Italy was giving visas, March 1991.
© Gani Xhengo

The U.S. government struggled to follow the fast-breaking news. The United States had cut its diplomatic relations with Albania forty-four years before and had no CIA presence in Tirana. Analysts had to rely on party speeches, newspaper articles, and Western countries with embassies in the capital. In the 1980s, a State Department desk officer covered both Albania and Bulgaria, and that work hardly filled the day. "So little is known about Albania's younger leaders or about any factions within the Albanian leadership that no predictions about the future direction of Albania's foreign policy can be made with any sense of confidence," a 1983 State Department report had said.[3] Another report from that time complained that "information on the inner workings of the Albanian leadership has always been extremely difficult to obtain."[4]

With information scarce, Washington relied heavily on the head of the Albanian program at the Voice of America, Elez Biberaj, whose family had fled Albania in 1951. Biberaj had earned a doctorate in political science at Columbia University and written three books on Albanian affairs. His visceral hatred of communism and relationship with Sali Berisha impacted U.S. policy in the years to come.

The rest of the Albanian American community, clustered in Boston, New York, and Detroit, also held fierce anti-communist views. The Free Albania Committee, funded by the U.S. government, and the Albanian American Civic League were talking with Washington. By late 1990, their members were traveling to Albania and returning with information and advice.

The key issue for Washington, and the driving policy prerogative over the next ten years, was not Albania as a country but Albanians in the Balkans. Yugoslavia was disintegrating and the U.S. wanted to contain the war. Tumult in Albania, the U.S. feared, could destabilize the mostly ethnic-Albanian regions in Kosovo and Macedonia.

So far the Democratic Party had not calmed Washington's nerves. The Bush administration wanted the last communist regime to fall, but it noted the DP's nationalist rhetoric about Albanians in other lands. The Democratic Party's first program said the party "fights for the realization and century-long aspirations of the Albanian nation for independence, unification and progress in accordance with the spirit of international documents."[5] Sali Berisha was equally strong. "The Democratic Party cannot accept as eternal the division of the Albanian nation," he told a Tirana crowd in January 1991.[6] By no means, the U.S. said, should an Albanian national movement rise in communism's place.

* * *

By late 1990, negotiations on Albania-U.S. diplomatic relations had gained speed. In the U.S., policy makers were of two views: to establish relations with Albania immediately or to wait for parliamentary elections, which had been postponed until March 1991. The first group thought it best to establish relations before the elections, because a diplomatic presence in Albania could monitor and encourage a fair vote. It was not likely the DP would win, the thinking went, so it was better to get in and take a long-term approach. The other group argued that establishing relations before elections would lend credibility to Alia and the Party of Labor. It was better, they said, to keep the leverage of diplomatic ties to encourage reform.

The Albanian side also had different views. Muhamet Kapllani, by then promoted to foreign minister, wanted to reestablish diplomatic relations as soon as possible, but others worried about having the U.S.

in Albania before the elections. Alia agreed to move quickly, and the Albanians decided in January 1991 to resume relations in early March. When the student hunger strike began in February, they requested a delay. Both sides finally agreed to a ceremony at the State Department on March 15, 1991, two weeks before the elections.

At the same time, the U.S. government was getting to know the DP. On February 21, one day after Hoxha's monument fell, a DP delegation had visited Paris and Brussels to meet French, Belgian, and U.S. officials. The sympathetic governments asked the visitors what the DP needed for the electoral campaign. Two weeks later, Arben Imami and Aleksandër Meksi traveled to Bulgaria to meet that country's anti-communist opposition. At the U.S. embassy in Sofia, they spoke with an official named Doug Smith, who later worked at the U.S. embassy in Tirana and in 1993 advised me and my friends to stay calm after our student newspaper was closed. Imami and Meksi presented the DP platform and, in contrast with the DP's conciliatory public statements, called Ramiz Alia "flatly communist" and "incapable" of reform, according to a report Smith sent Washington about the meeting.[7] Imami and Meksi "seemed sincere, intelligent and articulate; however, they also came across as politically naïve," Smith said.

In these meetings, the U.S. and other goverments wanted to know the DP's position on Kosovo and Albanian-Yugoslav relations. The U.S. wanted to help Albania's democratization and it saw the DP as a natural partner, but it rejected changes to borders. Gradually the DP understood that Albania was a small actor on a large stage. The country's struggle was linked to regional concerns.

Albanian foreign minister Muhamet Kapllani arrived in Washington on March 14, 1991, the day before the resumption of diplomatic ties. He was surprised to learn that the State Department had invited two leaders from the Democratic Party to the signing ceremony, Sali Berisha and Gramoz Pashko, who were in the U.S. on a "private visit." The foreign minister scrambled to reach Tirana for consultations—should he attend the ceremony with opposition members present? Because it was already late in Albania, nobody answered at the offices of the prime minister or the president. Unable to consult, he continued as planned.

The State Department's Hall of Treaties had about one hundred guests, many of them emotional Albanian Americans who had dreamed of this day. The protocol office did not have an Albanian flag for the ornate wooden table, so a State Department official had to bring a personal flag someone had given as a gift.

After the ceremony, Kapllani did the rounds. "What will you do if the Democratic Party wins the elections and you are no longer foreign minister?" Kapllani remembered one U.S. official asked. "I will teach English at the University of Tirana," Kapllani replied. His answer was half-correct. After the DP took power in 1992, Kapllani went to the United States and became an English teacher at a technical college in New York City. He retuned in 2003, when the former communist party retook power, as a foreign policy advisor to the president.

The DP leaders Berisha and Pashko also had meetings in Washington. "We are concerned by the Democratic Party's past endorsement of the annexation of Kosovo with Albania," a State Department memo on their trip said.[8] Berisha and Pashko traveled to New York, where they met members of the Albanian American community. The reception was cool. The community mostly sympathized with the monarchists or nationalist Balli Kombëtar. They questioned Berisha's long-term membership in the Party of Labor and they disliked Pashko because his father had served as chief prosecutor and minister under Hoxha. They criticized the DP's tolerance towards the communists, its reluctant relationship with political prisoners, and the policy of "national reconciliation," which they considered soft.

Despite their pedigrees, influential Albanian Americans gave Berisha and Pashko a chance. "We knew the movement had to come from inside," said Idriz Lamaj, who was active in the Free Albania Committee. "This was not 100 percent to our satisfaction but we had no choice."

At the same time, Berisha made a good impression. He was articulate, charismatic, and strong. Like much of the New York community, he came from the north. Over time, he won the community's trust, especially when they saw that the Democratic Party could defeat the communists. Within one year, Albanian Americans gave the doctor their full support.

* * *

Sali Ram Berisha was born in 1944 in the village of Viçidol in the poor and mountainous Tropoja region of northern Albania. In winter, snow sometimes cut Tropoja from the world. In summer, access was via a treacherous road or a rusting ferry, until the U.S. company Bechtel built a four-lane highway in 2010. One friend joked that Tropoja is where "Albanians stick a pin to hang the map."

As a teenager, Berisha won a scholarship to study diplomacy in the Soviet Union, but it was cancelled when Albanian-Soviet relations soured. Instead, at fourteen years old, Berisha left the mountains to study medicine in Tirana. The two hundred-mile journey took twelve hours.[9]

Berisha graduated in 1967 with a specialization in cardiology. He became a doctor at Tirana Hospital and an assistant professor at Enver Hoxha University. He met his wife Liri, a pediatrician, while she was his student, and they started dating after she finished the class.[10] People who studied and worked with Berisha say he was disciplined and hard working. He learned Russian, French, Italian, and English. He spent a lot of time by himself, voraciously reading books. As an outsider in the city, he was driven to succeed.

Berisha joined the Party of Labor in 1968, the year Hoxha banned religion, and for a while served as party head at Tirana Hospital. In 1978 he spent nine months in Paris for advanced studies, a privilege that few enjoyed. In 1989 he became a full professor at the university and was one of Albania's most respected cardiologists.

As a doctor, Berisha treated top officials, most importantly Hysni Kapo, who stood behind only Enver Hoxha and Mehmet Shehu in power and rank. Berisha was slated to join the team treating Shehu before the prime minister died in 1981. The next year, the doctors treating Hoxha expanded their team due to the Leader's deteriorating health. Berisha emerged as a candidate. Hoxha's security chief, Sulo Gradeci, voiced concern about Berisha's trustworthiness because Berisha's mother-in-law was a Serb. Gradeci approved Berisha nevertheless because, he told me, Berisha had served Kapo and was friendly with Hoxha's youngest son, Sokol. Hoxha's wife, Nexhmije, had a different view, doctors on Hoxha's medical team recalled. She refused to trust Berisha because of his wife's family, and she chastised Gradeci for letting him pass.

Berisha has avoided discussion of his past, and he refused multiple requests to be interviewed for this book. When an Albanian journalist asked him in 2004 whether he had served on Hoxha's team, Berisha said no, because Hoxha "chose his own team and he never asked me to visit."[11] Had Hoxha asked, Berisha said, he would have agreed because the Hippocratic Oath obliges doctors to treat everyone in need. A BBC interviewer later asked the same question, and Berisha replied that Hoxha "had his own criteria, and I didn't meet his own criteria."[12] He elaborated a bit in 2010 with the same Albanian journalist. "It had to do with some of his standards in connection to abroad, or with the geographic position of my home in Tropoja," he said.[13]

Berisha's career as a doctor came to an end when the Democratic Party was born. He became a full-time politician, and he brought to that role the same focus and determination. Unlike other DP leaders, mostly intellectuals from Tirana, he did not stop for coffee on the way to work. He always worked late. He did not drink. He had the drive and seriousness that other party leaders lacked. "It was great fun to go to Pashko's house and listen to the Dire Straits and drink whisky—he was so much more like us," said the U.S. diplomat Chris Hill, who helped open the new embassy. "Berisha had a kind of austerity."

From the start, Berisha also projected himself as the man to lead. He made decisions and took control. He exuded authority. And he challenged those who tried to take charge.

Eager for a strong leader, a person to answer the phone, international visitors lavished Berisha with praise. "Berisha exudes confidence and strength," said former U.S. congressman Jack Buechner, head of the International Republican Institute when the DP was born, and later a paid consultant for the Berisha government. "He was one of the most charismatic people I've met." Human rights groups were not immune. The current head of Human Rights Watch met Berisha in 1991 and called him a "sturdy, powerful man with a winning grin."[14]

Like Hoxha, Berisha had a finely tuned political sense. In 1990, with Ramiz Alia peddling gentle reform, the doctor published articles that criticized the system but did not directly challenge the one-party state or Alia's role. As the opposition strengthened, Berisha grew bolder but still declared himself in December 1990 as "a friend of the Democratic Party." He kept his Party of Labor membership until February 1991, after the DP's trajectory was clear. By 1992, he spouted anti-communism with a vicious snarl. As president, he had Alia arrested and used the specter of communism to silence dissent.

Former friends and colleagues of Berisha all commented on his dramatic switch. "He changed with the beginning of the movement," said one fellow doctor, who studied medicine with Berisha. "I was surprised how angry he became. I would expect extremism from those who suffered." Others expressed less surprise, seeing in Berisha the student and doctor an exceedingly ambitious man. Berisha has a "pathological ambition," said Sabit Brokaj, who served on Hoxha's medical team and said that he had proposed Berisha for membership in the Party of Labor. Brokaj and others who worked with Berisha as a doctor and a politician told me about his intense jealousy, his anger, and his paranoia. Above all, he hungered to rule.

* * *

The government set elections for March 15, 1991, and Sali Berisha led the charge. He and other DP leaders preached democracy and the market economy. They respected Alia but portrayed the Party of Labor as the source of economic woe and past abuse.

Berisha and Pashko tried to capitalize on their trip to the United States, suggesting that the Democratic Party had helped reestablish diplomatic relations. They said U.S. economic aid was "conditioned on the victory of democratic forces in Albania."[15] A DP slogan was "We Lead, They Give."

In contrast, the Party of Labor warned against rapid change. The party said it would guide Albania towards Europe with cautious reform. Ramiz Alia promised to resign as head of the party if the new parliament reelected him as president.

Despite their enthusiasm, the DP leaders faced a steep climb. The party leaders had no experience in politics, let alone elections. None of them had drafted policy or run a campaign. And the party lacked funds. Albanians in Kosovo and the U.S. gave money, as did the New Democracy Party in Greece and the Konrad Adenauer Foundation in Germany, but the DP could not afford posters and other supplies. The government first gave one car, a Romanian Aro, and later four more.

In these conditions the DP had to win over the conservative rural areas, where 60 percent of Albanians lived and state television gave most of the news. People outside the cities generally disliked the communists but they feared losing the little they had. The DP struggled to convince poor farmers and rural workers that they stood to gain from change.

Election night at DP headquarters had an electric feel. Laughter and applause reverberated through the halls as the first positive results trickled in. But the tallies came from Tirana and other cities, where victory was assured. By evening, the poor showing in rural areas became clear, and by nightfall the Democrats saw their defeat. Party members hugged and shed tears.

In the final results, the Party of Labor won just over two-thirds of the vote and the DP took slightly under one-third, mostly in the cities, with smaller opposition parties like the Republicans and Social Democrats taking the remaining seats. Alia lost his seat in Tirana, the traditional zone for the party's first secretary. Voter turnout across the country was a remarkable 98.9 percent. International monitors, including the U.S. International Republican Institute and Helsinki Commission, saw procedural flaws as well as some violence and intimidation. But neither deemed the problems significant enough to invalidate the results.

Berisha and Pashko gave the results a positive spin: we won the most emancipated sectors of society. No one could have expected that within four months the ruling party would face such a challenge, they said. The DP had shot from 0 to 30 percent, while the Party of Labor had plummeted from absolute power. The writer Ismail Kadare called the communists' victory "a miserable win" because it came from "the poorest and most backwards parts of the country."[16]

The spin aside, the results shook the DP. Supporters wondered whether communism would ever fall. The week after the elections saw a sharp rise in Albanians crossing the mountains into Greece. Violent demonstrations shook Durres and Tirana, where the police beat a fourteen-year-old boy to death. On April 2 in Shkoder, angry crowds protested what they considered electoral fraud. Army units opened fire on the protesters, killing four people, including the student leader Arben Broci. The crowd set fire to police cars and burned the Party of Labor offices. It was an inauspicious start to Albania's multi-party life.

* * *

The first session of Albania's first multi-party parliament took place without the country's first opposition party. To protest the four deaths in

Deputies from the opposition Democratic Party stand in parliament on April 10, 1991, to honor four anti-government protesters killed by the army. © Gani Xhengo

Shkoder, the seventy-five Democratic Party deputies stayed home. When they arrived two days later for the second session, emotional supporters waited outside to shake their hands and wish them well. In parliament the new deputies stood for a minute of silence to honor the dead.

Some in the DP had suggested not recognizing the election results because of the manipulation. But the United States urged the party to participate in the interest of stability. With a two-thirds majority in parliament, the Party of Labor easily reelected Alia as president. As promised, he resigned as Party of Labor head. The PLA formed a government run by a young, reform-minded economist from Tirana named Fatos Nano, who had grown up in the communist elite. This man would vie with Berisha for power over the next fifteen years.

Despite the loss, the DP quickly surged. The Party of Labor was old and uninspired. The DP presented a youthful team. The parliamentarians showed passion and verve. They analyzed and critiqued the government. And given Albania's frail economic state, they had much to say. The public, watching parliamentary sessions on television like sports fans, cheered the underdog.

Members of the first pluralist parliament, Fatos Nano of the Albanian Party of Labor (L) and Genc Ruli and Sali Berisha (R) of the Democratic Party, on May 3, 1991. © ATA

Gaining confidence, the opposition began to attack. In speeches and interviews, DP deputies criticized Alia for hindering their work and destabilizing the country. Gradually able to walk on its own, the party was casting away its political crutch.

Sali Berisha led the team. He accused the party and Sigurimi of fomenting instability and blocking reform. He warned about remnants of the regime. And he courted the former political prisoners and persecuted classes that the DP had initially kept at bay. This unfortunate group, ragged and dehumanized, joined DP branches around the country and gravitated towards the charismatic Berisha. They shouldn't have accepted him due to his past, but desperation and emotion overwhelmed fact. Over time Berisha developed two languages: a moderate, democratic appeal with foreigners and DP leaders, and a tough, anticommunist push with the formerly persecuted. To the former he urged reconciliation and collective responsibility. To the latter he promised destruction of the dictatorship.

In May 1991, Berisha made his second trip to the United States, together with Azem Hajdari and the writer Ismail Kadare. Albanian history "reminds one of the American writer Helen Adams Keller, deaf and blind from infancy," Berisha told a congressional hearing on Albania. "Her cure went through difficult phases, just like Albania, which after sixty-five years of dictatorship is now in the process of its reawakening."[17] Kadare added an eloquent description of Albania's aspirations. "The Albanians have pinned their hopes on the United States," he said, in case the DP's affinity for the U.S. was not abundantly clear. "The Albanians are among the nations that respect and love this nation, meaning the United States, more than anybody else."[18]

The Bush administration was impressed. It was ready to throw its full weight behind the democratic opposition and defeat Eastern Europe's last ruling communist party. But who in the DP should Washington support?

Ismael Kadare was writing in France. Azem Hajdari was young and brutish. Gramoz Pashko lacked seriousness. But Sali Berisha was disciplined, smart, charismatic and—a crucial point for the U.S.—spoke good English. As one congressional staff member who dealt with the visiting Albanians said, with Berisha "you didn't have to explain things more than once."

The U.S. also appreciated that Berisha hailed from the north because that region had family and cultural ties with Kosovo, the troubled province of Yugoslavia across the border. Washington hoped Berisha would encourage Albanians in Kosovo to remain peaceful so the Yugoslav conflict did not spread. Just as Alia had summoned Berisha to quiet the protesting students in December 1990, the Americans hoped he would keep the Kosovar Albanians patient and calm.

* * *

Back in Albania, the situation got worse. Long lines stretched from bakeries. The police stopped working and criminals looted stores. At the end of May, the recently established Independent Trade Union went on strike to demand higher wages and the government's resignation. The DP supported the workers' demands. "Up until then, we were leading the process," said Genc Ruli, one of the influential DP deputies at the time. "But then the process began to lead us."

On June 4, the government of Fatos Nano resigned. The DP and Party of Labor agreed to hold new elections in nine months. As a transition, they formed a "Stability Government." The Party of Labor named the prime minister, as well as the ministers of internal and foreign affairs. The DP contributed seven people to the government, including three party founders: Gramoz Pashko as deputy prime minister, his brother-in-law Genc Ruli as finance minister, and Preç Zogaj as minister of culture.

Berisha cleverly resisted the temptation of a post. If the government succeeded, the ministers could be accused of collaborating with communists. If the government failed, the ministers would sink with the ship. In addition, his main rival in the party, Pashko, would be forced to deal with government affairs, leaving Berisha to focus on the party. The doctor understood that political strength grows from the roots, and he spent the next six months forging ties in the districts, promoting his allies, and expanding his reach.

On the other side, the Party of Labor tried to show a moderate face. Some leaders endorsed the creation of a new party, but Alia rejected a definite break. He wanted a reformed party, which would allow the powerful PLA to keep its substantial property, structures, and electoral base.

On June 10, 1991, the Party of Labor held its tenth congress, which it called the "Congress of Renovation." The goal was "to create a party with a new physiognomy," explained Xhelil Gjoni, who had became first secretary after Alia resigned, adding that it was important "to preserve all good values that have been achieved."[19] When fourteen hundred party delegates converged on Tirana, it remained unclear which of Gjoni's statements would have the upper hand—change or preservation. Berisha predicted the party would split into hardline and reformist factions, like a "two-headed monster."[20]

Gjoni opened the congress with an ambiguous two-hour speech. He criticized Hoxha's self-reliance, which led to splits with Yugoslavia, the Soviet Union, and China. He condemned the extreme collectivization of land and the persecution of intellectuals. At the same time, he stressed that "Enver Hoxha is an indispensable part of our history." The delegates rose to their feet, shouting "Party-Enver!"[21]

That night saw nine hours of heated debate: How much of the old to keep and what from the new to include? By morning, the Alia-backed reformers had prevailed. The congress expelled a host of former Politburo members from the party and barred others from the Central Committee for having abused their privileges. Alia ordered them to leave their government villas.

The Party of Labor renamed itself the Socialist Party and took as its symbol the red rose of the European left. After initially refusing, Fatos Nano accepted the nomination and was elected party head. The reformers manipulated the voting to ensure the presence of more liberal views in the leadership, party leaders said. On June 13, 1991, the party's newspaper, *Zëri i Popullit*, published the decision to change the party name. For the first time in the paper's forty-seven-year history, the front page did not feature the communist hammer and sickle.

* * *

By now the U.S. was watching from the ground. The Italians still occupied the embassy, so the Americans worked from the Dajti Hotel. They quickly grasped the massive pro-Americanism among Albanians and proposed that Washington send a senior official. Washington agreed and on June 22, 1991, Secretary of State James Baker's plane touched down in Tirana as part of a Balkan tour. His few hours in town set the stage for U.S.-Albanian relations over the next twenty years.

Baker's convoy drove in from the airport around 9:00 a.m. through empty streets. "I assumed it was going to be a disaster," said the American diplomat Chris Hill, who already was in Tirana. Then, on the outskirts of Tirana, an ecstatic mob engulfed the cars, hoping to glimpse the guest from the West. Men threw flowers, kissed the windshields, and tried to carry Baker's limousine into town. "People were literally jumping on the hood of our car," Hill said. American security agents jogged along the vehicle, sweating in their suits. "In fifteen years I had spent in national politics I had never seen anything like this," Baker later wrote about the trip.[22]

The delegation drove to Skanderbeg Square, where more than three hundred thousand people had crammed every corner and nook despite oppressive heat, waving small American and Democratic Party flags. A large banner with the Statue of Liberty holding an American flag hung from the Palace of Culture. Spectators clung to lampposts and tree branches. They dangled off rooftops and balconies to get a better view. Someone raised a sign that read, in English: "Welcome Mr. Baker, Albania Has Been Waiting for You for 50 Years." The famously unflappable Baker was overwhelmed. "I have never felt more privileged to represent my country," he wrote.[23]

Baker and his entourage dipped into the Et'hem Bey Mosque on the southeast corner of the square to regroup. Someone needed to calm the crowd. A U.S. official turned around, saw Sali Berisha, and pulled him into the mosque.

"What should I say?" Berisha asked, according to a U.S. official who was present.

"Just calm them down," the Americans implored.

Berisha climbed the rostrum that had been constructed in front of Skanderbeg's statue, stepped to the microphone, and addressed the sea of faces.

"The American way of greeting friends is quieter than ours," he said in his booming voice. "So please, let him speak."[24]

U.S. secretary of state James Baker addresses a massive crowd in Skanderbeg Square on June 22, 1991. © ATA

U.S. secretary of state Baker meets President Alia. In back are future U.S. ambassador Bill Ryerson (L), VOA Albanian service head Elez Biberaj (C), and Albanian foreign minister Muhamet Kapllani (R). © ATA

Berisha then declared Baker to be an honorary citizen of Tirana. The crowd went wild.

American security cleared a path from the mosque and Baker made his way to the microphone, kissing a baby along the way. Berisha slipped to the back of the stage as Baker raised his hands in the two-fingered victory salute—the symbol of the Democratic Party.

"On behalf of President Bush and the American people, I come here today to say to you: freedom works!" Baker said through his interpreter, the VOA Albanian service chief Elez Biberaj. "At last, you are free to think your own thoughts."[25]

From the awestruck and hopeful faces—those of true believers—Washington understood it was dealing with a small and desperate country full of fans. The U.S. had a chance to win the last battle of the Cold War and to establish a trusted ally in a volatile region. Baker announced $6 million in aid and left for meetings with the prime minister and President Alia.

That afternoon at the Dajti Hotel, Baker met representatives of the Democratic Party and the other recently established parties, as well as from a group working on women's issues and another working on human rights. The Albanians sat around a long table with Baker at the center and Elez Biberaj by his side. Berisha sat across from Baker, wearing a fresh suit after the mob scene in the square. On the table in front of each seat was a small American gift: a necklace for the one woman present and a pin and cufflinks for the men—all of them with the bald eagle.

The Albanian delegates had agreed beforehand that each of them would have ten minutes to speak. Berisha took the floor first and spoke for twenty-five minutes in Albanian, with Biberaj translating, two of the Albanian participants recalled. "Mr. Secretary, communism is dead but its toxicity remains," Chris Hill remembered Berisha said. One of the participants, a former political prisoner from an interfaith initiative called the Christian Islamic Party, complained that the government had refused to legalize his party.

"What's happening?" Baker asked.

"Pure communist chicanery," another U.S. official replied. The official was right. Alia had allowed only those opposition parties that he felt he could control, like the Social Democrats run by the trusted former education minister Skënder Gjinushi.

From the hotel, Baker went to address parliament, where he underlined U.S. support for Albania's democratic reform. In case it was not clear to anyone by that point, he pinned the final star on Berisha's shoulder.

"Dr. Sali Berisha invited me to come to Albania," he told members of parliament. "I came here as soon as I could."[26]

Back at the airport, Baker waited in the VIP lounge with a U.S. diplomat named Bill Ryerson, who had come to Tirana with the advance team.

"Now Bill, you let me know if you need anything out here," Ryerson remembered Baker saying. Ryerson answered that they needed an ambassador and full embassy staff as soon as possible.

"Remind me on Monday to talk with [then deputy secretary of state] Larry [Eagleburger] about staffing," Baker told an aide. At that point, a U.S. diplomat named David Schwartz had been pegged as the first ambassador, but Baker apparently thought Ryerson had organized his successful trip. Despite Ryerson's lack of experience—mostly consular posts in places such as Barbados, Poland, Germany, and most recently Yugoslavia, where he learned Albanian—President Bush appointed Ryerson the first U.S. ambassador to Albania since 1939.

"Baker lost his cool and I was the result," Ryerson joked as he ground coffee for me with a traditional Albanian hand-grinder in his Virginia home near Washington, D.C. Large American and Albanian flags fluttered outside the front door. In the foyer hung the Albanian Order of the National Flag—First Degree, presented by President Sali Berisha on October 4, 1994.

Of course Albanians knew nothing of the historical twist. For them, Ryerson became the envoy of the strongest nation on Earth, and with that came incredible might. Despite being in consular affairs most of his life, Ryerson became one of Albania's most influential men.

At the same time, Washington and the Albanian political leaders realized that someone else was needed for the delicate work. While Ryerson maintained his symbolic importance, his newly appointed deputy, Chris Hill, undertook the complex tasks. The son of a diplomat, the thirty-nine-year-old Hill was smooth, smart, and ambitious. He quickly assumed responsibility for dealing with the president, political parties, and regional affairs.

"I wrote the stuff and I supervised the stuff, and he [Ryerson] did the public diplomacy," Hill told me in 2012, after he had ended his foreign service career, which included ambassadorships in Korea and Iraq. "The notion that I was the substantive guy kind of played to an old communist notion that it's the guy behind the scenes doing it all. But that's not quite fair to Bill. He spoke the language and really worked at it. Albanians loved that."

Ryerson was more blunt. "Berisha and I were on a first-name basis. He called me in on occasion," he said. "But the substance was with Hill."

* * *

The Stabilty Government performed well, given the country's desperate state. With an influx of foreign aid, it focused on privatization and land reform. In July 1991 the government opened the forbidden Block in Tirana where Enver Hoxha, Ramiz Alia, and the party elite had lived. Curious pedestrians meandered down the tree-lined streets they had imagined but never seen. Six weeks later, workmen in T-shirts used hammers and chisels to destroy the great white statue of Hoxha that sat in the Enver Hoxha Museum on the boulevard.

Government ministers traveled abroad, some of them for the first time. On one trip, Gramoz Pashko led a delegation to Vienna for negotiations on Albania's national debt, accompanied by two experts and the writer Teodor Keko. Knowing neither economics nor English, the witty Keko occupied himself during the meeting by scribbling poetry on scraps of paper, which he passed to his Albanian friends. At the end of the visit, Austrian officials expressed their thanks with a collection of gifts. Pashko and the others received opera binoculars, while Keko got an ornate Swarovski clock. The Austrians thought he was the boss. Ten years after the trip, I asked Keko if he recalled the poetry he had written during the meeting. "Here we write with lead and wood," he answered from his daily perch in Tirana's Café Europa. "Across from those with golden pens."

As the Stability Government assumed a modicum of control, Berisha sharpened his attacks against the newly renamed Socialist Party and what he called its "crypto-communists." He questioned how the Socialists had inherited property from the Party of Labor. He argued that the Socialists were benefiting from the Democrats' participation in the government.

"The DP is attacked first and foremeost today by the red nomenklatura and all those who lost their privileges and their tyrannical power," he told *Rilindja Demokratike*, using language Albanians would come to know well. "Enverist followers of the dictatorship are attacking. In this group, the Albanian criminal political police, state security, and hundreds and thousands of its spies have been very active."[27] The Socialists countered that Albania was facing a possible "right-wing dictatorship."

Again, Berisha had sensed the mood. Many Albanians wanted to blame someone for their plight, especially former political prisoners and their families. Accostomed to strong leaders, they sought a forceful character to assert control.

The U.S. government fed into this trend. The first elections could be written off as a "warm-up exercise," as one State Department official put it. But by summer 1991, Berisha and the Democratic Party had earned Washington's trust.

"We feared the DP would share the blame if it stayed [in the Stability Governent]," explained Jack Buechner, head of the International Republican Institute at the time, which was active in Albania. "There was more pressure to pull out of the government than to stay."

A CIA analysis from the time confirmed Buechner's view. Because the DP held key economic portfolios, a secret report said, the opposition "must share the blame if—as is almost certain—they cannot ease Albania's bleak economic prospect in the short period before the election."[28]

Later that summer, the DP held its first party congress, and the agenda included two contentious points: the election of the party chairman and the party's participation in the Stability Government. The Steering Committee voted 14–5 to empower itself with electing the party chairman but Berisha objected. The party congress, as the more representative body, should elect the chairman, he argued, knowing that he controlled the congress more than the Steering Committee. The party's National Conference, a body larger than the Steering Committee but smaller than the congress, agreed.

The first Democratic Party National Congress took place on September 27 and 28, 1991, in Tirana. Neritan Ceka and Preç Zogaj defended the Stability Government's record and supported the DP's participation. In his speech, Zogaj condemned creeping authoritarianism in the DP. "The people support us because they aspire for democracy," he implored. "But they can abandon us if we disappoint their aspirations."[29] The delegates applauded when Zogaj was done, but Berisha stood up demonstratively in the balcony, marched downstairs, and took the stage. A chant rose from the audience—"Ber-i-sha, Ber-i-sha!" Some of the delegates rose to their feet.

Nexhmije Hoxha is still powerful, Berisha proclaimed. The communists control the police and they want to sabotage the Democratic Party. The delegates applauded. From that moment, the party leadership was sealed. Berisha won about three hundred votes, followed by Neritan Ceka with around one hundred. Azem Hajdari won seven. The cardiologist had assumed control.

* * *

Following the DP congress, the Stability Government was doomed. On October 5, the DP organized a demonstration in Tirana called

"Democracy Will Succeed to Eradicate Communism in Albania." The rally called for the arrest of Nexhmije Hoxha and former Politburo members, and accused Ramiz Alia of stalling reform. In parliament, the DP began to criticize the Stability Government. Sali Berisha accused the DP ministers Genc Ruli and Gramoz Pashko of corruption.

On November 27, the DP Steering Committee had a meeting with the party's parliamentary group. Berisha argued that the government was paralyzed and the DP should withdraw. The Socialists gave the DP co-responsibility for governing but kept political power for themselves, he said. Others called for continued cooperation to smooth the transition. In the end, the committee reached a compromise. The DP would withdraw from the Stability Government if the government did not meet four conditions within one week: (1) try those responsible for the four killings on April 2 in Shkoder; (2) replace the director of state television; (3) commit to new elections in February 1992; and (4) arrest Nexhmije Hoxha and a group of former communist leaders. Two DP members were appointed to present the demands.

The two men achieved some success. Parliament accepted a draft law that would free the state television from political control. The proseuctor agreed to expedite the Shkoder investigation and Alia committed to new elections. The sticking point remained Nexhmije Hoxha's arrest. One of the DP representatives, the archeologist Neritan Ceka, visited President Alia to plead his case. "If you start to arrest the former Politburo, where will it stop?" Ceka remembered Alia asked.

With the one-week deadline pressing, Alia reluctantly agreed to Nexhmije's arrest. Ceka rushed to parliament with the news. The police had not yet arrested Nexhmije, but Alia had promised that they would do it soon, he told the DP group. The party agreed to extend the deadline one more day, when Berisha would hold a press conference to announce the results. In Ceka's mind, the Stability Government had been saved.

The next morning Ceka went to the prosecutor's office to confirm Nexhmije's arrest. He watched three unmarked police cars arrive with the seventy-year-old former first lady. Satisfied the police had Nexhmije in custody, Ceka went to the press conference. Berisha sat alone at the front of the room, reading a prepared text. Ceka sat beside him and slid a note across the table. "Nexhmije and the others are under arrest," it said. Berisha read the note and continued to talk.

"Today will be marked as the day when the communists in power, through their flouting of the law, intolerance and general misconduct, obliged the Democratic Party to withdraw from the Government of National Stability," he said.[30]

Gramoz Pashko was in London for meetings with the European Bank for Reconstruction and Development when he heard the news. Incensed, he called the decision a historic mistake and complained publicly of a split within the DP.[31] One week later, he decided it was wiser to maintain a common front before elections. "There are no divisions inside the DP," he told a press conference in Tirana. "What unites me with Berisha is stronger than what divides us."[32]

Neritan Ceka, who had negotiated Nexhmije Hoxha's arrest with Ramiz Alia, was less accommodating. At a meeting with Chris Hill, Berisha and Ceka screamed and cursed at each other in English, blaming each other for provoking a crisis. On December 6, President Alia called a meeting with the political parties to discuss a technical government until new elections. Ceka and Berisha attended for the DP. State television covered the event. Before the cameras, Ceka declared the Stability Government still alive because the DP had not been unanimous in pulling out. He announced his resignation from the party and called on Berisha to leave politics. Berisha hardly blinked. Taking advantage of the cameras, he dealt Ceka and Alia a decisive blow.

"This is a plot between the two of you," he insisted, storming out of the room.

Alia understood immediately what Ceka had done.

"They will use this against you," the wizened communist told the neophyte politician. He was right. The DP responded that Ceka's "declarations, interviews and letters have served Ramiz Alia and the communist Albanian rulers."[33] DP election rallies soon rang with shouts of "Neritan-Alia" and "Gramoz-Hoxha." The disgruntled DP leaders had been outplayed.

* * *

The collapse of the Stability Government thrust Albania into a downward spiral of lawlessness that some have called the "time of dark forces."[34] The outgoing prime minister, Ylli Bufi, strangely announced that Albania had only one week of reserves for bread, causing frantic mobs to storm bakeries, warehouses, and shops. An estimated forty-five people died between December 1991 and February 1992 from riots and street violence. The all-powerful communist state had collapsed and nothing had taken its place.

Some villages organized the systematic dismantling of community centers and cooperatives, distributing the windows, roof tiles, wooden beams, and electric wires. But in many cases, thieves yanked up railway track, uprooted water pipes, and stole manhole covers. They ripped bars from Albania's prisons. They felled the stately poplars that lined national roads and burned them for heat. "The trees are nice," one man told a journalist. "But if we don't cut them, the bandits from the next village will do it first."[35]

* * *

The second elections contrasted sharply with the first. The Party of Labor, now called the Socialist Party, was backpedaling while the Democrats advanced. The new United States embassy gave the DP its full support. More than fifteen U.S. consultants provided advice, including Bush campaign staff and members of the Heritage Foundation. The International Republican Institute and National Democratic Institute gave expertise and aid. IRI donated nine white jeeps that rolled into desolate villages like royal steeds. Conservative parties from the U.K. and Germany assisted the courageous Democratic Party to slay the communist beast.

U.S. and Western European enthusiasm had multiple roots. First, these governments felt a genuine sympathy for this discarded but enchanting nation—the East's last red star. Even hardened diplomats felt touched by Albania's emergence from a haunted past. Ideologically, Albania was a contagious drama that stimulated the cold warrior's sense of justice. With its small size and eager population, Albania represented a chance to convert the most rigid Eastern European state into the modern West.

More practically, Albania offered a strategic base of operations in a region on the brink. With the Gulf War over, the U.S. was turning its attention to the dissolution of Yugoslavia. Albania offered an outpost in the southern zone. In the coming years, Washington used Albania to house spy planes, to base troops, and to exert a moderate influence on ethnic Albanians in neighboring Kosovo and Macedonia.

The U.S. embassy in Tirana openly campaigned for the DP, with Bill Ryerson and Chris Hill appearing on the podium at rallies. "I believe that neither the U.S. nor any European state is interested in building socialism in Albania," Hill told a DP rally in Kuçova, until recently known as Stalin City.[36] At a rally in Korça, a DP supporter asked Ryerson what he thought of the communists. "I wish them good health, long life . . . and unemployment after the elections," Ryerson remembered saying.

"You could argue you shouldn't go," Hill said, when I asked years later if he had gone too far. "Yes, we're being accused, but you'd have to be kind of a curmudgeon not to."

Ryerson's cables to Washington reflected the revolutionary mood. "As they see their political fortunes waning, the Socialists, all 'former' communists schooled in the works of the dictator, seem to have reverted to what they know best—manipulations of statements, appeals to xenophobic fears, and attacks on the U.S.," he reported. "All these point to desperation by leaders trying to cling to power."[37] Regarding Berisha, Ryerson's praise was effusive. The DP leader was "charismatic, able to communicate well with any group from any strata of society, with a keen sense of judgment."[38] Socialist head Fatos Nano, in contrast, was "an ineffectual leader who cannot make major decisions on his own."[39]

When I asked Ryerson whether he had let himself get swept away, he admitted not knowing enough about Albania at the time. But he still believed he had done the right thing. "Maybe I was used by Berisha," he said, "but only to promote democracy and the free market."

Under U.S. guidance, the DP moderated its stance on Kosovo and the region. In contrast to earlier statements about "extreme sacrifices"[40] for Kosovo and even union with Albania, the 1992 electoral program said the DP "intends Albania to fulfill a stabilizing and pacifying role in the Balkan region."[41]

Domestically, the DP concentrated on the villages they had lost in 1991. In IRI jeeps, candidates traveled the country to spread the good word. The Socialist Party presented itself as a safe continuation of Albania's social traditions: education, full employment, and health care. It attacked the DP's land policies, warning that prewar landowners would reclaim property at the peasants' expense.

These policy debates constituted a small part of the deep chasm between the two sides. With most Albanians equal in their poverty, the parties did not represent economic classes or interest groups. The election was a battle between new and old, open and closed, future and past.

* * *

On election day, March 22, 1992, U.S. ambassador Ryerson traveled the country inspecting polling stations. At a school near Elbasan a soldier guarding the station turned to the ambassador and gave him a knowing wink. "Don't worry, Ambassador," Ryerson recalled being told. "They're all for Sali."

The soldier's claim was a bit exaggerated, but not far off. With voter turnout at approximately 80 percent, the DP won 62 percent of the vote, garnering ninety-two of 140 seats in parliament. The Socialist Party won 25.7 percent, or thirty-eight seats. Together with the Republicans and Social Democrats, the opposition had one hundred seats. An ethnic Greek party, the Union for Defense of Human Rights, won two seats. International monitors claimed the vote "legitimately reflected the will of Albania's citizenry."[42]

The DP and its supporters celebrated their victory like soccer fans at the World Cup. Cars with men on the roofs waving DP flags rolled up and down Tirana's boulevard blaring their horns. A crowd outside the U.S. embassy unfurled American flags and chanted, "Long live America! Long live George Bush!" A DP brochure published in 1992 aptly summarized the mood: "Albania had voted to break once and for all with communist rule, with fear and with poverty," it said. "Albania had voted for its future."[43]

PART III

Red to Blue

Democratic Party Rules, 1992–1996

7

Rebuild the State

For forty-five years, elections in Albania had been a farce. Ballots listed one candidate from the Party of Labor, and a folded paper without marks constituted a valid vote. Now Albanians had secrecy and choice.

Albanians overwhelmingly chose to usher in a new generation of politicians who promised to break from the past. In what was largely a referendum on communism, Enver Hoxha lost. Albanians wanted to own jeans, travel abroad, and speak their minds.

A political prisoner for twenty-eight years, Pjetër Arbnori, became speaker of parliament. On April 4, 1992, he opened the first session:

> The great honor to declare open the proceedings of the first post-war democratic parliament belongs not only to me but to all democrats who have suffered in jails, internment and emigration, to all the persecuted, to all the martyrs of the darkest period our homeland has lived with.[1]

The entire assembly, in the presence of the new government and foreign ambassadors, stood and sang the national anthem.

Now Berisha and the Democratic Party had to deliver. Destroying the old system was far easier then building something new. The government had to reform banks, revise curricula, and revamp defense. And the new power holders had no experience in running a state. Doctors, writers, scientists, and men straight from prison were forced to cultivate a democratic revival without tools. The ministries lacked computers and copy machines. The intelligence agency needed audio tape.

As undisputed leader of the Democratic Party, Sali Berisha called the shots, and the first question he faced was to become president or prime minister. By law, the prime minister enjoyed more power, but the president was the traditional head of state and the post Alia had held. Berisha decided to be president but the law forbade the head of state from belonging to a political party, and Berisha did not want to lose control of the DP. His supporters accommodated him by proposing that the limitation apply only to the president heading a party. Enough new members of parliament agreed, setting a precedent for legislative subservience to the executive. Parliament elected Berisha Albania's first post-communist president later that day, and he stayed in the Democratic Party as an active member of the important Steering Committee. Eduard Selami became party chairman, but Berisha remained the unchallenged party head.

The Democratic Party, like the Party of Labor before it, immediately had more power than the organs of state. Party leaders told ministers what to do. Albanians seeking jobs or promotions joined the party and followed the party line.

"Sali wanted to apply this model—the party above the government—because the party was him," explained Genc Ruli, who was finance minister in 1992 and held key posts under Berisha after that. "Through the party, he controlled the members of parliament and the ministers. It was a communist model."

As prime minister Berisha proposed fifty-three-year-old Aleksandër Meksi, the short, bespectacled archeologist with a reputation as a consensus builder who had helped form the Democratic Party. Meksi was mild mannered and unassuming. He was also an Orthodox Christian for religious balance among the heads of state (Berisha is Muslim and Speaker of Parliament Arbnori was Catholic). Many DP leaders disliked the proposal, fearing Meksi lacked the strength to counter Berisha.

That fear proved to be justified. During Berisha's tenure as president, from 1992 to 1997, Meksi stood in the doctor's shadow, never seriously challenging him, even as the country slid towards violence. His obsequiousness is perhaps why Berisha proposed him in the first place. Although no concrete evidence has emerged, Meksi is dogged by allegations of corruption, leading some Albanian observers to conclude that the two men had an unwritten deal: Berisha ruled and Meksi stole.

In contrast, Berisha denied his rivals important positions, with the exception of Genc Ruli, who stayed to deal with finance. Democratic Party founders Gramoz Pashko, Preç Zogaj, and Arben Imami sat in parliament but held no other posts. Azem Hajdari, the first DP head, was denied his request to be interior minister and settled for head of the parliamentary commission on state security. Relations between Hajdari and Berisha deteriorated over the next year, even forcing the former student to spend time in the United States after the police threatened him with arrest.

At the same time, the DP got depleted as intellectuals and professionals took jobs in government and state institutions. Berisha filled the void with grateful supporters: ex–political prisoners, anti-communist militants, and people from his region of Tropoja. Familiar with this style, many Albanians joined the party because they got sholarships, jobs, and business deals.

* * *

As Berisha consolidated power, the DP and government struggled to run the state. Bandits stopped drivers for their money, cars, and even clothes. Gangsters were better armed than the police. In April, Prime Minister Meksi declared that crime and poverty were "the gravediggers of the new democracy."[2] Lawlessness and rampant individualism were the dark genies inside the democratic bottle. With the fear of Enver gone, Albania lost its glue.

Desperate to show authority, the government publicly hung two brothers convicted of bludgeoning a family of five to death in the town of Fier. Authorities left their bodies swaying in the square for a day.

The government tried to reform the police, but that mostly meant replacing communist-era officers with a new cadre from the north. The Albanian military struggled with rusting Chinese hardware and an annual budget of less than $50 million. The soldiers needed uniforms, jackets, and socks. The U.S. embassy called it "the worst equipped military in Eastern Europe."[3]

Under guidance from the World Bank and International Monetary Fund, the government liberalized prices and controlled spending. Given the desperate situation, the government had success. Inflation, estimated at 250 percent in early 1992, fell to 10 percent by year's end. According to the IMF, the economy grew 11 percent in 1993, the most of any country in Europe.[4] As time would show, those numbers, if indeed accurate, masked deep-seated economic flaws that would eventually cause a disastrous crash.

Across the country, families sent a relative to work in Italy or Greece, and remittances became a pillar of the new economy. Other Albanians traveled to Bulgaria or Turkey to buy clothes, electronics, or bathroom supplies. Tirana's streets became sprawling bazaars of fake Adidas, light switches, and faucets. Restaurants and cafés opened, first with hand-ground Turkish coffee and then espressos and cappuccinos from Italian machines. Albanians fixed their homes by tiling bathrooms, getting sit-toilets, and installing hot water heaters. Electric stoves replaced the gas cookers. Enterprising businessmen advanced from faucets to sinks, and from sinks to showers. Corrugated metal kiosks sprouted up in neighborhoods selling trinkets and humanitarian aid. Without regulation, they grew awnings, laid concrete patios, extended side rooms, and built second floors. Tirana's once green Rinia Park on the boulevard became a warren of kiosk pizza parlors and cafés.

In the chaos, corruption boomed. Inexperienced officials at first accepted three-figure bribes, but they quickly learned the proper scale. When British Petroleum signed a contract to provide fuel at Rinas Airport, a person familiar with the deal told me, Albanian officials wanted pilots to pay by the tank with cash, like cars at the pump.

The sanctions imposed by the U.N. on neighboring Yugoslavia because of the war offered special opportunities for smugglers, and Albania had the perfect combination of remote borders and a weak state. In the coming years, the Democratic Party and others would get rich from illegal oil sales to Slobodan Milošević's regime. The sanctions busting drove a black economy, created a class of criminalized businessmen and damaged the already fragile institutions of state.

To help the transition, Western advisors poured in, as the Yugoslavs, Russians, and Chinese had done before. Great Britain got the offices of the president and prime minister, although Berisha's closest relations remained with the United States. The U.S. took the ministries of defense and finance. The Germans got the agency for privatization.

Starved for contact with the outside world, Albanians treated the foreigners like gifts from above, and swallowed advice with indiscriminate zeal. "People thought Maggie Thatcher had kissed me on both cheeks and sent me off," recalled Guy Roberts, a young British advisor sent by the Westminster Foundation to help the prime minister. "In fact it was a departmental researcher in the basement."

The lessons started with the basics, Roberts and other advisors said: how to operate a computer and copy machine, set agendas and draft budgets. In 1992, the government wanted to establish diplomatic relations with Libya, and it drafted a letter to Muammar Qadhafi, at the time scorned as a terrorist by the West. A western advisor gently suggested they drop the idea. That same year, the foreign ministry received a "diplomat" from the Republic of Sealand who wanted to establish diplomatic ties. When ministry staff could not locate the country on the map, they asked a foreign advisor for help. He politely informed the minister, a doctor from a respected Catholic family, that Sealand was not a country but an abandoned anti-aircraft fort six miles off Britain's eastern coast that had declared itself a principality. That same minister discovered a hidden button under his desk which, he was told, turned on the recording equipment in the ministry's negotiation room. Such recordings were normal to create transcripts of meetings with foreign states. The next day the minister held a press conference and accused the communists of bugging the ministry to undermine the Democrats' work, and he even took the case to court. "The minister apparently doesn't know the difference between a microphone and a stethoscope," an expert witness testified.

In 1992 an Albanian delegation flew to Rome to negotiate diplomatic relations with the U.K., which had broken in 1946 after the two British destroyers struck mines near Corfu. Hoxha refused to pay compensation and the U.K. withheld the 2.5 tons of Albanian gold that it had confiscated from Germany. The delegation met their counterparts at the British embassy, a member of the Albanian delegation told me, sitting on one side of a long table across their interlocutors with Albanian and British flags alternating down the middle.

"Her Majesty's Government is willing to accept a less substantial amount as compensation," the British announced. "Can we agree on that point?"

"Yes," the Albanians quickly replied.

"Her Majesty's Government is willing to accept the amount of two million U.S. dollars," a British official said.

The Albanians were thrilled because Berisha had authorized them to concede the larger sum of two million British pounds, but they strategically asked for time to consult. The British ambassador offered his office and only behind closed doors did they chuckle and shake hands. They enjoyed the Rome view for five minutes before returning to the table with serious looks to accept.

Setting up diplomatic missions in London and other countries proved more complex, even where embassies had existed before. Virtually none of the new ambassadors had traveled abroad. Many had never flown, stayed at a hotel, or ridden an escalator. Around the world, Albania's new diplomats lived in cramped quarters above the embassy. They ate in cafeterias and arrived at state functions on the public bus. Diaspora communities had to buy them clothes.

To save money, the government asked the prewar ambassador to the U.K., an émigré living in London, to resume his job. He declined due to age, but his son took the job as honorary counsel. "We put a brass plate on my house and worked from the sofa," Alexander Duma told me with a smile. He and his father designed a visa stamp in the garden and had it made down the street. A full ambassador came one year later and the government upgraded the Duma house to embassy.

* * *

In late March 1992, President Sali Berisha and Democratic Party head Eduard Selami sat in the Dajti Hotel on the boulevard. With them were U.S. ambassador Bill Ryerson, his chief political officer, Chris Hill, and the CIA station chief for Albania.

"What do you need?" the Americans asked.

"A meeting with Bush," Berisha replied.

The relationship was close. The men were on a first-name basis. The Americans had helped the Democrats sweep to power and now they would help them rule. Chris Hill visited Berisha's office a few times a week.

As promised, the next month Berisha, Selami, and Foreign Minister Serreqi traveled to Washington for high-level meetings and an audience with President Bush, who was in the midst of an electoral campaign. The International Republican Institute bought Selami a new suit for the trip.

The three excited Albanians entered the Oval Office on June 15 to meet Bush, along with Secretary of State Baker, National Security Advisor Brent Scowcroft, and Ambassador Ryerson. That morning, Bush had requested Congress to grant Albania most favored nation status, which Congress later approved. "I just want you to know that I took great pleasure in doing that, and I want you to have a pen," Bush said, handing

Berisha the pen with which he had signed the congressional request. "You get a free pen there."[5]

"It is for Albania and Albanian people a very historical signature," Berisha replied in English. "We appreciate also very much the attitude of United States adopted toward ex-Yugoslavia. And I could assure you that the heartiness of your attitude and the statement that Mr. Baker did in London was very important to slow down the activity and to stop the shifting of the war to Kosovo and other regions."

"Well, we want to talk a little more about that when we have our private meeting," Bush replied. "Because we are very anxious to be helpful where we can. But you're so close to it, I want to get your views on Kosovo and see where we go."

That Kosovo became the central theme was no surprise. U.S. policy makers in Washington had one overriding concern: war in the former Yugoslavia. By that time, fighting was raging in Bosnia and Croatia, and the Bush administration feared the war's spread to Kosovo and also Macedonia, where roughly 25 percent of the population was ethnic Albanian. As James Baker had told Berisha about the region in a congratulatory letter when Berisha became president: "We know you will understand our view that a prudent approach is called for in this regard."[6]

In the private conversation, talk quickly turned to the region. "We welcome you into the democratic family," Selami told me Bush said. "We'll do what we can to help you and to help Albania prosper. But things are heating up over there, so don't get involved in the conflict. You have our protection. Don't jump, just do the right thing."

The Albanians were thrilled. They had won support from the strongest nation on Earth, and all of them understood how important that was back home. They could easily support the moderate U.S. ally in Kosovo, Ibrahim Rugova, and block the sporadic and disorganized training of Kosovar militants that was taking place in Albania's north.

As the meeting closed, the Albanians said they hoped Bush would win the forthcoming presidential race. "I think I will," Selami recalled Bush saying, as he put his arm around the young Democratic Party chairman in the new suit. "But if I don't, our policy won't change."

The point about continuity did not sink in. The Albanians viewed U.S. policy through an Albanian lens, whereby alliances and strategies

President Sali Berisha and President George Bush in the Oval Office on June 15, 1992. From left to right are Ambassador Bill Ryerson, Democratic Party head Eduard Selami, Foreign Minister Alfred Serreqi, Secretary of State James Baker, and National Security Advisor Brent Scowcroft. © George Bush Presidential Library and Museum

change with every new government. They did not realize that, although policies shift, U.S. institutions have a momentum of their own and foreign policy largely stays on course.

That November, when Bill Clinton defeated George Bush, Berisha and the DP leaders were crushed because their ally had lost the White House. "We did not know the U.S. system," Selami recalled. "We thought in a Balkan style: we're out. If the Republicans lose, we've lost a friend."

The next month the outgoing Bush administration rewarded Berisha's moderation on Kosovo with what it called the "Christmas warning." The United States announced it was "prepared to employ military force against the Serbs in Kosovo and in Serbia proper" should their leader Slobodan Milošević initiate conflict in Kosovo.[7] The warning pacified Kosovo Albanians and allowed Berisha to show Albanian nationalists that he was addressing their cause.

Upon coming into office, the Clinton administration promptly reiterated the Christmas warning, proving the continuity of U.S. foreign policy that the Democrats had failed to grasp. The Faustian deal that underpinned the U.S.-Albania relationship—play nice abroad and rule at home—remained in effect.

* * *

Annointed in Washington, Sali Berisha tightened his grip. During the 1992 electoral campaign, he had stressed national reconciliation, coining the phrase "Together Responsible, Together Victims," which meant that all Albanians had played a role in the dictatorship and should avoid revenge. After the elections, Berisha jabbed his finger at the former communist leaders, whom he dubbed the "red mafia."

In early May, the government exhumed the bodies of Enver Hoxha and ten top communists from the Cemetery of the Martyrs, including Josif Pashko, the father of Gramoz, and reburied them in a public cemetery on the outskirts of Tirana. "The violent way in which the action was carried out was unnecessary," Pashko told the press. "I was not even informed."[8]

The next day, parliament amended the labor law to allow state enterprises and institutions to fire employees without explanation or appeal. Thousands of people lost their jobs in the ministries, universities, state media, and companies. While many of these work places needed change, the law's vague terminology and lack of an appeal process opened the door for a cleansing on political lines. Complaining of "Operation Extermination," the Socialists said 250,000 people lost their jobs. This number seems high, but Socialist supporters were dismissed en masse across the country, replaced by DP enthusiasts and their relatives, especially in the police, secret police, and customs offices.

According to DP officials from that time, the dividing line was not what a person had previously done, but whether he or she supported Berisha and the new regime. As ambassador to Hungary, Berisha chose Lisen Bashkurti, the former head of the communist youth organization, who had sat next to Ramiz Alia during the December 1990 meeting with the students. Mehmet Elezi from Tropoja, a former media chief for the Party of Labor and head of the communist youth, served as a presidential advisor. Berisha was ready to forgive these people for their pasts, so long as they pledged loyalty to his future. In fact, Berisha preferred people with a past, DP officials from that time said. It gave him a sword over their heads, especially those who had collaborated with the secret police.

"Sali divided people into good spies and bad spies, based on who supported him," then DP chairman Eduard Selami explained. "If you were a spy who shut up or supported him, you were fine. If you opposed him, you were revealed." When needed, *Rilindja Demokratike* or state television would "out" a person who was irking the government by providing juicy snippets from a Sigurimi file or revealing a code name from communist times.

To run the new intelligence agency, renamed the Shërbimi Informativ Kombëtar (SHIK, or National Information Service), Berisha appointed a math professor named Bashkim Gazidede, who quickly became one of Albania's most feared men. Born in 1952, Gazidede was a heavy smoker and devout Muslim who ran Albania's Society of Islamic Intellectuals. His faith opened him to allegations of relations with Islamic fundamentalists and terrorist groups, but no evidence has emerged to support those claims. More importantly, Gazidede was an ardent anticommunist who saw a red plot under every stone. He filled SHIK's ranks with Democratic Party supporters, many of them from formerly persecuted families, and many of them young men from the north. The 1992 salary of 2,500 lek per month was good pay, with additional income from illegal sources.

Most importantly, Gazidede was a Berisha devotee, faithfully running the president's political police. "SHIK never had relations with the party or the government, only relations with Berisha himself," said Tritan Shehu, a foreign minister, deputy prime minister, and Democratic Party head during Berisha's time as president, who said he was continually under SHIK's watchful eye. Then prime minister Aleksandër Meksi agreed, complaining of surveillance when he was in office from 1992 to 1997. When discussing sensitive matters in his office, Meksi told me, he winked at visitors and put his finger to his mouth, knowing SHIK was nearby.

Berisha and Gazidede developed close ties with the CIA. The American agency provided eavesdropping equipment and trained Albanian agents in surveillance techniques. "Total cooperation," was how Berisha described his relationship with U.S. intelligence at the time. "They worked in Albania as if they were in New York or Washington."[9]

The CIA's main interest was the foreign Islamist groups that were setting up cells in Albania, taking advantage of the corrupt and lawless state. But Berisha used the equipment and training to monitor his political foes. Opposition politicians and journalists got used to cars with scruffy minders idling outside their homes.

* * *

In mid-1992, the Democratic Party faced its first test as the ruling party. Local elections that July would mark the first time since 1944 that local authorities were elected and not appointed. After four months of democracy, Albanians faced shortages of oil, soap, and salt. The average monthly salary for a civil servant was between 1,000 and 1,200 lek ($10 to $12).

Despite these conditions, Berisha and the DP expected to win. No one wanted a return to the dark past, they thought, and a local victory would complete the democratic sweep. "Communism has been eliminated as an ideology but not yet as a practice," Democratic Party chair Selami said at the time. "And this election will mark the final departure from communism."[10]

On a hot July 26, the Albanian people spoke, and the Democrats disliked what they heard. Voter turnout was lower than expected, around 70 percent. More surprisingly, after a second round the Democrats won only 43 percent of the vote, compared to 41 percent for the Socialists. Just four months prior, the DP had won two-thirds of the vote.

The results looked even worse up close. The Socialists won the mayoral races in twenty-three towns and cities, compared to nineteen for the Democrats, although the Democrats won Tirana and other key cities. The Socialists won more communal chairmanships than the DP and more seats in the various municipal, district, and communal councils.

Publicly, the Democrats blamed the economic crisis. In addition, the Socialists had spread misinformation and even panic, the DP said, including rumors of another refugee exodus in early July. In a party brochure published after the loss, the DP concluded that the Socialists had "deftly capitalized on the present difficulties of the country, here and there helping them along to make them look more convincing."[11]

"I cannot imagine how any government could win popular support while in the midst of liberalizing prices," Berisha explained after the loss.[12] Diplomats and foreign officials tended to agree, seeing the set-back as the natural result of painful reform.

The Socialists applied a different spin, saying voters had rejected Berisha's authoritarian style. "This government has been characterized by revenge," the head of the SP parliamentary group, Namik Dokle, said. "Four months in power shows that the Democratic Party does not have contemporary values."[13] Party head Fatos Nano said voters disliked the "old dictatorial methods, which they saw in the new government."[14]

Both the Democrats and Socialists were probably right. The deterio-rating economy had frustrated voters who were starving for the *dolce vita* as seen on Italian TV. They increasingly associated democracy and the market economy with shrinking pensions, unemployment, and a fivefold rise in the price of bread. But Berisha's bullying style had also alienated many Albanians, and not just those loyal to the Socialist Party. Even some who had voted for the Democrats in the parliamentary elections turned against the party as a counterweight to Berisha. They believed that Albania needed a distribution of power, rather than an ac-cumulation of strength.

Within the Democratic Party, Berisha's critics tried to use the election loss. In an August meeting of the party's Steering Committee, party co-founder Arben Imami proposed a motion to evaluate the election result and the responsibility of the party head. The chairman was officially Eduard Selami but everyone understood the proposal took aim at Beri-sha. Berisha's main rival, Gramoz Pashko, as well as Preç Zogaj and six others endorsed Imami's request.

Berisha swiftly counterattacked, labeling the "motionists," as he called them, leftists and communist sympathizers. "It was clear right away that they would leave the party," one member of the Steering Committee from that time told me, referring to Imami and the others. "Sali was very strong. They could not bring him down."

Berisha called and chaired an extraordinary meeting of the party's National Council on August 13. Council members lambasted the "mo-tionists" for not campaigning hard enough in the local elections, for making left-wing speeches, and for being weak on communism. In the end, the council voted to expel Pashko, Imami, Zogaj, and four others from the party. Outraged at the expulsions, two others voluntarily joined the group.

At the time, Berisha explained the expulsions as the removal of an "anti-democratic faction opposed to democratic reform."[15] Later he claimed that Pashko, Imami, and the others were angry at being denied government posts. "What happened, actually, was that a handful of gentlemen found themselves without power and were very unhappy about this," he said.[16]

Arben Imami rejected the claim. "It was not a struggle for power," he told me in 2001. "There were two different approaches to ruling the country. We were liberal, he was communist—and it produced [*demokracia* plus *diktatura*] *demokratura*."

To the international community, the expulsions reflected the natural evolution of the DP from an anti-communist front to a political party. It was normal for the group to splinter when communism died. United States ambassador Ryerson bought Berisha's line. "Imami wanted to be speaker of parliament," he told me. "And no room is big enough for Pashko and Berisha."

Regardless of the reasons, Albania's democratic spirit had died. Backroom deals, jealous looks, and seedy plots prevailed as the new leaders schemed how to get and hold important seats. Revenge and accusations replaced reconciliation and debate. Preç Zogaj articulated it well. "It all happened so quickly, the return of a concept of power for the sake of power," he wrote days before his expulsion from the party. "And now in place of an exchange of ideas we have a fight between ideas, in place of the negotiating table we have faceless memos, in place of a respect for differences of opinion we have intolerance, banal campaigns in the press, purges and petty intrigues."[17]

Expelled and scorned, the ousted DP members formed a new party called the Democratic Alliance. Their aim, Arben Imami said at the time, was "to moderate Albanian politics and have an opposition with credibility."[18] The archeologist Neritan Ceka joined, as did the brother of the writer Ismail Kadare. Azem Hajdari wanted to join, but some members disapproved.

Berisha tried to discredit the Democratic Alliance at home and abroad, labeling them communists and spies. Throughout 1992 and 1993, the state press maligned the party and its leaders, SHIK agents monitored their lives, and provocateurs disrupted the party's work. On January 14, 1994, the Alliance held a rally with some six hundred people in Shkoder. DP supporters burst into the hall chanting pro-Berisha slogans and provoked a clash. In the melee, someone shot and killed a twenty-six-year-old Alliance activist named Gjovalin Cekini. Parliament formed a commission to investigate but the assailant was never caught. Six weeks later, the editor of the Alliance's newspaper was beaten in Shokder. A few days after that, the outspoken writer and Democratic Alliance member Teodor Keko exchanged harsh words in parliament with Berisha and SHIK head Bashkim Gazidede. On March 10, Keko was walking in the center of Tirana with his wife when two men struck him on the head with brass knuckles.

"The state is led by a communist mentality, according to which the opposition does not exist," Keko told me a few days after the attack, a gaping wound on his head. "Journalists will either shut down their papers or go to prison," he added. "These are the two best options, especially because our prisons are getting better thanks to the European Union."

8

One-Party Town

In this tense atmosphere I arrived, landing in Tirana in July 1993. My two friends and I started working on the student newspaper at Tirana University, funded by the Soros Foundation, with two computers donated by the International Media Fund, which the U.S. government had established to assist media in the former communist bloc.

Among the first people we met were the founding members of the Democratic Party, Gramoz Pashko, Arben Imami, Preç Zogaj, and Teodor Keko, who had just been kicked out of the party and formed the Democratic Alliance. They gathered every Friday night at the home of the Soros Foundation director. We watched as Albania's new opposition got drunk on bad wine and fake Stolichnaya, cursing Berisha. The men were funny and smart but also rude. They told dirty jokes and made fun of the wives who occasionally came, and especially those who did not. One night the group watched on television as Keko exploded against the Democrats' arrogance during a session of parliament until he was ejected. He appeared at the house ten minutes later with a frozen pizza. "I just left those pricks," he screamed when he saw parliament on TV. The group was astounded that he had found frozen pizza in Tirana.

The men also seemed depressed. They were upset by Albania's undemocratic turn, but some seemed to regret that they were not in charge. More than anyone, Gramoz Pashko gave me this impression. He looked more modern than the others, with distinguished gray hair and tortoiseshell glasses that gave him the appearance of an Ivy League professor. He spoke perfect English, Italian, and French. His house—around the corner from the Friday-night gatherings—where the DP had drafted its founding statute two and a half years before, had a desktop computer, a laptop, and a large CD collection—unheard-of in Albanian homes at the time. Photographs showed Pashko standing next to Mother Teresa and Václav Havel. He and the others complained about Berisha hijacking the democratic movement, but I sensed jealousy in their complaints.

On one of those Friday nights I had my first contact with the goons from SHIK. The foundation director and I stepped out to buy more wine and he tapped my arm. "Watch that car," he said, motioning to a white Mercedes across the street. On cue, the car rolled forward to keep us in sight.

I understood the politics better as I got to know the country's main human rights group, the Albanian Helsinki Committee. First the members forced out the secretary general, the former political prisoner Fatos Lubonja, because he was criticizing the Democratic Party. His seventeen years in prisons and labor camps did not suffice. Then the director came under pressure because his sisters were married to Politburo members. Such pressure was typical of the time, but I was stunned that Tirana's intellictuals, including staff at the Soros Foundation, were unwilling to defend these individuals or the independence of a human rights group. In private they disliked Berisha, but they lacked the courage to take a stand.

That summer, Berisha moved against his chief political adversary, Socialist Party head Fatos Nano. The state-run media accused Nano of corruption during his stint as prime minister in 1991. On July 27, a prosecutor asked parliament to lift Nano's immunity. Parliament agreed the following day.

Nano insisted on his innocence and condemned the "revanchist clan led by Sali Berisha." Going a step further, he accused the U.S. embassy of proposing his prosecution. In a speech on July 27, he charged that "'diplomats' like [Chris] Hill and [Ambassador] Ryerson . . . , after making their careers in the CIA and Belgrade, put the scenario on Berisha's desk."[1]

I asked Nano about these allegations ten years later, after he had returned to the top of Albanian politics. "It had nothing to do with Hill as a person or a diplomat or Ryerson," Prime Minister Nano told me from a decorative couch in his large office, sipping gin and tonic from a crystal glass. The U.S. position at the time—supporting the government and maligning former communists—was, he claimed, "a ready-made product offered to former communist countries."

On July 29, the Socialists held a large rally in Tirana's Dinamo Stadium. Most of the party's supporters were pensioners and veterans, but this rally drew about ten thousand people waving mass-produced signs against Berisha and the DP. In the dusty heat, word spread that Nano would not attend. He had been arrested.

The crowd chanted for Nano's release. Around 7:00 p.m., the stadium lights went out. The crowd filed into the street, onto the main boulevard, and down to Skanderbeg Square. Uniformed police watched from the periphery, but men in civilian clothes, probably from SHIK, intervened with batons. Government supporters jeered the crowd and threw stones.

The U.S. embassy in Tirana gave the protest a pro–Democratic Party spin. "Many pedestrians stopped at the square to watch and listen, but were not participants," Ambassador Ryerson reported to Washington on August 2. "Those taking part were for the most part older PS [Socialist Party] members, former Sigurimi employees and their families. Police were required to subdue a few ralliers and did make some arrests of demonstrators for disturbing the peace and trying to provoke skirmishes with police officers."[2]

Police blocked approaches to Tirana on the opening day of Nano's trial. Handcuffed and refusing to speak, Nano was charged with embezzlement "for the benefit of third parties" and the falsification of documents. He had illegally assisted an Italian businessman named Giuseppe Perniola, the prosecutor said, during the delivery of Italian food aid in 1991, squandering $9 million.

Nano's trial was rife with manipulations. The judge arbitrarily rejected evidence and witnesses from the defense. *The Economist* called it the "the last great political show trial in Europe."[3] In April 1994, Nano was sentenced to twelve years in prison and ordered to repay approximately $720,000 to the state. While Nano might have been guilty, and credible allegations of corruption have dogged him ever since, the prosecution never made its case. "We thought he was guilty," said then DP head Eduard Selami, who supported Nano's arrest. "But they convicted him before all the facts, and then pressed the judiciary."

Throughout the trial, the U.S. government remained silent, fueling rumors that it had agreed to Nano's arrest. Ambassador Ryerson denied that the U.S. had any involvement, but told me that he and Chris Hill "were persuaded that Nano was a crook." Ryerson's cables to Washington rejected any political motivation behind the arrest. "Claims that Berisha is superceding legal authority, instituting a police state and not respecting human rights have been a standard part of Socialist rhetoric for over one year now, and have no basis in fact," he reported in April 1993, when the accusations against Nano first emerged.[4]

The CIA was more careful, stating in an August 1995 report that Berisha had "the access and power to determine events" in Nano's case. But, the report concluded, "there is no evidence that Berisha was responsible for the irregularities associated with Nano's case." The agency considered Berisha's role in the arrest "possible but not provable."[5]

Chris Hill adamantly denied that Washington had proposed or encouraged Nano's arrest. "It is inconceivable that anyone in the USG would have said this was a good idea," he told me. The question, Hill said, was what to do about it. "Do you oppose [Berisha] publicly or reason with him privately?" he asked. "And mostly we thought we try to reason with him privately."

That decision had an impact on Albanians. They saw that Berisha could jail his opponents after bogus trials with no clear response from Europe or the United States.

Rather than erode Nano's status, the conviction boosted his popularity. Instead of weakening his control of the party, Nano exerted more influence from inside a cell. According to Jack Buechner, head of the International Republican Institute at the time, Nano's arrest "made a rag into a Gucci bag."

* * *

The first edition of our student newspaper, *Reporteri*, appeared on October 20, 1993. The students distributed the paper around town and started talking about articles for the next edition. Four days later, the university shut us down.

At first we thought the order had come from the deans. But I learned later from senior DP officials that Berisha himself had made the call. The president cared little about the student newspaper, but he was furious with our funder, the Soros Foundation, and in particular its director in Tirana. That man, Fron Nahzi, had begun challenging Berisha's democratic credentials, and he had the budget to give his challenge weight.

An Albanian American raised in the Bronx whose family had fled communism, Nahzi had opened the foundation for Soros in February 1992 and eagerly supported the Democratic Party. After the 1992 elections, the foundation gave the government fax machines, photocopiers, and computers. It bought newsprint for the struggling press. Nahzi had access to Berisha day and night.

The thirty-one-year-old Nahzi relished the power, holding staff meetings around his desk with a wooden carved "BRONX" on his computer. But he soon realized that Berisha was drifting from the democratic path. He watched from inside the palace as Berisha kept a list of his enemies, ordered arrests, and wrote anonymous articles for the party paper. Journalists who critized Berisha came under threat, and Nahzi helped some of them get abroad. In February 1993, the foundation organized a media seminar with foreign journalists. Afterwards, a British journalist from the *Guardian* wrote one of the first articles criticizing Berisha in the international press, calling him "clannish" and "dogmatic."[6] Berisha was furious at Nahzi for setting him up.

When the Democratic Alliance formed, Nahzi sided with its leaders, whom he considered more open-minded. He saw an urgent need for an opposition aside from the former communists, and he helped the Alliance as he could. Nahzi's home became the site of the Friday night events with fake Stolichnaya and bad wine. For Berisha, these parties and Nahzi's support of the Democratic Alliance amounted to treason. In the culture of the north, a friend's deceit is worse than an enemy's attack. "Between me and Sali Berisha was a deep hatred," Nahzi told me years later in New York, after we had become close friends. "I thought he was destroying the country and he thought I had betrayed him."

The deathblow came when our newspaper, *Reporteri*, criticized the government's new press law, and Berisha seized the chance. As the main funder, Nahzi took to the paper's defense. In a meeting at the university, he suggestively told the students that "there cannot be a university without the students," harking back to the student strike two and half years before. That night on the national TV news, the university deans launched a stinging attack.

"The time when the halls of faculties can be used by party organization and cells is finished once and for all," a statement by the deans said. It continued: "For this flagrant interference by the representative of the Soros Foundation, as it is not the first time that he prefers to be where he is not invited and not to be where he is asked to be, we are going to send a briefing to the multi-billionaire George Soros."[7]

From that point Nahzi's departure was a matter of time. Berisha wrote to Soros, complaining that his director in Tirana was pro-Serb and offering "a fresh start." Soros wrote back that, in his view, Nahzi had done nothing wrong. "I realize the tremendous obstacles you face both internally and externally," Soros wrote. "That is why I shall not be discouraged by petty and unjustified attacks."

Soros came to Tirana soon thereafter and met with Berisha, who called Nahzi a Serbian spy. Soros asked to see the evidence, which Berisha did not provide. Still, the foundation stood in a difficult place. Soros could either challenge Berisha, probably forcing him to close the foundation, or find a new director. He chose the latter, and Nahzi was dismissed.

The American embassy was relieved the thorn was gone. Ambassador Ryerson and Chris Hill were promoting Berisha in Albania and abroad, and Nahzi had become a disruptive voice. Ryerson later explained Nahzi's departure to me as the result of a personal rift with Berisha, just as he had described the creation of the Democratic Alliance. "It was personal," Nahzi agreed, when reflecting on that time. "If you take ideals and values personally."

Instructive for me was how Albanians reacted when Nahzi lost his job. He stayed in Tirana for a few weeks and, as with former political prisoners during Hoxha's reign, few people dared to go near a banished man. With a few exceptions, friends walked by while he drank coffee alone, giving him a shrug of the shoulders and a knowing look: "I'd love to join, but you know . . ."

* * *

For the next year, my friends from Columbia and I worked at the newly established Soros Media Center, which gave training to local journalists. Editors and journalists visited daily because we installed a satellite link with Reuters. In those pre-Internet days, only the state-run news agency had electronic access to the daily news. *Reporteri* published again, though with a tamer approach. The students wrote about the university and films.

I began sending information about human rights conditions to Human Rights Watch in New York. It started with the treatment of journalists and extended to pressure against the opposition and abuse by the police. I reported on constitutional reform and the work of the courts. I observed trials with judges who had no gavels or robes; cold wind blew through courtrooms where the windows had no glass. Some Supreme Court justices slept in their offices because they had no place to live.

A new law created the High Council of Justice to appoint, dismiss, and discipline judges and prosecutors, and the Democrats controlled the body from the start. Berisha chaired the council, which often held meetings in a room next to his office. No one doubted that abusive judges and prosecutors had to go, but their replacement was based on political loyalty, nepotism, and old-fashioned bribes.

Over the next year, Nexhmije Hoxha, Ramiz Alia, and other senior communists went on trial. The victims of the regime looked for justice, or at least information about the past. They got trials that focused on corruption by former elites.

Nexhmije Hoxha's trial had begun in 1992, and the charges centered on the illegal purchase of less than $100,000 in coffee, food, and other goods. The announcement of her nine-year sentence passed with little interest. When Hoxha appealed, the court extended the sentence by two years. Ten second-tier communists were charged with misusing up to $15 million of state funds. They had seven hundred workers for 131 villas, the prosecutor said, and access to special supplies of meat, cheese, milk, chocolate, beer, and raki. They used gold from the state archives to fill their teeth. They got sentenced to between five and eight years, and those sentences were later reduced.

The most high profile trial began in May 1994 with the appearance of Ramiz Alia and nine senior officials, known as "Blockmen" for the villas they had in the Block. Unlike the defendants in previous trials, the prosecutor charged this group with political crimes dating back to 1951. On a stifling hot day, observers crammed a small, third-floor courtroom painted pale blue. The Blockmen sat in two rows, their balding heads wet with sweat.

Alia stood out from the rest. He sat alert and erect, his thinning gray hair combed back in disciplined, straight lines, as if following a five-year plan. He was slightly pale, but his dark eyes beamed with confidence. The courtroom was oppressively hot, and people in the gallery cooled themselves with fans made from that day's news, but Alia did not flinch. An hour into the proceedings, he reached into his suit pocket, retrieved an ironed and folded handkerchief, and lightly dabbed his head. "When you know the result, there is nothing to sweat over," he told me eight years later when remembering that day.

A reel-to-reel camera filmed the event as the twenty-five-year-old judge began the proceedings with a bang of his pen on the desk. The prosecutor, twenty-eight, presented the charges for two hours in a monotone voice, lulling some lawyers to sleep. The defendants had supported shoot-to-kill orders, resulting in the deaths of hundreds who had attempted to flee the country, he said. The accused had collaborated in the ban on religion and the internal exile of government opponents, as well as the misappropriation of state funds. Guards served the defendants water from a tin kettle. The sounds of modern Tirana floated in, mostly the musical car horns of private vehicles once banned by the accused. A drummer banged on his drum to announce the end of the Muslim holiday Eid al-Adha—Kurban Bajram in Albania—which Albanians had once not dared to observe.

The judge announced the guilty verdict on July 2, the fourth anniversary of the storming of the embassies. Alia received nine years in prison. Hekuran Isai, minister of the interior in December 1990 when the police beat the students near Student City, got five. Most of the men were released after one year, but Alia stayed in prison until mid-1995, and he was arrested a second time after that.

The verdicts hardly made the news. By this time, many Albanians were disillusioned with the new government and worried about finding a job. They had neither time for nor interest in probing the past.

* * *

The work in the media center kept my focus on press freedom, and there was plenty to do. The Democratic Party had complained about the bias of state TV when it was in opposition, but it did little to reform the station when it took power, or to pass legislation to allow private stations. The nightly news, with graphics from the 1970s, showed Berisha speaking to adoring crowds at home or world leaders abroad. Announcers smeared opposition politicians as "communist sympathizers" or "foreign spies."

Radio and TV journalists were previously afraid of jail or worse, but under the new government they feared for their jobs. During one radio call-in show, a caller complained about government corruption. Editors fired the show's host for letting the caller speak, and the host's mother lost her job at a state institute.

Unlike in the past, Albanians had access to news from abroad, and they soaked it up. In addition to the Voice of America, which supported Berisha, Albanian-language services began at Deutsche Welle, Radio France International, and the BBC. Satellite dishes dotted roofs and balconies across the country, and even bunkers that were occupied by homeless families. In the far northern mountains, a family I visited cooked on an open hearth but watched Hollywood movies on a German station via satellite. ("Why do they always cut to a commercial at the best part?" the father innocently asked.)

The international programs were not immune from attack. In August 1993, the government accused the BBC of supporting the Socialist Party, labeling the radio the "British Bolshevik Corporation." A public letter from a group of journalists at the state-run Albanian Telegraphic Agency said the BBC Albanian program was "protecting the remnants of communism in Albania."[8]

That year, Berisha subverted U.S. government attempts to promote a free press, and the embassy stayed mum. The International Media Fund, which had donated two computers for our newspaper, had also given equipment for a radio station that was installed in the pyramid of the former Hoxha museum. Berisha had requested the gear before the March 1992 election, a person familiar with the deal said, with the understanding that it would be for independent use after the elections. Once in power, Berisha said Albania lacked legislation to allow private stations, which was true, so the donated radio stayed in government hands. Ambassador Ryerson defended the move and the government used the radio to broadcast VOA.

A similar problem befell a $1 million printing press, also donated by the International Media Fund. The Democratic Printing Press, as it was called—the only offset press in Albania at the time—was intended for use by seven of the country's non-party newspapers. Through legal twists and the arrest of the plant's manager, Berisha allies appropriated the press and charged the non-party papers higher rates to print.

The move did not stop the vibrant and provocative opposition and independent media. They poked Berisha at every turn with rumors, jokes, and snide remarks. The reporting was weak, but the criticisms resonated with people who increasingly disliked the doctor's black-and-white approach. Leading the pack was a provincial paper from the town of Lezhë called *Koha Jonë* (Our Time), which gained popularity as it published the Berisha critics who got kicked out of the Democratic Party. The first contributor was Frrok Çupi, the founding editor of the Democratic Party's *Rilindja Demokratike*, whom Berisha had forced from the job. "There are people who have adopted Enver's tactics very well," Çupi told *Koha Jonë* in August 1991. "It's not their fault, they cannot be different, they use the same methods."[9] In late 1992, the expelled DP founders Gramoz Pashko, Arben Imami, and Preç Zogaj wrote in the paper's expanding pages, and circulation grew. The government responded by harassing the paper with financial inspections. Printing and distribution costs rose.

"Enver Hoxha would not let anyone criticize him like that," the editor of *Koha Jonë* at the time, Aleksandër Frangaj, told me years later. "He [Berisha] considered it a weakening of his power."

On two occasions the government tried to silence *Koha Jonë* with a criminal case. The first came in March 1993 when Frangaj personally saw the military transporting tanks towards the north. Two days later, *Koha Jonë* published a three-paragraph article entitled "Tens of Tanks towards Northeastern Border." "Why were those tanks being transported to the Albanian-Serbian border?" the short article asked, implying that something in Kosovo was amiss.[10] International agencies picked up on the story, quoting a Ministry of Defense spokesman who said the movement was a normal part of the army's "restructuring."[11]

Unaccustomed to open reporting, the government was incensed. More importantly, Berisha saw a chance to slap the feisty paper. Frangaj was charged with disseminating false information to incite panic and placed under house arrest, even though the government had admitted the movement of tanks.

On March 27, *Koha Jonë* tried to clarify its position. A short statement sarcastically apologized for assuming the tanks were rolling to the "northeastern border" instead of to the "northern border." Rather than cause panic, the paper said, the article had calmed the public because readers learned that the army had tanks. "Many Albanians know that the former regime left the country without a capable defensive military capacity," the paper joked. "This news encourages people and raises their morale by informing them that we possess tanks and the ability to protect people in case of attack."[12] Circulation soared.

At Frangaj's trial, the defense presented two hundred signatures of people who claimed to have seen the tanks traveling north. One witness testified that the convoy had run over his pig.

"Are the tanks of Albania causing you panic?" Frangaj's lawyer, the flamboyant Spartak Ngjela, asked a Ministry of Defense official called by the prosecution.

"Yes," the official said.

"No!" boomed Ngjela. "The tanks are scaring Milošević and securing Albania!"

The prosecutor asked for a break. When he returned, the charges were dropped.

The next day, the prosecutor amended the charge from disseminating false information to revealing state secrets. In court, Ngjela weaved legalistic genius and vaudeville flair.

"The first charge was for disseminating false information," Ngjela said, waving his hand in the air. "And the Defense Ministry has submitted testimony that no tanks were in the north. Therefore, if the charges are changed to revealing state secrets, then it means the minister lied in court. Either both my client and Minister Zhulali go to prison or they both go free!"

The prosecutor dropped the charges again. But it was not the end of the paper's legal fight.

On January 12, 1994, *Koha Jonë* reprinted a Ministry of Defense document signed by the minister that ordered off-duty officers to keep their guns in the barracks. Next to the order was an article entitled "Disarming the Military," written by Martin Leka. The government claimed the paper had published a state secret.

On January 26, Frangaj arrived at the *Koha Jonë* office and saw it surrounded by police. He slipped over a wall in the back and met the agitated staff. The telephone rang and an unknown caller said the staff would go to jail. Teodor Keko, a frequent contributor to the paper, calmly replied, "You will eat our shit." The next day's edition ran banner headlines: "Threats against *Koha Jonë*" and "Democracy, Freedom, Free Press and Human Rights in Danger." Below was a subtitle from Keko: "I

Am Answering Politely: You Will Eat Our Sh——."[13] The paper sold out by 9:00 a.m. The police arrested Frangaj and Leka four days later.

The Defense Ministry had issued forty-four copies of the order and, to make its case, the government demanded that each order be returned. By checking the stamps with the document published in *Koha Jonë*, investigators narrowed the culprits to four possible officers. The police arrested them all until the guilty officer admitted giving the document to Leka, whom he knew from Lezhë, because he disagreed with the order.

Frangaj and Leka were held on the third floor of Tirana's main prison, together with the ex–interior minister Hekuran Isai and Enver Hoxha's bodyguard Sulo Gradeci. On the second floor sat Ramiz Alia and imprisoned Politburo members, as well as Socialist Party head Fatos Nano.

The February 1994 trial I observed made absurdist theater look sane. Scruffy judges presided over an unruly court with policemen in baggy uniforms. Frangaj and Leka arrived each day from prison in a paddy wagon to the cheers of family and friends, raising their shackled hands in victory. "The changes in Albania smell like food gone bad," Leka told the court. The judge sentenced him to eighteen months in prison, but acquitted Frangaj. The two officers who had leaked the document got jail terms of four years. An appeals court convicted Frangaj and sentenced him to five months in prison, but he had fled abroad.

Throughout the trial, Western governments stayed silent. One U.S. official in Tirana tried to justify the arrests by telling me that *Koha Jonë* was a "left-wing scandal sheet." The lack of professionalism in the Albanian media was very real, but the U.S. and other governments were more interested in supporting their ostensibly democratic partner than in defending a free press or fair trial.

As with Fatos Nano's arrest, the *Koha Jonë* trial backfired on Berisha. Albania was now open to the world and he could not silence critics by locking them up. The convictions got reported abroad, including in statements by Human Rights Watch and the Committee to Protect Journalists, based on information I sent. Under pressure, Berisha pardoned Frangaj, Leka, and three other journalists that May 3, World Press Freedom Day.

* * *

Despite the revanchist politics, Albania's economy seemed to grow. I watched Albanians buy cars and fix their apartments. They opened cafés and traveled abroad. But I could not understand from whence the money came. Industry had collapsed and Albania was importing basic goods. Unemployment was higher than the government said. Remittances from workers abroad no doubt helped, but could they keep the country afloat?

The answer became clear when I visited the area around Lake Shkoder on the northern border with Montenegro, at that time still part of Yugoslavia. A narrow two-lane road with potholes and a weak shoulder ran to the border crossing. During communism, only rumbling government trucks or a clopping mule had interrupted the asphalt's sleep. By 1994, the road had become an active strip, with goods worth millions rolling through every month.

The boom began in 1992, when the United Nations imposed sanctions on Yugoslavia because of the war. Formal trade ceased with Yugoslavia's neighbors—Romania, Bulgaria, Macedonia, and Albania—but clandestine trade quickly soared, especially for oil. Albania's far north became a booming commercial zone; smugglers calculated their money by weight. According to the sanctions coordinator for the European Union and the Organization for Security and Co-operation in Europe (OSCE), Albania supplied more fuel to Yugoslavia than all other countries combined.[14]

The U.S. and European governments knew about Albania's illicit trade. Border monitors sent regular reports. In November 1994 the U.S. embassy told Washington that, "a select few in and outside of the political class reportedly get rich from influence peddling, payoffs, Serbian sanctions-busting, drug-running and other unsavory activities."[15] A secret U.S. report from April 1995 said that "significant volumes of oil is now imported through Albania's Adriatic ports and shipped overland to Montenegro." Albania "lacks the political will and enforcement capabilities to stem this traffic," the report said.[16]

Occasionally a Western official confronted the authorities with satellite images or photographs, and the Albanian government would shut some of the smaller smuggling rings. But neither side took serious steps. The international community understood that Albania needed the business. Concerned with cooperation on Kosovo and Macedonia, it tolerated illegal acts.

The business began with Albanian companies importing oil and fuel from Italy and Greece to the ports at Vlora and Durres, former Albanian government officials and financial police told me. Albania's domestic fuel use had jumped with the legalization of private cars in 1991, but imports soon far exceeded what Albania consumed.[17] By one count, in 1994 Albania imported double the amount of oil that it used.[18] Once in Albania, the importers sold the fuel to smugglers who transported it north. Tankers deposited the fuel in one of the many gas stations that had sprung up near the border. Day and night, trucks brought feul from the stations to Lake Shkoder, where smugglers loaded it onto boats for transport to Montenegro on the other side.

At first men loaded barrels onto dinghies. Soon they pumped gasoline and diesel through rubber hoses onto small barges. Eventually smugglers installed underground pipes. Because the Yugoslavs purchased oil and fuel with German marks, a correlation developed between Albania's oil imports and the Albanian lek's exchange rate with the mark: as imports increased, the lek climbed.

One of the main oil importers in Albania was a company called Shqiponja (Eagle), which belonged to the Democratic Party. The law allowed political parties to run businesses, and the Socialists had a similar company called Progress. Shqiponja's top officials were Tritan Shehu, who later became head of the party and then foreign minister, and Mitro Çela, another senior party official. The company imported oil, mostly from Italy and Greece, and sold it to "distributors" in Durres, Shehu told me in 2002. The company closed in late 1995, he said, partly due to pressure from smugglers who wanted to control the imports.

Shehu said the company worked legally and transparently, but a person who worked in the Democratic Party's financial department during that time bristled uncomfortably when I asked about Shqiponja. The company's huge profits skirted normal party accounting, the person said, wishing to remain anonymous. When employees asked Shehu about missing funds, he said the DP needed money for elections.

While some got rich, honest Albanian policemen grew frustrated that Albania was breeding a generation of traffickers. "Two boats with a machine gun could have stopped it had there been political will," a former officer in the financial police told me. In 1994 and 1995, the police frequently released the smugglers they had arrested, he said. In one case, the police confiscated a tanker full of airplane fuel and brought it to the customs office. The next day, someone had replaced the tank with water.

In early 1995, the U.S. and European governments wanted to pressure Milošević into a deal on Bosnia so their tolerance for the smuggling waned. At a meeting in Washington on March 28, senior U.S. officials decided to "limit fuel being smuggled to Serbia and Montengro through Albania." Among other steps, they agreed to "press the Albanian government to improve enforcement."[19] Albania responded by requiring gas stations to have licenses and by banning fuel trade within three miles of the lake. To import fuel from Italy and Greece required pre-verification that it was for domestic consumption. To apply pressure, a Western diplomat talked with the media about jet fuel flowing from Albania to "the Serbian war machine."[20] Berisha called the allegations "absolutely not justified."[21]

Apparently dissatisfied with Albania's progress in stopping the trade, someone leaked U.S. intelligence reports about smuggling to the *New York Times*. The amount being smuggled from Albania had tripled in the first three months of the year, the reports said. As of March 1995, Albania was importing nine thousand more barrels a day than it consumed, mostly from Greece. The smuggling reportedly provided Yugoslavia with almost half its fuel.[22]

In addition to fuel, the Albanian government was also making money by selling ammunition and weapons from the old regime. For years under Hoxha, a factory in the town of Poliçan had produced bullets and hand grenades. Factories in Gramsh and Mjekës had made Kalashnikovs and explosives. The communist government sold these products abroad through a company called Makina Import. Production slumped with the transition in 1990, but the depots stayed full and foreign demand was high. During the Stability Government of 1991, the Ministry of Defense established a firm called MEICO (Military Export-Import Company) to sell the arms and ammunition that the communist government had piled high. When the DP came to power in 1992, MEICO's business flowed. The overcrowded warehouses offered a seemingly endless supply.

One recipient was the Bosnian Muslims, who were fighting Serbian forces, despite the U.N. arms embargo in place since September 1991. Former DP and Albanian government officials told me Berisha offered

Albania as a gateway to Bosnia for arms and foreign fighters. Berisha later admitted that Albania offered arms during the war to "friendly nations."[23] He did this with the knowledge of at least the United States, which was eager to arm the Bosnians and reach a balance of power between the warring parties.

In June 1995, Amnesty International published a report on the sale of Albanian and Israeli arms to the Rwandan army in violation of U.N. sanctions against that country.[24] Two months later, Taliban forces in Afghanistan intercepted a cargo plane destined for Kabul, forcing it to land in Kandahar. Inside they reportedly found a crew of seven Russians and three million rounds of ammunition from Albania bound for the Afghan government.[25]

The minister of defense, Safet Zhulali, a hard worker and heavy smoker who died of a heart attack in 2002, denied wrongdoing, but ministry staff during his tenure told me he aggressively tried to sell arms. According to a retired colonel from the U.S. Army who served as Zhulali's military advisor from May 1995 to December 1996, the ministry's inspector general investigated "only those he is ordered to inspect and generals and special 'friends' of the minister seem to not be subject to inspection."[26] Another report from the advisor discussed the corrosive effect on the military of "corruption, nepotism and the centralization of power."[27]

* * *

As Albanians spoke of "Salinism," Western diplomats and politicians praised the Democratic Party as the golden apple of Europe's East. They called Berisha the Václav Havel of the Balkans for his courageous battle against the communist wraith. No one denied the bumps and turns, but supporters said such problems must be expected from the region's most closed and repressive state. Some said Albanian democracy was too fragile to withstand a harsh critique. "[Chris] Hill and I thought Albanians had been through so much that they were willing to endure a lot in the transition," Ambassador Ryerson told me. Indeed, the ambassador's reports from Tirana praised Berisha's DP for bold reform, minimized criticism, and lambasted the Socialists who, he noted in cables, had "changed their name—but little else."[28]

Chris Hill said he was aware of Berisha's democratic failings but policy makers were looking at the bigger picture. "Senior people were saying, 'We have meltdown throughout the Balkans, but this crazy little place Albania is kind of holding it together,'" he said. "And who's doing that? Oh, it's Berisha. Let's help him."

International financial institutions like the World Bank and International Monetary Fund lauded their faithful student for cutting state spending and containing inflation. Economic growth was the fastest in Eastern Europe, they said, even if GDP was still below 1989 levels. The optimistic forecasts concealed the structural weaknesses and widespread corruption, as the 1997 pyramid schemes would soon show.

In return for good behavior, Western countries provided aid. In October 1993, Albania and Washington signed a military memorandum of understanding "to broaden and expand defense and military relations."[29] It was the first such agreement Washington signed with a former communist country. Berisha and Defense Minister Zhulali became favorites of U.S. secretary of defense William Perry, who sent advisors and training for the Albanian armed forces and helped build a military hospital, training compounds, and a radar station in the north. In February 1994, Albania joined NATO's Partnership for Peace and soon opened its ports and runways to NATO ships and planes. In June 1995, the CIA announced the deployment of Predator drones in Albania for surveillance flights over Yugoslavia, although U.S. drones had flown from Albania since at least early 1994. The two countries conducted nine joint military exercises in 1995. Minister Zhulali told U.S. officials that they had "no better friend in the Balkans, even among your allies."[30]

Western aid and praise impressed the population of a small and vulnerable state. Although Berisha's support in the country was waning, few Albanians went against the man with backers in the world's strongest capitals. Most Albanians did not know that, for Europe and the United States, Albania was a speck in the larger scene. From the perspective of Washington, Brussels, and Berlin, what happened inside Albania was of little consequence, so long as Kosovo and Macedonia stayed calm. Berisha could be a wolf at home, but he had to play sheep abroad.

Berisha understood the deal, former advisors said, but his character prevented him from sitting still. He craved to be a player in the region and he felt neglected by the Clinton administration. He also sensed the growing gap between his popularity at home and abroad. The Socialists had won local elections, the Democratic Alliance had taken part of the liberal intelligensia, and a newly formed Democratic Party of the Right was courting the former landowners. Eager for a spark to mobilize support, he started to play in the one place he wasn't allowed, like a child drifting to the deep end of the pool. In December 1993, Berisha began to support a radical ethnic Albanian group in Macedonia, backing off only under pressure from the United States. In April 1994 the Albanian police arrested five ethnic Greeks on charges of espionage. The arrests infuriated Greece and Washington, too. It did not seem so at the time, but it marked the beginning of Berisha's fall.

9

The Fall

Early in the morning of April 10, 1994, around 2:00 a.m., a small group of armed men crept towards an Albanian army outpost near the southern village of Peshkopia, not far from the border with Greece. It was the last night of a three-month training course for Albanian border guards, and the soldiers slept in the simple barracks. The intruders approached silently and opened fire without warning, killing two soldiers and seriously wounding three, before slipping into the dark.

The Albanian government quickly blamed a "Greek terrorist commando" and demanded the Greek government take responsibility. One of the attackers spoke Albanian with an accent of the Greek minority in Albania, the government said.

The Greek government condemned the attack and vehemently denied a role. An obscure organization called the Northern Epirus Liberation Front, which had fought in World War Two, claimed responsibility. The irredentist group sought annexation of southern Albania, which it considered the rightful Greek land of Northern Epirus.

On April 18, Albanian police arrested more than thirty members of the Greek minority. They released most of them but charged five ethnic Greeks from the organization Omonia with espionage, though they were not linked directly to the attack. Berisha wanted to charge as many as thirteen people, then DP officials told me, but his advisors suggested he stick to five.

Even that number enraged the Greeks. In retaliation, Greek police rounded up and expelled twenty thousand Albanian immigrants working illegally in Athens and other cities. Tirana ordered Greece to cut its diplomatic staff in Albania by almost half, provoking Athens to respond in kind.

The Greek government, with its powerful lobby in Washington, asked the U.S. government to intervene. Discrimination against Albania's Greek minority was already an issue for Athens, mostly concerning

Greek-language education and the return of church property, but these arrests went too far.

Washington said it would try. The U.S. government still adored Berisha, but the Albanian leader could not jeopardize relations with a member of NATO and the European Union.

The U.S. government dispatched a top official from the National Security Council, Richard Schifter, to speak with Berisha. They had known each other since 1991. Berisha sent holiday cards and the two men stayed on friendly terms. "I was really impressed with Sali Berisha," Schifter told me in 2002, recalling his early impressions of the man. "I was amazed to see such a strong personality and clear commitment to democracy come from the benighted system of Albania." His opinion soon changed.

Schifter arrived in Tirana on August 8, 1994. To his dismay, the indictments against the five Greeks were riddled with unsubstantiated claims. In a private meeting, he urged Berisha to tolerate the Greek community's activities, as long as its members did not advocate violence. Berisha promised to look into it, Schifter recalled.

A few days later, Ambassador Ryerson called Schifter in Washington. Berisha said the Omonia Five, as the defendants were known, would get eight years in prison instead of the death sentence, Ryerson reported. Schifter was livid. He made immediate plans to return to Albania with Ryerson's former deputy, Chris Hill.

Back in the region in early September, Schifter gave the Albanian government a letter from President Clinton that asked for détente. "It is in the interest of both countries, as well as all the world to avoid the creation of another big conflict in the dangerous region of the Balkans," the letter said.[1] The key moment of the trip came on September 2, when Schifter had dinner with Berisha and his aides. In retrospect, the meal turned the tide of Albanian-American relations. Berisha refused to be interviewed for this book, but Schifter called it "the most unpleasant dinner I've ever had."

The Albanians sat on one side of a table across from Schifter, Ambassador Ryerson, and Chris Hill, Schifter recalled. The NSC official repeated his call to free the five Greeks, stressing the importance of good neighborly relations. Berisha argued that the men had threatened the security of Albania, and he had evidence to prove it. As Schifter pushed,

Berisha got increasingly mad, accusing the U.S. envoy of siding with the Greeks.

"He was furious that I had dared to ask for less than eight years," Schifter said. "Right then and there I came to the conclusion that he was unstable psychologically."

According to Berisha's then advisor Genc Pollo, also present that night, Berisha felt ambushed, having thought the meeting was about foreign aid. "It was a very strange dinner with Schifter insisting and insisting and Berish refusing and refusing," Pollo said. "The other U.S. diplomats were staring at each other." Schifter returned to Washington and recommended that the U.S. distance itself from Berisha. "He would fall and we should not be associated," Schifter said.

The evening sparked a split between Schifter at the National Security Council and the State Department, CIA, and Pentagon, which saw Berisha as a stabile force in a fragile region. It became Schifter's personal fight, what Genc Pollo called "a private guerilla war," to convince Washington that Berisha was undemocratic and, more importantly, not trustworthy.

Some U.S. officials who worked on Albania think the influential Schifter reacted personally to Berisha's rebuke. "I think it had to do with Berisha, in Shifter's view, not fulfilling a promise," said Chris Hill, who attended the fateful dinner. "He gets very upset when he feels he hasn't been treated well." Bill Ryerson's successor as ambassador, Joe Lake, was more direct. "The problem was Dick Schifter's personal animosity of Sali Berisha," he said. "His goal was to bring Berisha down." Schifter responded that it had nothing to do with individuals but rather about human rights. "[Berisha] talked a democratic game but he was basically a Leninist," he said.

Regardless of Schifter's motivations, Berisha had developed a powerful enemy in Washington, and Schifter would play a central role in the Albanian leader's demise.

Berisha pressed on with the Omonia trial, despite protests from Greece and the United States. In September, a judge sentenced the men to between six and eight years in prison. Greece expelled seventy thousand more Albanians, and the police beat men as they tossed them across the border. The European Union and Council of Europe publicly criticized the trial and launched diplomatic efforts to resolve the row.

In Washington, Schifter turned up the heat. Throughout 1995 and 1996, he expanded contacts with the Albanian opposition and became what one Berisha advisor called "a real scourge for all of Berisha's friends in Washington."[2] Hill said Schifter had "kind of a hunting license with Albania," and his actions emboldened Berisha's opponents. "Berisha is not a saint," Hill said. "But he's not quite the bad guy the Greek lobby portrayed him to be."

From Berisha's perspective, the criticism proved that the Clinton administration was not a friend. He lamented the loss of his Republican allies in Washington, and maybe thought he was doing them a favor by giving Clinton and Schifter a hard time. George and Barbara Bush came to Albania on a private visit in November 1994, perhaps to talk Berisha down, and Berisha awarded the ex-president the Order of Skanderbeg for "liberating the peoples of Eastern Europe."[3]

In October 1994, an appeals court reduced the Omonia Five's sentences and released one of the defendants. In February 1995, Albania's Supreme Court ordered the four remaining defendants released. Berisha seemed to have relented but it quickly emerged that the court's chief justice, Zef Brozi, had acted without consultation. SHIK head Bashkim Gazidede telephoned Brozi, calling him a "traitor" and "Greek spy," Brozi told me.

Greece responded positively to the decision and diplomatic relations slowly improved. In spring 1995, the Greek police arrested five militants from the Northern Epirus Liberation Front in connection with the Peshkopia attack. Washington expressed relief.

"I was pleased to hear that the Omonia four were released in an orderly and appropriate manner," then assistant secretary of state Richard Holbrooke wrote privately to Berisha in February 1995. "I realize the many difficulties you are facing, and I know that things often look quite different from the outside than they do on the inside, but this is an important moment for you and your country internationally, and should not be lost."[4]

But Berisha's ties with the U.S. failed to improve. More than restrictions on the press or judiciary, U.S. policy makers cared about Balkan stability, and some beyond Richard Schifter began to doubt whether Berisha could be trusted to keep his word. If he reacted so aggressively in response to a small attack, what might he do if really provoked?

* * *

I returned to New York in summer 1994 to resume graduate school and was shocked to see President Berisha hailed as a democratic chief. My experience in Tirana had left a different taste, and I knew many Albanians felt the same. Based on material collected during the year, I wrote a report for Human Rights Watch on the Greek minority, which was getting attention after the Omonia arrests. The report cited discrimination against the Greek community but concluded that the main minority under threat was the democratic-minded citizens of Albania.[5]

That fall, Berisha organized a referendum for a new constitution. Despite being advised to let the Democratic Party run the campaign, Berisha led the campaign, visiting remote villages and losing his voice, television crews in tow. Without access to state media, the opposition had trouble presenting their views. The police blocked their meetings and rallies.

The voting on November 6, 1994, went smoothly, with approximately 84 percent of eligible voters taking part. But the government and Democratic Party were shocked by the outcome: the constitution had suffered a stinging defeat.

That night Berisha stayed up to the early morning making calls, his advisors told me. The cabinet and Democratic Party leadership debated whether to doctor the results. Never had they pondered a loss, let alone one this large. "Berisha was so convinced he'd win, he didn't bother to fix it," said the British advisor Guy Roberts, who was working with Prime Minister Meksi at the time.

At first Berisha, who saw the vote as a personal defeat, thought about resigning. In the end, he chose to fight. As a State Department analysis from the time correctly assessed, "Initially devastated by the defeat, Berisha has regained his balance and is not likely to accept early elections," as the opposition was demanding.[6] Under pressure from the U.S. embassy, the government finally released the official results: 54 percent had voted against.

The problem was not the proposed constitution, which largely met European standards. Rather, Albanians had rejected the manner in which the constitution was sold. Berisha's booming voice on television, leading the nightly news, reminded them of a time gone by. His visits to the countryside surrounded by supplicants evoked images of an era that the new constitution was supposed to replace.

At first the State Department missed this point. An internal analysis attributed the loss to "economic discontent, concern over tensions with Greece, and a feeling that parliament should debate the constitution."[7] A later report from the embassy was more astute, adding as reasons "the government's high-handed pro-constitution media campaign, the overly incestuous relation between the government and the Democratic Party, and the perception of widespread government corruption." It is possible, the report said, "that some voters were alienated when they saw a future that too closely resembled the past."[8]

The Albanian opposition and some independent analysts were less equivocating. For them the defeat showed the extent of popular discontent with Berisha's rule. Because he had campaigned so personally, voters saw it as a referendum on his leadership, rather than on the constitution. On this point, the U.S. embassy eventually agreed. "Berisha was clearly as interested in an endorsement of his presidency as he was in giving Albania a constitution," a December cable read.[9]

In an open letter to the president, the well-known painter Edi Rama summarized the result:

> The vote against the draft constitution was a protest vote against the party of Sali Berisha, the television of Sali Berisha, the newspapers of Sali Berisha, the government of Sali Berisha, the coffee-cup trials of Sali Berisha, the Security Service of Sali Berisha, the intellectuals recruited by Sali Berisha, the Kosovar president of Sali Berisha, the sclerotic fogies of scientific communism and the bards of Sali Berisha's Writers League, the Canon of Lekë Dukagjin and the *çiftelis* [Albanian lute] of Sali Berisha, and the Enverist mass actions of the democratic groupies of Sali Berisha, who mobilized even toddlers to take their places at rallies. It would not be any exaggeration, Mr. President, to say that the vote against the draft constitution was a protest even against the hoarse voice of Sali Berisha.[10]

Berisha said the defeat was the understandable result of tough economic reform. He also blamed corruption and reshuffled the government. Eight ministers lost their posts and were replaced by even more loyal supporters.

As with previous losses, the referendum defeat threw the Democratic Party into disarray. For four years, party chairman Eduard Selami had supported Berisha, dutifully presenting a moderate face abroad, but after the referendum he tried to make a move. He called for a government change and, after the reshuffle, said that the prime minister should also be the party head. Directly opposing Berisha, Selami then supported the opposition's call for parliament to approve the new constitution.

Berisha shot back with vitriol, calling Selami the "Iago of democracy." But unlike Othello, it was only a question of time before the master dispatched his treasonous aide. At an extraordinary DP conference in March, party members denounced Selami for treason and ousted him as party head. United States ambassador Joe Lake told Washington it was "a negative milestone in the history of democratic Albania."[11]

Selami left Albania soon thereafter, and got asylum in the United States. "Berisha started falling into the old mentality," he told me from a Starbucks in Norfolk, Virginia, where he was living with his family. "The opposition is the enemy."

* * *

The referendum debacle cast Albania into a dangerous phase. Berisha and the Democratic Party felt the sting of defeat. They saw their popularity dipping and got nervous about parliamentary elections that spring. The Socialist Party, meanwhile, rode the seesaw's other end. Only four years after losing power, they saw a chance to bounce back.

In this atmosphere, the repression increased. The police arrested more journalists and secret police harassed the opposition. When I visited Albania for Human Rights Watch in 1995, SHIK stayed close at hand. Eager to annoy Berisha, the Socialists antagonized and provoked.

In Washington, Richard Schifter was telling everyone that Berisha was a dangerous man. Still, the State Department, CIA, and Pentagon were not willing to cast the doctor aside. The U.S. embassy followed a middle path. Ambassador Lake broke Ryerson's practice and started to meet with the Socialists, which he said incurred Berisha's wrath. But he also disagreed with Schifter's hardline approach. "If we wanted to change Albania, to bring democracy to the table, we had to seek to influence Berisha to pursue that goal, and we had certain levers we could use," he told me. "The main one was the tremendous respect and influence the U.S. had in Albania."

Lake's approach did not go over well with Schifter, who thought Berisha had to go. "I thought Joe Lake would be understanding but he wasn't," Schifter told me. In March 1996, Lake resigned because, he told me, he did not feel he could properly do his job.

That fall Berisha visited the United States. The relationship had soured but he still enjoyed support. The Bosnian war was ending and everyone knew the Albanians in Kosovo were the Balkans' unresolved mess. The U.S. wanted to ensure that Albania did not stir the pot.

"Our decision to invite President Berisha to Washington reflected the important role Albania has played in promoting stability in the former Yugoslavia," President Clinton explained to members of Congress who questioned the visit. "Tirana has worked effectively to encourage moderation on the part of Albanians in Kosovo and the Former Yugoslav Republic of Macedonia and, in so doing, has been instrumental in preventing the further spreading of the Bosnian conflict to the south Balkans."[12]

Berisha met Clinton on September 12, 1995, and had what the White House called a cordial meeting. The only public criticism was about treatment of the Greek minority.[13] Back in Albania, nine days after the meeting, Berisha engineered the illegal removal of the chief justice of the Supreme Court, who had shown the audacity seven months before to release the four Omonia prisoners and was about to review the case of Socialist head Fatos Nano. The move reminded Albanians of Enver Hoxha, who conducted purges after trips to the Soviet Union or China to suggest the cleansing was sanctioned from above.

Washington was furious. The State Department issued démarches in Tirana and Washington to protest what it considered a politically motivated purge. A pointed statement said the justice's dismissal had taken place "under circumstances which do not appear to comport with democratic procedures."[14] Fearing arrest, the justice, Zef Brozi, left for the United States, escorted to the airport by an official from the U.S. embassy.

* * *

Just after his trip to Washington, I met Sali Berisha for the first and only time. He came to the Council on Foreign Relations in New York, where he gave a radio interview. As the Human Rights Watch researcher for Albania, I was asked to respond. In confident spurts, Berisha defended his government's work. "We will have elections early next year," he said. "And definitely I will win."[15] His use of the first person struck me at once. The elections were for parliament, which would not elect the president until the following year.

Human Rights Watch issued a large report on Albania a few months later, based on research conducted during my year in Tirana. It documented police abuse, press restrictions, and the lack of independent courts. It acknowledged the monumental changes since the fall of communism but criticized the government for reestablishing a one-party state. "Critics of the ruling Democratic Party are often regarded as critics of 'democracy,'" I wrote.[16]

As we released the report, I went to Washington to testify in Congress at a hearing on Albania. I naïvely thought policy makers knew the Albanian government was straying from its democratic path, but the other panelists had different views. The head of the Albanian VOA program, Elez Biberaj, praised Berisha as "an effective president, shaping the nation's agenda during a period of momentous political, economic, and social changes." An American lawyer working in Tirana was critical but struck a balanced tone. They read their testimonies and I took a deep breath. Maybe I had it wrong. But my statement was printed and I lacked the courage to change it on the spot. I adjusted my glasses and started to read, gaining confidence as I recounted my impressions from the previous year. Parliamentary elections were planned for spring 1996, I said, and "I must express my deep concern that these elections will be neither free nor fair."[17]

That spring I got a telephone call from Richard Schifter, who asked for information on human rights abuses in Albania. I was surprised, because I did not know Schifter's position on Berisha at the time and I questioned the motives of his call. Surely the U.S. government knew what was happening on the ground. I gradually realized that U.S. policy on Albania, as on most countries, was influenced by different institutions and groups, and Schifter was gathering ammunition for his fight.

* * *

The May 1996 parliamentary elections were Albania's first serious democratic test. The Party of Labor had manipulated the 1991 elections and
the 1992 campaign was a vote against the repressive past. These elections
would show whether voters and politicians could address the pressing
issues—the economy, the judiciary, foreign relations—and, more importantly, whether the new rulers would peacefully step down if asked to
leave. Had Albania established institutions in four years that were strong
enough to withstand a transfer of power?

It quickly became clear that the answer was no.

The Democrats entered the campaign feeling insecure. The 1993 local
elections and the 1995 referendum had showed their support was in de-
cline. They looked at Eastern European countries such as Poland and
Hungary, where former communist parties were returning from the
grave. Moderate Democrats argued that they needed another four years
to implement reform. Hardliners said the elections must be won at all
costs.

In September 1995, the DP-controlled parliament passed a law that
tilted the field. Cumbersomely named the Law on Genocide and Crimes
against Humanity Committed in Albania during Communist Rule for
Political, Ideological, and Religious Motives—better known as the
"Genocide Law"—it banned former high-ranking officials from holding
positions in parliament, the executive branch, the judiciary, or state-run
media until 2002. The law banned people on the basis of positions they
had held rather than acts they had committed.

Two months later, parliament approved the equally lengthy Law on
the Verification of the Moral Character of Officials and Other Persons
Connected with the Defense of the Democratic State, sarcastically called
the "Virginity Law." The law regulated the opening of the Sigurimi files
to determine who had collaborated with the secret police and defined
more precisely who should be banned from office. It established a commission of seven people to review the files, six of them appointed by
the executive branch and one by parliament. The commission met in
private and kept its findings unknown, unless the candidate refused to
withdraw. Candidates could appeal, but they were not allowed to see
the evidence against them. Defending the laws, Berisha claimed they

affected "people who were responsible for the murders of some 600 to 1,000 people on Albania's borders in 1990 and are still in power."[18]

The U.S. embassy in Tirana saw through the ruse. "The PD [Democratic Party] has set the stage for a nasty campaign, beginning late last year with personal and legal attacks on opposition figures and the judiciary, and continuing with the recent passage of the 'Genocide' law," Joe Lake reported to Washington before his departure.[19]

As intended, the laws hit the opposition. The "Virginity Commission" declared 139 people ineligible to run in the election, although seven successfully appealed. Of those banned, three came from the Democratic Party. The DP paper *Rilindja Demokratike* ran the names of the banned candidates on April 13 under the headline "Red Front, the Front of Spies."

In late November, the authorities exhumed the remains of more than forty people from a mass grave outside Shkoder, possibly the bodies of political prisoners. The man who found the grave said he had known of it for ten years but was too afraid to speak. More mass graves were revealed the next month, allegedly of former political prisoners or people shot trying to cross the border. Later that winter, the police arrested twenty-four former communist officials, some of them for the second time, including Ramiz Alia, who had been released from his first prison term after two years.

To ensure a DP win, parliament then passed a biased election law. According to the U.S. International Republican Institute, until then a strong DP supporter, the ruling party gained "complete control over every level of the process."[20]

None of these developments went down well in Washington, where Berisha had promised President Clinton a proper vote. Schifter and other critics were gaining strength. But Berisha still enjoyed support at the Pentagon, which viewed a judge's removal and draconian laws as bumps in the road. From the military's perspective, regional security remained the top concern, and authoritarianism would not break an otherwise fruitful bond.

In April 1996, Defense Secretary William Perry spent three days in Albania for a meeting of south Balkan defense ministers. "You have made tremendous strides in integrating Albania into Europe as a whole," he told a press conference while announcing an increase in military aid. "This has taken great courage and great determination. Do not stop now—see this change through."²¹ Berisha responded by giving Perry the Order of Skanderbeg.

After Perry's visit, a senior State Department official arrived to clarify Washington's view. Albania and the Democratic Party still had U.S. support, Undersecretary of State for Global Affairs Timothy Wirth told Albanian officials, but free and fair elections were central to maintaining good ties. He warned in private meetings against the "arrogance of power."²² At a meeting and dinner with Berisha, he stressed how closely the elections would be watched.²³

In April, a Socialist Party delegation visited Washington on a private trip to meet U.S. officials, including Shifter at the NSC. American officials asked three questions, in this order, one of the visiting Socialists recalled: (1) What is your position and influence in Kosovo? (2) How are your relations with Greece? (3) What is your position on communism and democratization?

On May 8, 1996, with elections approaching, Albanian foreign minister Alfred Serreqi met U.S. secretary of state Warren Christopher in Washington. According to Serreqi, Christopher reiterated a willingness to cooperate with the Democratic Party, but stressed that a mono-party parliament would be a destabilizing force. Serreqi said he promised Christopher that the elections would be fair. According to a State Department memo on the meeting, Serreqi assured Christopher that Albania had "taken all possible measures to see that the elections are conducted properly, and promised to respect the results."²⁴ After the meeting, the State Department told the press that Serreqi had "assured the Secretary that the elections would be free and fair."²⁵

* * *

The Democratic Party opened its campaign with dancers, singers, models, and politicians at a huge Tirana rally and concert, featuring a speech by Berisha, broadcast on television at prime time. That kicked off a series of concerts across Albania, with the motto "With Us, Everybody Wins."

The Socialists had trouble getting permissions for rallies, and retreated to smaller halls and peripheral fields. The International Republican Institute later called the approval process for public meetings "arbitrary and biased."²⁶

President Berisha at an election rally in Berat on May 21, 1996. © Reuters

Traveling tirelessly around the country, Berisha warned of unrepentant communists and former spies who would drag Albania back to the dark ages. He trumpeted the economy's stellar growth. The Socialists spoke of a new dictatorship and said the economy had nowhere to go but up. Between the two rivals was a smattering of smaller parties. The most formidable were the Democratic Alliance and Social Democratic Party, which joined in a coalition called the Center Pole. According to the new election law, the coalition had to clear 8 percent of the vote to enter parliament.

During the campaign, Washington took a cautious approach. In contrast, some Western European groups gave Berisha their full support. Former Austrian foreign minister Alois Mock, head of the conservative European Democratic Union, attended a Democratic Party meeting. The Konrad Adenauer Foundation of Germany's Christian Democratic Union gave electoral advice. One of Berisha's most vocal supporters was Leni Fischer, a German politician little known at home who headed the

Council of Europe's Parliamentary Assembly. Fischer praised the Genocide Law, saying that similar legislation was needed for East Germany. Berisha later awarded her the Gold Medal of Mother Teresa.[27]

Election day was tense. Some parts of the Democratic Party, particularly members of the secret police, were not going to allow a DP defeat. They feared losing the benefits of power. They also understood Albania's tradition of revenge. A Socialist government would kick them out of their jobs, and probably throw them in jail.

"Unfortunately, something began a few days before," said Tritan Shehu, who had become head of the Democratic Party. "Attempts from some sectors of the security service and police began to create problems. The Socialist Party was provoking and they were not able to avoid these provocations."

As the day progressed, stories of harassment and ballot stuffing flooded in from observers. They saw tampered ballot boxes, premarked ballots, and multiple ballots folded together. At a polling station in Berat, voter turnout reached 105 percent. In Kukes, an Albanian-speaking observer overheard the local election commission head apologize to someone on the phone because observers had made it impossible to "deliver the required results."[28] In the afternoon, Berisha unexpectedly extended the close of voting from 8:00 to 10:00 p.m.

Around 6:00 p.m., the Socialist Party had seen enough. Citing massive irregularities, they announced they were boycotting the election. Their members on the local election commissions withdrew. The other opposition parties followed suit.

It remains unclear whether the boycott was a spontaneous reaction to the irregularities, as the Socialists claimed, or a premeditated tactic to disrupt the vote, as the Democrats and Berisha backers in Washington argued. Regardless, with the opposition removing itself from the process, DP supporters went wild. Without opposition observers, they gleefully stuffed ballots at voting centers from north to south.

Years later, top DP officials admitted to me that their party had committed widespread fraud. "Short of direct ballot stuffing, the problem was the massive involvement of the officials and state apparatus," said Genc Pollo, a close Berisha aide at the time. "The administrative resources were in favor of the ruling party—that was rather obvious."

That night, Democratic Party supporters hit Tirana's main boulevard and Skanderbeg Square to celebrate with young men hanging out of cars, waving party flags, honking horns, and shooting guns. A red coffin symbolizing the death of communism rode up and down the boulevard atop a car. Inside the ministries, raki flowed. Official results were far from complete, but the DP announced winning more than 60 percent.

Inside Tirana's hotels, the scores of international observers were not convinced. They sat together comparing notes of intimidation and fraud. For many these were the worst elections in Europe since 1989. The next morning, observers from the OSCE's Office for Democratic Institutions and Human Rights (ODIHR) gathered in Tirana to debrief. While some reported minor irregularities, the majority had seen major vioations. They drafted a critical statement and sent it to OSCE headquarters in Vienna for review. To their surprise, headquarters answered that they should tone down the criticisms, a person involved in drafting the statement told me.

The OSCE had a second group of monitors in Albania from the Parliamentary Assembly, comprised of European parliamentarians. That group issued a cautious statement that highlighted problems but generally approved the vote. "Officials at polling stations, in general, performed their duties in an orderly manner," the statement said.[29]

The U.S. embassy's initial report lay somewhere in between the two versions from the OSCE. "There is little doubt that the May 26 Albanian parliamentary elections were fraught with numerous irregularities," a May 27 cable to Washington reported. "Most of these were practical, administrative and procedural in nature. As such, they were generally insignificant, although their sheer volume speaks poorly of the organization of the process and will serve only to increase general voter distrust."[30]

That night Berisha gave a victory speech in Skanderbeg Square, saying the opposition had boycotted the vote to conceal its defeat.

Some of the OSCE's ODIHR monitors were deeply troubled. They feared that the mild report by their colleagues from the Parliamentary Assembly and censorship from Vienna would lead to the approval of a fraudulent vote. "We were very upset with what we had seen," Aage Borchgrevink, a Norwegian observer with ODIHR, told me years later. "So many of the observers were giving positive or featureless statements—they were spreading this lie." In response, Borchgrevink and eight observers from Norway sat down to prepare an alternative view. They drafted a statement condemning the violations and convinced two British monitors to join their dissident group. On May 28, they held a press conference in the lobby of Hotel Tirana on Skanderbeg Square.

"The elections did not meet international standards for free and fair elections," their statement began. After summarizing the problems, from politicized commissions to "an atmosphere of intimidation and coercion," the statement concluded that "the will of the Albanian people was not expressed in a free manner."[31]

As the renegade observers read their statement, the situation outside the hotel got worse. The police had denied the opposition parties permission for a demonstration in Skanderbeg Square, warning they would use force to disperse a crowd. Opposition politicians and their supporters were gathering nevertheless. At midday a pouring rain began, beating down on the commanding statue of Skanderbeg. Police reinforcements arrived, some in riot gear. Two armored trucks guarded the Ministry of the Interior. "Well, it's time to get beaten," Neritan Ceka from the Democratic Alliance told his colleagues and a foreign diplomat as he finished his coffee and set out for the square.

International observers, diplomats, and journalists watched from the veranda of the Tirana Hotel as the police moved in with batons against the opposition leaders and the crowd. The police were "clobbering people without regard," one U.S. observer said.[32] They beat six opposition leaders, including Democratic Party founders Gramoz Pashko and Arben Imami, who lost his front teeth, and dragged them away in vans. Paskal Milo from the Social Democrats, later Albania's foreign minister, broke his arm.

"May 28 was absolutely out of control," then Democratic Party head Tritan Shehu admitted to me years later, after he had split with Berisha. He attributed the violence to extreme forces in the intelligence service and police, calling it "the most stupid, crazy and anti-democratic action."

"Definitely it was unwise to club protesters in front of the cameras," Genc Pollo told me, after he had broken with Berisha (and before he had joined him again). "It was like a modern-day Coliseum."

Even former SHIK agents remember the day with regret. "I was happy when the DP won in 1996," one former agent told me. "But then I saw it was maybe the biggest mistake we made."

The police denied that anyone had been hurt, claiming that Sigurimi agents in the crowd had "called for war, violence and massive exodus to neighboring countries."[33] Berisha called on Albania's citizens not to "fall prey to the decisions of the Albanian former secret police leaders, today's Socialist Party leaders, who, after their total defeat, withdrew from the free elections."[34] He called the outspoken OSCE observers supporters of Enver Hoxha. "Marxist-Leninist organizations from Norway have old ties since the sixties with the Party of Labor of Albania (SP's predecessor)," an item in the rabidly pro-government *Albania* newspaper declared.[35]

On May 29, the Central Election Commission released the initial results. The Democrats had won ninety-five direct seats, and the Socialists had won five. The winner in nine zones remained unclear, so a runoff was called for the following week. There would also be a revote in four zones due to irregularities, the commission said. "The Albanian democracy today is surer than ever in its history," Berisha declared. "On May 26 it received through the free vote the blessing of the whole Albanian people, the blessing of God."[36]

In the following days, the various observer missions began to release their reports. The International Republican Institute said in a preliminary statement that, "while not widespread, observed voting irregularities raise serious questions about the conduct and integrity of a number of Albania's 1996 Parliamentary contests."[37] The same day, IRI released the results of its exit poll, which predicted the DP had won 56 percent of the vote, compared to 22 percent for the SP.[38] Berisha's defenders in Albania and abroad pointed to the poll as evidence that the DP would have won the elections regardless of any rigging.

After some delay, the OSCE issued two reports that reflected the divisions within the organization. Continuing the tone set by the Norwegians and Brits, the Office for Democratic Institutions and Human Rights issued a critical report, although weaker than initially proposed, that highlighted intimidation, voter list manipulation, and ballot stuffing. The OSCE's Parliamentary Assembly was critical but more reserved.

The U.S. government, which had been promised free and fair elections, was not restrained. On June 1, the State Department declared the elections "a significant step backward" from previous votes and urged that some races be rerun.[39] In Tirana, U.S. diplomats met with the Democrats and other parties to discuss a solution, but Berisha was unwilling to bend. DP officials open to compromise told U.S. diplomats that the president would not back down. He wanted his victory to be absolute.

As if nothing had happened, the Albanian government held the runoff vote on June 2 without the opposition. The intransigence made outside pressure increase. International institutions and foreign governments had sent observers to the elections, and it was unacceptable to embarrass them in this way. Berisha was forcing the international community to approve a deeply flawed vote, widely condemned in the world press.

Looking for a compromise, the State Department offered Berisha a way to save face: rerun thirty-seven zones. Even if the DP lost them all, the party's victory would be secure. Berisha summoned Prime Minister Meksi and party head Tritan Shehu to discuss the idea. Both men accepted the proposal, they told me separately, seeing it as a way to win the elections and satisfy international demands. Berisha criticized them for selling the Democratic Party's vote. "His idea was not to win the elections but to completely destroy the opposition," Shehu said.

The U.S. proposal insulted Berisha's hardline approach. For him, compromise showed weakness. In addition, former DP officials told me, the president never thought the United States would push him too hard. For years Washington had overlooked Berisha's indiscretions—the arrest of Fatos Nano, restrictions on the media, and the removal of Chief Justice Brozi. In Berisha's mind, this too would pass. Certainly, he told advisors at the time, Washington would not turn its back on a man so central to stability in the region.

Berisha also had practical reasons to stand firm. Although the U.S. proposal would allow the Democrats to hold parliament, a two-thirds majority was needed for Berisha's reelection as president the following year. His plan, then prime minister Meksi and DP head Shehu told me, was to get reelected, and then amend the constitution so the president would henceforth be elected by direct popular vote. This would secure an additional two terms.

Under growing international pressure, the Central Elections Commission declared a revote in an additional thirteen zones, bringing the total number of revotes to seventeen—still below what the international community desired. Washington, the European Union, and the OSCE proposed an international team to investigate irregularities and make recommendations. Berisha rejected all allegations of fraud and said Albania would hold new elections only after four years. He refused to see an envoy from the OSCE.

In an attempt to break through, the U.S. government asked former president George Bush to take time from a holiday in Greece to meet with Berisha. On June 16, Bush traveled by yacht with his wife, Barbara, and future Secretary of State Colin Powell to Vlora from nearby Corfu. After lunch at a government villa, the three men retreated for a conversation aboard the yacht, but the discussion seemed not to help.

"Albania continues to be a stable country that will consolidate democracy despite efforts by ex-communists to destabilize it," Berisha said after the meeting.[40]

The limited revote took place on June 16 without the opposition. The DP won all seventeen zones. The final results looked like a parliament from the time of Enver: Democratic Party, 122 seats; Socialist Party, ten seats; Republican Party, three seats; Union for Human Rights, three seats; and the National Front Party, two seats.

Relations with the United States got worse. In mid-July, Undersecretary of State Timothy Wirth wanted to meet Berisha again, but the Albanian president refused. Shocked, embassy officials urged Defense Minister Zhulali to convince Berisha to change his mind. They summoned Tritan Shehu to explain. "We're sure you'll win the elections and you're better than the Socialists," Shehu remembered an embassy official saying. "But don't make artificial problems."

"I didn't like him from the beginning," Wirth told me in 2010, referring to Berisha. "I thought he was lying to me."

The U.S. embassy tried to convince Berisha directly. He responded that the elections were a "matter of sovereignty" and Albania's "institutions must be respected."[41] United States congressman Eliot Engel, chairman of the Albanian caucus in Congress, tried to visit but Berisha refused to see him too.

The new parliament convened on July 1 with 87 percent of the seats held by the Democratic Party, more than enough to reelect Berisha president and to amend the constitution. In protest, the U.S. embassy did not send a representative to the opening session. "Ceremonial contacts are not encouraged and may be prohibited in the future," a directive from Washington said.[42] An embassy spokesman said the U.S. "did not want to give the impression that we consider this matter closed."[43] The electoral manipulation, the beating of the opposition, and the unwillingness to negotiate were not only bad signs—they had embarrassed the United States.

At a congressional hearing in Washington, a senior State Department official cited "serious irregularities" in the elections despite "repeated assurances by Albanian officials" that they would be free and fair. Most significantly, he called for new parliamentary elections to "restore the faith of the Albanian people and the international community in Albanian democracy."[44]

* * *

The elections poisoned Albania's political scene. The opposition felt robbed and the ruling party felt under attack. The Democrats knew they had manipulated the vote, and this bred a sense of insecurity that made Berisha more sensitive and scared. The secret police cut the phone lines at the Socialist Party headquarters, *Koha Jonë* newspaper, and the Albanian Helsinki Committee. The Ministry of the Interior fired seven policemen for the post-election violence in Skanderbeg Square, but six of them got transferred to other jobs. The prosecutor charged the opposition leaders with having organized an illegal demonstration.

On June 15, a group of prominent intellectuals published a declaration that urged the international community to stop the resurgence of dictatorship. "President Berisha's unfettered power beyond all democratic control is violating all the standards set by the OSCE, despite all promises to the contrary, and he has no reason not to also break his two-faced promises connected with international and regional policy," the statement said, showing an understanding of the West's concern for wider stability. "Just as he is sacrificing the rights and freedoms of the citizens of the Republic of Albania for the sake of personal power, he may with the same motives trifle even more dangerously with the fate of Albanians across the border."[45]

As much as people grumbled privately about Berisha, many public fig-ures refused to sign their names to the statement out of fear. The twenty-seven people who did sign got lambasted in the pro-government media for being "power-hungry charlatans, perverts and spies."[46] They got ha-rassing phone calls at home and were threatened with losing their jobs.

To mute the criticism, Berisha announced a new government. Despite rumors of corruption, Aleksandër Meksi remained prime minister. The loyal Tritan Shehu, a critic only after breaking with Berisha, got pro-moted to deputy prime minister and foreign minister. Safet Zhulali re-mained minister of defense, perhaps because of his good relations with the United States. Halit Shamata replaced Agron Musaraj as minister of the interior but the powerful heads of the police and secret police, Agim Shehu and Bashkim Gazidede, remained. Both men would play major roles in Berisha's fight to survive.

* * *

Five months after the troubled elections, Albanians had to vote again. Local elections were set for October 1996 and, given the May fiasco, the campaign assumed great value to both Albanians and the outside world. Particularly the Democrats wanted to show that they could organize a proper election. A clean win would convince doubters of their mandate from May.

In Washington, an interagency working group coordinated U.S. pol-icy. The NSC and State Department felt the Pentagon was being too soft. The unified position, as articulated to Foreign Minister Tritan Shehu in October, was that Albania must restore its democratic credentials by holding free and fair local elections, passing a new constitution through a referendum, and holding parliamentary elections within the new con-stitutional framework. "This is a USG-wide policy," Shehu was told, ac-cording to a State Department cable from October 1996.[47]

With parliament under his control, Berisha acquiesced to some oppo-sition and international demands. He established a permanent Central Elections Commission and revised election procedures. Still angry at what he called the OSCE's communist sympathies, he limited the num-ber of monitors the organization could send. Rather than accept limits, the OSCE refused to send monitors at all. In contrast, the Council of Eu-rope sent its observers, despite OSCE pleas to maintain a common front.

To everyone's relief, the local elections went well, and observers considered them acceptably fair. The State Department called them "sufficiently democratic," but repeated its call for new parliamentary elections.[48] Berisha supporters in Washington argued that Albania was back on track.

The Democrats won 326 of 374 local posts, or more than 87 percent, suggesting that it would have won the May 1996 elections without resorting to fraud. Even loyal Democratic Pary supporters began to wonder why the May victory had to have been so complete.

Despite the improvement, Berisha's critics in Washington had gained the upper hand. The uncompromising president had shamed his patrons. As one State Department official told me at the time: "We are not going to tie our horse to Berisha."

Berisha also distanced himself from the United States. He expelled an American advisor to the minister of defense, declaring him persona non grata, and sent Albanian military officials to Germany for training. Still angry with the OSCE, Berisha offered the Council of Europe a more prominent role.

The final break with Washington, however, came when Berisha played across the border. In December 1996, as tension in Kosovo was rising, he supported calls for Kosovo Albanians to take matters into their own hands and rely less on international support—a clear reference to the United States.

By this point, even Berisha's supporters in the Pentagon felt he had gone too far. The friction with Greece could be contained. Stolen elections can be tolerated. But a threat to regional stability, with American troops in Bosnia and Macedonia, was too much. "Berisha didn't switch state policy but he suggested a change," a U.S. official working on Albania told me about Berisha's shift on Kosovo. "By that point, even his backers had lost all justifiable reasons to support him."

The Albanian who probably sensed the shift more than anyone was Defense Minister Safet Zhulali, who had what his U.S. military advisor called "a single-minded devotion to the United States."[49] In an interview in April 1997, after the Democrats lost power, Zhulali accused Berisha of using Kosovo to distract Albanians and foreigners from the domestic crisis. "President Berisha's last political move to transfer attention towards Kosovo, in trying to radicalize the situation, failed," he said. "This also brought about his final isolation from the outside world."[50]

PART IV

Blinded by Gold

Crash of the Pyramids, 1997

10

Profiteers' Pact

The International Monetary Fund and World Bank could not have been more thrilled with their pliant client in Albania. Since 1992, Tirana had followed their formulaic diet of liberalizing prices, cutting government subsidies, and containing inflation. "We do not cure a foot, we cut it off," an IMF official told a shocked meeting of the government in spring 1992, one Albanian minister recalled.

At first the formula had success. After the calamity of 1990–91, inflation decreased and production rose. Albania emerged from chaos to tentative calm, and IMF and World Bank officials lavished praise. Albania was the "success story" of the region and a "star pupil," they said. When growth reached a reported 11 percent in 1993, they declared Albania the fastest growing economy in Europe.[1]

"Your government deserves our deepest congratulation for the success it has achieved against chaos, inflation and economic crisis," a top World Bank official told Berisha in 1994.[2] In December 1994, IMF head Michel Camdessus said Albania had made "prodigious efforts and remarkable results have been seen in this small country."[3]

On the surface, the praise seemed apt. The country that had banned private cars was clogged with Mercedes. Espresso sippers lounged in cafés, surrounded by new shops. High-rise apartment buildings were filling Tirana's exclusive Block.

A closer look revealed deep fissures and cracks.

First, the government doctored the data. Officials at Albania's statistics institute, INSTAT, told me that ministers inflated numbers to please the president. "He wants to see what looks good," then INSTAT director Milva Ekonomi remembered one minister told her. The World Bank and IMF knew of the ruse but refused to speak. "I know inflation was 5% in July, but the government reported it at 1.3%," the World Bank representative in Tirana told the U.S. ambassador in September 1996, according to an embassy report. "In August it was reported as 1.9%, but who knows?"[4]

Second, the privatization of farms and cooperatives complicated accurate data collection. Determining agricultural production required
guesswork, and some Albanian economists believe the government
vastly overstated the growth. In apparent agreement, the IMF retroac-
tively revised GDP figures downward in 1997.

Third, even if the numbers had been accurate, the astonishing growth
was less impressive when compared to the past. The economy was expanding, but Albania remained Europe's poorest country. Absolute GDP
did not pass the 1989 level until the year 2000. The economic miracle
was Albania bouncing off the rocky floor.[5]

From 1992 to 1996, the economy stood on three pillars, each of them
weak. First were remittances from Albanians working abroad, mostly
young men in Italy and Greece. As Greece had shown after the Omonia
arrests, it could expel those workers when tension flared. Second was
foreign aid from Europe and the United States, which was substantial
but still below the country's need. Third was illegal trade: the smuggling
of oil, arms, and drugs. Albania did not produce. Unemployment stayed
high. Foreign investment was scant. The center of Tirana had water cuts
in summer and brownouts in winter.

The IMF and World Bank overlooked these essential facts. Similar to
Albania's political patrons in Europe and the United States, who focused
on short-term Balkan stability over building institutions, the international financial institutions concentrated on immediate success without
addressing structural flaws.

* * *

By 1993, Albanian mattresses were full with bills. No one trusted the
state-run banks. Guest workers were sending money for their families
to open cafés, buy satellite dishes, and refurbish apartments. Businesses
worked with cash and people hid their money at home.

Three years later, the banks had not improved. Payment times lasted
five to six days, and three times that for interbank transfers. ATMs,
checks, and credit cards did not exist. As the U.S. ambassador reported
in 1996, the banking system was "a relic of the past."[6]

The lending side looked even worse. A high default rate forced the
national bank to impose credit ceilings, on advice of the IMF. In 1994, on
IMF and World Bank advice, the government restricted the state banks

to lending only the amount repaid on existing loans.[7] These restrictions crippled Albania's fledgling small businesses. New ventures could not start and existing companies could not expand. "Without support from the bank, actually no decent businessman can make money and survive," the director of the state-run savings bank said in 1993.[8]

In response, an informal credit market emerged. With individuals looking to invest their savings and businesses in need of capital, entrepreneurs filled the void. Small operations that often started as currency exchanges began to accept deposits and provide credit. They grew over time, taking deposits from legal and illegal sources with interest rates from 4 to 6 percent per month. Albanians began to sell their apartments and parcels of land. Workers in Italy and Greece provided a steady stream of cash. The de facto banks looked for a wider pool of depositors, and Albanians jumped at the attractive rates. The pyramid schemes were born.

Later, some foreigners called Albanians "naïve" for having invested in the fraudulent schemes. But the pyramids grew due to the economic conditions of the time. They resulted from an unregulated market and the need for functioning banks. As the 2008 collapse of Bernie Madoff's $50 billion Ponzi scheme in the U.S. showed, the most sophisiticated financial systems can fall prey to monumental scams when the conditions are right.

In Albania, some of the schemes were regionally based, but the largest of them worked nationwide. Most had branches in the southern city of Vlora because more men from the south were working in Italy and Greece, sending money home. A speedboat ride from Italy, Vlora had also become Albania's center of organized crime. The smugglers needed a place to invest and launder their loot.

By 1997, Albania had seventeen known pyramid schemes. A family that invested $1,000 could earn up to $60 per month, just below the average monthly wage. As pyramid schemes function around the world, interest was paid from the principal of new investors. The schemes relied on an ever-growing number of investors willing to play the game, plus steady input from smugglers and workers abroad.

Some of the schemes functioned as pure pyramids, based on getting more investers. Others tried to build legitimacy by purchasing businesses or making investments. A public face lent credibility to the scam, giving investors the impression that their interest payments came from the company's profit, rather than from someone else's principal. In Albania, some of these investments were legal, and at times profit making. But many were worthless, like rundown mills and empty fields. Some of the investments were tied to criminal groups. Many details remain unclear and Albanian government commissions since 1997 have failed to reveal the true face of what the *Wall Street Journal* called "murky empires," but some of the pyramid schemes were apparently involved in money laundering and the smuggling of oil, arms, and drugs.[9] Legal activities by pyramids "could hardly have paid the unrealistic interest rates they promised their clients," a head of the World Bank in Albania later wrote.[10]

The largest scheme was VEFA Holding, run by a portly man with a pudgy face and a flock of wild, gray hair named Vehbi Alimuçaj, who one journalist described as "a night-club bouncer who had won the lottery."[11] Registered in October 1992, VEFA began as a currency exchange because, Alimuçaj said, "Albania was lacking the private second category banks."[12] VEFA claimed to have invested in a spectrum of businesses, from brickyards to poultry farms, and within three years boasted of having branched into tourism, supermarkets, light industry, mining, hotels, soccer teams, factories, shipping, and a folk group called My Labëria. VEFA said it had amassed $6 billion in assets, sixty-five hundred employees, and seventeen branches abroad. It hosted flashy inaugurations and advertised at Formula One races around Europe. Alimuçaj, a former sergeant in the army who had managed an artillery warehouse during communism, took pride in calling himself Albania's first millionaire.[13]

VEFA's criminal ties are suspected but still unproven. On February 26, 1996, a car bomb exploded in front of a VEFA supermarket in Tirana, killing four and injuring twenty. Berisha denounced the incident as a "barbaric and fascist attack organized by members of the former secret police."[14] He promised the government would track down and execute those responsible.[15] The police reportedly arrested a man with links to the mafia.[16] They also questioned staff at the critical newspaper *Koha Jonë*.

The most common allegation against VEFA was that Alimuçaj used his old army connections to sell arms. The company's name

Head of the VEFA pyramid scheme Vehbi Alimuçaj
in his Tirana office, February 1997. © Reuters

stood for Veprimtari Ekonomike Forcat Armatosur (Economic Ventures
of the Armed Forces), some said. Alimuçaj said the name stands for four
members of his family: Vehbi, Edmond, Flora, and Artan.[17]

* * *

Up until 1996, the pyramid schemes worked. They paid their investors
in full and on time. Competing with one another, their rates slowly
climbed, but most returns hovered around 6 percent per month, supported by a gradually expanding investment base and income from
illegal trade. Albania's factories lay still but the cafés thrived.

Foreigners invested too. Some flew into Tirana, paid an Albanian
$100 to stand in line to make a deposit or to collect interest, and then

flew home. Foreign diplomats, missionaries, and aid workers were not immune from the pyramid craze.

Technically all the "companies" were illegal because they did not have banking licenses. But the authorities allowed them to function because they said they were not officially banks. Both the government and international financial institutions tolerated their activity to supplement the struggling state banks.[18] When a new banking law in February 1996 mandated that only licensed banks could manage deposits, the governor of the national bank said the pyramids should be closed. The chief prosecutor replied that the new law did not apply.

Berisha had no intention of stopping business. In part, some individuals in the Democratic Party and government were profiting. As an IMF official later wrote, "there were corrupt relationships between the companies' operators and the highest levels of the Albanian government."[19] More importantly, the president could not stop what had become many Albanians' means of survival, especially with elections coming in spring 1996. Berisha told this to the IMF and World Bank, who were beginning to warn him that the schemes had grown out of control.

U.S. officials also raised the alarm. "I simply can't deal with that before the elections," Berisha told a U.S. diplomat who said he raised concerns about the pyramids.

On the contrary, Berisha supported the schemes. Throughout most of 1996, the larger pyramids advertised on state television. Senior officials attended parties thrown by VEFA and another large scheme called Gjallica, which sponsored the forty-ninth Miss Europe pageant, attended by Berisha and Prime Minister Meksi. In Vlora, the Democratic Party candidate in the 1996 elections had posters with the pyramid schemes VEFA, Gjallica, Cenaj, and Kamberi listed under the slogan "P.D. Everything for Vlora." Albanians interpreted all of this as signs of government support—a kind of insurance.

In addition, Albanians believed that Berisha had international support. Until the May 1996 elections, Berisha had visited the White House, seen the chancelleries of Europe, and been praised by powerful financial institutions. Surely these leaders knew how Albania was surviving, many Albanians thought. Even those who understood the fragility of pyramid schemes believed the government and its international supporters would not let the schemes fall, at least not before the elections. As one

Albanian economist wrote, "Albanians believed in the steadiness of the system."[20]

The government's willingness to close the pyramids weakened further as Berisha's domestic support declined. He feared losing power after the constitutional referendum defeat in November 1994 and the fear intensified after the controversial 1996 elections, former advisors and Democratic Party leaders said. "He knew he was weak, and then he didn't feel strong enough to close the pyramids down," explained Mero Baze, a close Berisha confidant at the time who later turned against him.

In 2001, I asked Ridvan Bode, minister of finance in 1996–97, whether political considerations had affected the government's willingness to close the pyramids before they crashed. "I cannot accept that nor can I find the argument to deny it," he replied. "The attitudes of the DP were linked to the political environment."

At the same time, the opposition parties and Albanian society as a whole gladly played the game. Some Socialist Party leaders had ties to the schemes. Even without those links, the Socialists feared closing the pyramids for the same reason as Berisha: they were helping so many families to survive. "Our position was to be suspicious, but not to be against them," said Arben Malaj, a top Socialist official who was an advisor to the Cenaj pyramid scheme and, after Berisha's fall, became minister of finance. "It was an election period." The Democratic Alliance took the same view. "We would be perceived as being against the people," explained Arben Imami. "To go against them [the pyramids] was to go against everyone."

Eager for cash over principle, the Albanian media failed to investigate the schemes or to warn Albanians about the risks. The irreverent *Koha Jonë*, Berisha's antagonist since 1992, made VEFA president Vehbi Alimuçaj its Man of the Year in 1996. That September, the paper began a daily section on the schemes that listed the day's attractive rates. Articles such as "How Does Kamberi Function" and "The Mechanism of Profit at VEFA Holding" did not explain how these schemes made money, but rather where and when people could invest.[21]

To question the pyramid schemes was like speaking against communism during the time of Hoxha: everyone thought you were insane. It was a confederacy of collusion, a societal secret, a profiteers' pact. And soon it would end.

* * *

By late 1995, the Bosnian war was coming to a close. The presidents of Bosnia, Croatia, and Yugoslavia signed the Dayton peace accords in December and the United Nations lifted sanctions on Yugoslavia. Overnight, Albania lost its lucrative oil market to the north. Albania had always maintained that its fuel imports only met domestic need, but with the sanctions busting gone, oil imports dropped.

One month later, the pyramid schemes began to shake. Without a steady income from smuggling, the schemes were forced to recruit an ever-growing number of investors. To attract new principal, they raised their monthly rates, setting in motion a downward spiral that ended in their dramatic crash.

Some Albanians believe that foreign governments eager to undermine Berisha may have expedited the pyramids' fall by shutting down their other illegal operations. The Democratic Party's first finance minister, Genc Ruli, who later held a variety of economic portfolios under Berisha, told me that "outside factors" had blocked money laundering operations to "accelerate the collapse." Bode, finance minister in 1996–97, said he did not "exclude any influence of specific circles." He stressed, however, that the "main responsibility for what happened is with Albanian politicians and Albanians."

All of the U.S. officials I interviewed denied a hand in what they called the pyramids' inevitable collapse. "When I saw the pyramids, I realized he would self-destruct," said Richard Schifter, speaking of Berisha. Then U.S undersecretary of state Timothy Wirth, whom Berisha had refused to meet following the elections, concurred. After his first visit to Albania in 1996, he said, he thought the "whole house of cards is going to come down." Joe Lake, the U.S. ambassador until March 1996, also said the pyramids fell under their own weight. "There may have been some pushing," he conceded, but he had "seen no evidence of this."

Against IMF advice, Berisha increased wages during the election campaign and postponed the imposition of a value-added tax. Inflation rose, as did the budget deficit, although this was also due to reduced tax revenue from fewer oil imports. To entice investors, the pyramids increased their rates to 8 percent after the May elections. Soon two new schemes appeared, offering up to 10 percent. The "companies" Xhaferri and Populli, run by two brothers-in-law, quickly attracted thousands of new investors, which forced other schemes to compete. The Albanian intelligence service later accused these two schemes of having ties to the opposition and of getting funds from the United States.

By the summer of 1996, the investment craze had boomed. Interest rates rose to 20 percent and then 30 percent, with ever-shortening repayment times. People sold family treasures to invest. Peasants sold their livestock and farm equipment. Educated Albanians told me they knew it was a scam, but the profits could not be ignored. Most understood the end would come, but they thought Berisha would tolerate the schemes until parliament reelected him president in March 1997.

In September, Populli offered more than 30 percent per month. In November, Xhaferri jumped to 44 percent. A scheme called Sude said it would double a person's investment in two months, and then announced a special rate of 170 percent for pensioners and poor people who deposit their money for five months. By some accounts, investments jumped from $500,000 to $3.5 million per day at the beginning of July.[22] The bigger it got, the less people wanted it to end.

The total figures are difficult to assess because records are poor, the schemes overvalued their assets, and pyramid operators stole millions. Conservative estimates say one-third of the population invested $1.2 billion in the schemes, which amounted to 50 percent of Albania's GDP. Others say 60 percent of the population invested up to $2 billion. By any count, the pyramid schemes reached into virtually every Albanian home.

By the summer of 1996, the IMF and World Bank could no longer ignore the craze. Although they had warned the Albanian government since 1994 about corruption in general and money laundering in particular, it was not until an IMF mission in early August that international experts understood the schemes' breadth and depth. They left a letter for Berisha advising him of the danger the pyramids posed.[23] A World Bank mission in September 1996 repeated the warning, telling Berisha that they worried about the rising budget deficit, the slow pace of institution building, and the unchecked growth of the pyramid schemes. "The president laughed," the World Bank director for Central Europe and Asia told the new U.S. ambassador, Marisa Lino, at the end of his trip. "They are not taking this seriously."[24]

Ridvan Bode told me he first learned of the pyramids' "real dimensions" in July 1996, just after he became finance minister. Two months later he had meetings with the IMF and World Bank in Washington, where officials told him the schemes must stop. He returned to Albania in early October and announced on state TV that the IMF and World Bank wanted the pyramids closed in order to "avoid later and inevitable harm."[25]

The reaction was immediate and sharp. "It was the IMF which, after it was kicked out of other former eastern communist countries, applied its schemes in Albania and felt proud of the 16 percent growth of the Albanian economy in the previous year," opined the pro-government newspaper *Albania* (though growth in 1995 was about 6 percent).[26] Even government critics did not understand why the international financial institutions were changing direction after years of praise.

Two days after Bode's remarks, VEFA head Alimuçaj went on state television to reassure his depositors. VEFA's investments worth tens of millions of dollars were "a guarantee for us to pay back our creditors," he said.[27] The next month, Prime Minister Meksi and Speaker of Parliament Pjetër Arbnori accepted medals in celebration of VEFA's fifth anniversary. On December 11, Berisha weighed in with a a bold claim that confirmed the government's unwavering support. "There is one thing I can vow here in front of you and in front of everyone," Berisha said at a press conference broadcast on state television. "That the money of the Albanians is the most honest and the cleanest money in Europe and the world." In case it wasn't clear, he added: "The serious Albanian companies have serious investments and I congratulate all the Albanians who invest."[28]

Five years later, Bode told me that his warning did not have impact because it "did not have the support of academic circles or the government and ruling party at the time." Other members of that government were more direct. "Berisha blocked us from blocking them," then prime minister Meksi told me. "He wanted to keep them until the 1997 elections." Then Berisha advisor Genc Pollo mostly agreed. "After the general complications of the May elections it was difficult to do things," he said. "One needed the same results or similar results in the local elections and that's what complicated our dealing with the pyramids."

On January 15, 1997, the Sude scheme—already closed for more than a month—declared bankruptcy, reportedly owing $38 million. Police arrested the operator, Maksude Kademi, who said she had started the scheme in the shoe factory where she worked.

The next day, the government froze accounts from the schemes Populli and Xhaferri, reportedly worth $250 million. The government returned the money over time, but the move sparked protests in the schemes' hometowns, Fier and Lushnje. The pyramids VEFA, Cenaj, Kamberi, and Silva agreed to lower their rates to 5 percent, but it was too late. The first of the larger schemes, Gjallica, went under next, and the others followed suit.

Albanians took to the streets. The pyramid managers had deceived the public and absconded with millions, but Albanians mostly directed their rage at the government, especially its powerful chief. Partly this focus came from Albania's paternal politics, in which the leader sits atop the country with people looking for guidance from above. Fifty years of Enver Hoxha had cultivated a culture of passive care, with citizens expecting to get provisions from on high. But mostly Albanians felt duped. The government had given the impression that their investments were safe. Berisha had said the Albanians' money was "the cleanest money in Europe and the world." He encouraged them to invest. They could tolerate his arrogance and authoritarianism so long as they made money. Now they had no reason to accept his lies.

The government promised to return what it could. "Not even a penny from these deposits will be used for other purposes besides their reimbursement," Berisha said, promising distribution on February 5.[29] By then anti-government demonstrations had spread across southern and central Albania, including Tirana. When the police responded with violence, the people's anger swelled.

11

Revolt

To residents of the dusty and dilapidated town of Lushnje in central Albania, the pyramid boss and former army officer Rrapush Xhaferri was a saint. Known as "the general," he renovated the stadium and brought world-class players to the local soccer team. More importantly, he helped thousands of Lushnje residents survive. His pyramid scheme Xhaferri, which he called a "charitable foundation," provided income in the town of crumbling concrete homes.

The Albanian government had a different view: "the general" was a leftist sympathizer with Socialist Party ties. His "charitable foundation," along with the other newer scheme, Populli, were pure pyramids without business investments, and therefore easier to close. On January 23, 1997, the police arrested Xhaferri and more than one hundred people connected with the two schemes.

Lushnje erupted. An angry mob shouting "Down with Sali!" broke through police lines and set fire to city hall. Protesters surrounded the police station, demanding Xhaferri's release. "Ask me for something I can do," the police chief told the crowd, witnesses recalled. "Release the others arrested from Lushnje," the crowd screamed back. Some policemen jettisoned their caps and joined the crowd.

* * *

Albania's foreign minister, deputy prime minister, and head of the Democratic Party, Tritan Shehu, answered his office phone the next morning at 9:30. On the line was Agim Shehu, the powerful deputy interior minister.

"The situation is dangerous in Lushnje," Tritan Shehu recalled being told. "The people are about to attack the police. The police will shoot and cause many victims."

Agim Shehu said the demonstrators wanted to meet a representative of the government and someone should go there by helicopter with the recently arrested men from Lushnje to calm the crowd. The police would provide protection as the delegation landed in the stadium to divert attention from the police station. Tritan Shehu said he would think it over.

Five minutes later Berisha called. "You are the only one to go," he told Shehu, stressing the need to avoid violence. "I was nervous but I also wanted to avoid bloodshed," Shehu recalled. "I said yes." It was a decision he would ruefully regret.

Two helicopters took off, one carrying Shehu, his bodyguard, and the minister of justice, the other with a group of Lushnje detainees. The pilots unloaded their cargo in the stadium, as planned, and started to leave. As dirt swirled under the rotors, the Lushnje crowd converged. They waved leeks in the air—the lone vegetable in shops during communism's latter years—as a symbol of their poverty. The Lushnje detainees lifted their shirts to show the welts and bruises they had received in custody. As the only means of escape disappeared over the stadium seats, the crowd swarmed on Shehu like sharks to bloody meat.

Shehu tried to calm the crowd but an iron bar struck the back of his head. Angry men beat him with fists and leeks. That night rumor spread through Lushnje and Tirana that demonstrators had stuffed Shehu's mouth with leeks. Whipping through the cafés, the story became leek sodomy. Because Albanian myth is stronger than fact, Shehu lives with that shame today.

SHIK officers in the crowd and DP supporters from a nearby village dragged Shehu inside the stadium and into a locker room. Thirty to forty people crammed inside, behind a locked door, as the mob raged outside.

"If Xhaferri doesn't come, Shehu is dead!" they screamed.

The men protecting Shehu had weapons but no one could figure out how to escape. Shehu was bleeding from the head, staining the back of his shirt.

Two hours later, Tirana sent another helicopter with twelve police. As they landed in the stadium, the crowd stripped them of their weapons and beat them, witnesses said. Three of the police escaped into the locker room. The others begged for mercy. They said their commander had forced them to come.

By nightfall the crowd had dispersed. A doctor came to the locker room and stitched Shehu's head. Then the stadium lights went out. Either the police cut the lights to cover an escape or the electricity died as it did most nights. A scrum of men surrounded the blood-soaked Shehu and hustled him onto the playing field and out the back of the stadium.

Back in Tirana, Shehu downplayed the incident. "I was faced with anger by part of the population, which was peacefully solved among us," Shehu said on that night's television news.[1] But as much as he or the government tried to play it down, the leek beating was a watershed in the government's response. It showed that the state was unable to confront the crowds.

"Not using the police from the beginning created the idea among the rebels that the state was weak and could be toppled," deputy head of SHIK at the time, Bujar Rama, told me years later. "The deputy prime minister was trapped and the answer from the police was not to respond but to withdraw."

Berisha's then advisor Mero Baze agreed. "The state did not grasp the extent of the anger," he told me. "When Shehu was kidnapped, they should have saved him to show strength."

Despite being beaten and trapped in a stadium, even Shehu failed to grasp the extent of people's anger. "We did not understand the reality," he told me in 2002. "The best would have been to declare new elections in January, but none of us recommended that."

Just as Ramiz Alia and the Party of Labor had failed to grasp the extent of anger in 1991, Berisha and the Democratic Party were blind to the fury of 1997. The arrogance of power had pushed them out of touch.

Violence quickly spread to other parts of the south. Mobs in Berat and Fier stormed government buildings, burning down the town halls and Democratic Party offices. On January 26 in Vlora, demonstrators scaled city hall and ripped the flag off the balcony. The independent-minded Vlora, center of Albania's smuggling rings, quickly became the physical and spiritual heart of the revolt.

The Socialists distanced themselves from the violence, calling it a spontaneous outburst against the government. At the same time, they held a rally in a Tirana stadium, blaming the government for the people's financial loss. Thousands of opposition supporters and defrauded investors marched towards Skanderbeg Square, where water cannons dispersed the crowd. Parliament authorized Berisha to deploy the military to guard government buildings and clear roads. It was not a state of

Protesters in Vlora burn copies of the Democratic Party newspaper *Rilindje Demokratike* on February 14, 1997. © Reuters

emergency, the government stressed, but a necessary step to maintain order. Prime Minister Meksi announced that the government would begin paying back the money it had seized on February 5.

Meksi's announcement had little effect. Across the south, crowds sacked court houses and town halls while police used truncheons to disperse the crowds. Berisha called the violent protesters members of "the criminal police of the communist regime, some individuals from fraudulent foundations and some ordinary paid ill-doers."[2]

In Tirana, the police and secret police tried to crack down. In the evening of January 22, the painter and outspoken Berisha critic Edi Rama was walking near his apartment with friends when thugs in dark coats beat him in the face and head with brass knuckles. Five days later, a Socialist Party official named Ndre Legisi got pistol whipped on a Tirana street.

Pyramid investors waited eagerly for February 5, when the government said it would return their funds. To their dismay, the opposite occurred. Instead of reimbursement, the large-scale Gjallica scheme declared bankruptcy. The government might have been able to contain problems with Xhaferri and Populli to the smaller cities where these schemes were based, but Gjallica had businesses and property across the country.

In Vlora, one thousand people marched from the city's Flag Square to the port with Tirana politicians Skënder Gjinushi from the Social Democrats, the last communist-era minister of education, and Neritan Ceka from the Democratic Alliance. On February 7, demonstrators there clashed with police. Three days later, a demonstration was planned in Vlora for 10:00 a.m., but police blocked the main square. An open trench ran along the boulevard where the city was laying a telephone cable, providing protesters with ammunition. "Straight to Tirana!" they cried, throwing stones and overwhelming the police.

In the melee, police shot and killed a young man named Artur Rustemi, who had lost more than $5,000 in the schemes. The next day, thirty thousand people escorted the coffin down the boulevard and someone set the Democratic Party office in town on fire. The mentality of Vlora and the region, known as Labëria, is strong-willed and proud, and the government had succeeded to wake its wrath.

In Tirana, the Socialists and other opposition parties formed an anti-Berisha alliance called the Forum for Democracy. The government denied the group permission to protest in Skanderbeg Square on February 12, but the leaders marched anyway. Riot police blocked the streets and intercepted the leaders as they walked to the square. Police threw them into a van and beat some of them with brass knuckles and batons. Prime Minister Meksi threatened more force. "The Democratic Party has organized to respond with our forces, not only the police," he reportedly warned.[3]

Two days later an article appeared in the British press that rattled Tirana. Under the title "The Gangster Regime We Fund," the *Independent* newspaper claimed to have seen evidence from intelligence sources of collusion by ministers and DP members in organized crime. The Berisha government had been "drug-smuggling, gun-running, sanctions-busting and money-laundering," the article said. "Yet it is still enjoying the support of Western democracies, including Britain."[4]

* * *

February 20 is an important date in Albania's history, and Vlora's citizens were keenly aware. Seven years before in Tirana, crowds had toppled Enver Hoxha's monument in Skanderbeg Square, marking the symbolic end of the dictatorship. To commemorate the event in 1997, Vlora demonstrators raised three fingers in the air on February 17—two fingers and the thumb—as a sign that Berisha had three days left. The three-fingered salute, an evolution of the Democratic Party's two-fingered victory sign for freedom and democracy, quickly spread through Albania as a symbol of anti-government rage.

For ethnic Albanians in Kosovo watching the revolt on television, the three fingers were a confusing and offensive shock. Kosovars knew the sign as a Serbian nationalist salute that police waved aggressively in their faces every day. "Is this Albania or Angola?" a stunned friend in Kosovo asked as we watched the Vlora protests on television. "Don't they know what that means?"

When the three days expired, fifty-seven students at Ismail Qemali University in Vlora entered a school auditorium and declared a hunger strike, just as the Tirana students had done seven years before. Their key demand was less idealistic than their predecessors', but it reflected the protest's main goal: give our money back! Government officials declared the strike illegal and the students' assumed a more political stance: the government must resign! Out of touch in Tirana, the Democratic Party held a rally the same day in Student City to commemorate Enver Hoxha's fall.

Solidarity with the Vlora students spread through Vlora and the south. On February 22, some forty students at the university in Gjirokaster filled a classroom on the second floor with mattresses and started a hunger strike of their own. Four days later, four buses from Shkoder arrived in Vlora to support the strike. Although Berisha's stronghold was the north, people there had lost money too.

Vlora residents accepted the Shkoder buses but they viewed unknown men in town as Berisha spies—evil SHIK agents bent on crushing their revolt. Berisha's men vandalized shops, harassed women, and stoked violence, people said. They blamed any problem from sporadic electricity to bad food on what they called "Chechen spies," meaning Democratic Party supporters from the mountainous north. Some even believed Berisha was training fighters from Kosovo for deployment in the south.

On February 28 protesters gathered at Vlora's university, believing that SHIK agents were trying to break the students' strike. SHIK agents had stabbed a student, some said. A white van had abducted a student, others replied. Unsure what had happened but determined to blame the secret police, an angry horde set out for SHIK's headquarters on the edge of town, demanding their money and cursing Berisha. What happened next is a matter of intense debate with mutual accusations of unprovoked attacks and macabre deaths. Only the violent result is clear: three protesters and two SHIK agents dead.

According to Vlora residents present that night, when the crowd arrived at the two-story SHIK headquarters, the agents inside opened fire, killing three protesters. Only then did the protesters storm the nearby navy base, seizing ammunition and arms, and returning with pistols, machine guns, and grenade launchers, which they fired into the SHIK facility.[5]

According to SHIK agents in the building at the time and officers in Tirana, the Vlora mob launched a coordinated attack and the agents inside fired in self-defense. The armed crowd arrived around 9:00 p.m., they said, as the twelve SHIK agents inside were debriefing and getting ready for bed. "Suddenly we heard explosions in front of the building entrance," one former agent told the press. "Without any warning, bullets burst through the windows and doors."[6] Unit commander Besnik Hidri called headquarters as the assault began. "They are attacking us, send backup!" he yelled, according to a former SHIK agent in Tirana who worked communications that night. "Everything is okay, the helicopter will come," Tirana replied. The helicopter never came.

"The state had died. The only part of the state still functioning was state security," said Bujar Rama, deputy head of SHIK at the time. "In those conditions, it was impossible to defend and secure them."

The crowd threw Molotov cocktails and fired machine guns and grenade launchers at agents in the building. Each of them had only two rounds of ammunition, the former communications officer told me. Three of the agents got pinned on the ground floor because the route upstairs was under fire. At one point, Commander Hidri went to the window to look at the crowd and was shot in the throat. He died the next day.

After a two-hour standoff, the demonstrators brought a dump truck and rammed the front door, both former SHIK and Vlora residents recalled. Agents on the second floor jumped out a window in the back. Some found shelter in Vlora homes. Others ran to nearby villages, eventually reaching Tirana.[7] Three agents were captured, one of whom died.

With the Vlora SHIK under the protesters' control, military garrisons in the area continued to fall. Albanian conscripts were underpaid, unmotivated, and largely sympathetic to the furious crowds who stormed their gates. Vlora residents easily looted machine guns, ammunition, grenades, grenade launchers, and anti-tank missiles. From that day, sunny Vlora grew dark. Armed men set up checkpoints to keep out Berisha's "Chechens." Nobody knew who the men were—hoodlums or members of a political group.

Anticipating the worst, the former Argentinian soccer star Mario Kempes, working as coach in Lushnje, left Albania with two of his Brazilian players. "It was difficult," Kempes told a journalist. "We were in good shape and in the semi-finals of the Albanian Cup."[8]

* * *

Back in Tirana, Berisha consulted with Prime Minister Meksi and Foreign Minister Shehu throughout the night. They agreed that Meksi and Shehu should ask the opposition leaders to calm the Vlora crowds. Around midnight, four Socialist Party leaders and Skënder Gjinushi from the Social Democrats came to the prime minister's office. "They asked us to help calm Vlora," one of the Socialists in the meeting, Namik Dokle, recalled.

The Socialists agreed to try. They called their party head in Vlora and asked him to intervene on behalf of the captured SHIK agents. Gjinushi made a similar plea, Meksi recalled. "Don't desecrate the bodies," he remembered Gjinushi said.

Early the next morning, Berisha spoke with Meksi and Shehu again. He was nervous and upset, the men separately recalled. Vlora residents were armed and building roadblocks outside the city. Berisha surprised them by saying he was ready to resign and call new elections. Shehu said the Democratic Party leadership should approve new elections, but Berisha argued there was no time. "It's an emergency situation and we will bear responsibility for this decision," Shehu recalled Berisha said. Forty-five minutes later, Berisha called Shehu back to say he had changed his mind. "I rethought it," Berisha said, according to Shehu. "And I decided to declare a state of emergency and no new elections."

At around 10:00 a.m., a reinvigorated Berisha met a delegation of Socialist Party leaders. "We tried to find a channel of communication, to find a solution and calm the situation," said Namik Dokle, who met Berisha that day. The Socialists were calling for the creation of a technical government and for Berisha to withdraw his candidacy for president. In a remarkable case of bad timing, Berisha's five-year term was due to expire in one week.

Berisha promised nothing, Dokle said, especially about his reelection. Years later, Berisha's advisors and Democratic Party leaders told me that preserving power was Berisha's foremost goal. Partly he thought strong leadership was required to guide Albania in a time of need, they said. But above all, he was determined to remain as president. He could compromise after his reelection was secure.

At a government meeting later that day, Berisha surprised many of the ministers by announcing that the Meksi government should step down. That night on state television, looking tired, he announced that, "to resolve the problems that have been created, the leaders of the political parties . . . came to the conclusion that the Meksi government will resign."[9]

Berisha presented the government's resignation as a compromise—the government was responsive to people's needs. But few southerners accepted the move, least of all the gunslingers of Vlora, for whom only Berisha's resignation would suffice. "While Meksi leaves, the crime remains," Berisha's journalistic nemesis Frrok Çupi wrote at the time. "Only Berisha was and still is prime minister, minister and so on and so forth."[10]

* * *

On March 1, 1997, I arrived in Tirana with a colleague from Human Rights Watch to monitor the crisis. I was nervous. The government hated me after my critical reports and advocacy in the United States. Some in the Democratic Party thought I was vilifying Berisha abroad, and there was truth to that claim. For me, it was about his policies and not the man. Friends picked us up at the airport and took us to the new Rogner Hotel, a fancy Austrian-owned establishment on the main boulevard, across from the president's office.

Business in the hotel boomed as foreign journalists scrambled to understand the year's most bizarre tale. Albanian politicians and foreign diplomats stuffed the lobby café, talking conspiratorially in huddles amid the twang of American country music. Cigarette butts overflowed the plant holders. The Albanians left in the evening to meet an 8:00 p.m. curfew but the foreigners sat around the pool eating barbeque while the country burned. A German journalist tried playing tennis but stopped when a bullet landed on the court. "And it was in," he announced with flair. Strange characters came every day. A British businessman in a pinstriped suit sat next to me in the café drinking beer. "When the bullets fly, people buy," I overheard him say. That afternoon I saw a dark-haired man who I was told worked at the Russian embassy. When he rose from the table, I saw a silver dagger hanging from his belt.

My colleague and I met the U.S. ambassador, Marisa Lino, an Italian-speaking career diplomat who had arrived in September 1996. To talk in the hotel lobby gave us a degree of credibility and protection. At the same time, I was shocked how Lino and her staff were interpreting events. Berisha had "good intentions," one senior embassy official told me. Another believed that the January beating of the artist Edi Rama was probably because of a dispute over a woman. Lino never made such claims but she avoided blaming Berisha and took what I considered to be an artificially evenhanded stance, equally blaming all sides.

We also visited the Forum for Democracy, the coalition of opposition parties and groups co-run by the former political prisoner Fatos Lubonja. The simple office had one sign on the wall that read, in English: "A neat desk is a sign of a sick mind." In contrast to Lino, Lubonja argued that Berisha would destroy the country to preserve his power. "Ramiz Alia gave signs he would change," he said, referring to 1990. "But Berisha gives no signs."

The day after my arrival, looters emptied the Koshovicë military base near Vlora. In Tepelena, armed men stormed the police station and freed prisoners. In Saranda, rioters set fire to the library and state bank. Across the south, army depots had been guarded by three to six soldiers, most of them nineteen-year-old boys who were poorly equipped and barely paid, some using rags as socks. Overcome by rabid crowds, the conscripts let people take guns, ammunition, and grenades.

In Vlora, armed protesters said they would storm Tirana if Berisha ran again for president. That afternoon, the DP-dominated parliament voted 118–0 to impose a state of emergency. SHIK head Bashkim Gazidede was named commander to "quell the bands of armed terrorists."[11] The loyal Gazidede was Berisha's only choice, former military and SHIK officials said. The police and army had failed. Across the south, and increasingly in the north, soldiers had shed their uniforms, abandoned their posts, and even escorted looters to arms.

"The political leaders of the state and the president of the republic had fully lost their confidence in the army and its general headquarters," Berisha's military advisor at the time, Major General Adem Çopani, later said. "For them the army would serve as an accessory, while to carry out operations they needed the loyal forces of SHIK."[12]

"Only the SHIK functioned," then SHIK deputy head Bujar Rama told me in 2002. "He did not trust anyone else—only Gazidede."

Berisha also removed the head of the army's general staff, General Sheme Kosova. According to the Ministry of Defense, he was fired for his "incapability and inactivity in defending some military units, which were attacked from the armed rebel groups."[13] General Kosova told me he quit because he disagreed with the state of emergency.

"The soldiers had family and friends among the protesters," Kosova told me in a Tirana café six years after the events. "Who would defend the officers and soldiers if we had opened fire?"

Berisha replaced Kosova with his military advisor, Çopani, a competent professional and former Alia advisor, but Çopani could not resuscitate a gutted force.

On television that night, I watched Berisha promise to crush the communist revolt:

> Through this message I want to inform the Albanian people, all Albanians wherever they are, and the whole international public opinion that a communist armed rebellion organized by former Albanian communists and former Albanian secret police in cooperation with foreign intelligence agencies burst [sic] in Vlora and some nearby zones last night. . . . The armed communist rebels, helped and financed by for-

eign intelligence agencies, have launched military operations to over-throw the government by force and to establish their own rule across the country.[14]

That same night, government thugs ransacked the Tirana office of *Koha Jonë*, which the government called a mouthpiece of the revolt. My colleague and I inspected the office the next morning and saw black streaks stretching upwards from the windows and bullet marks on the outside wall. Carbonized paper and smashed computers littered the floor. Witnesses said armed men came three times, despite the curfew, shooting at the walls and then lighting the office on fire.

Koha Jonë's staff went into hiding. Some of the younger journalists sought refuge in the Rogner, and I spent an evening trying to convince foreign journalists to house them for the night. Their fears were stoked by an opportunistic publisher who hoped to win reconstruction funds, but not wholly misplaced. That night, the police detained and beat a *Koha Jonë* journalist and driver. Police in Fier detained another journalist from the paper, Alfred Peza, who later showed me eggplant-colored bruises across his arms and legs.

The U.S. embassy helped to arrange a meeting for me and two colleagues from the free speech group Article 19 with Arian Starova, the deputy foreign minister. Late in the evening we sat with him in an uncomfortably large room at the ministry. *Koha Jonë* had incited people to violence with its anti-government diatribes, Starova said. But he insisted the government was not behind the attack on the office.

Berisha supporters were also afraid, believing that fanatical communists would storm Tirana, like the Volunteers of Enver had threatened in 1991. Rumor ripped through the Rogner that rebels had compiled a hit list of pro-government journalists, mostly people from the newspapers *Rilindja Demokratike* and *Albania*.

Around the same time, someone cut the FM signals of the BBC and Voice of America and transmissions of the European Broadcasting Union, which was feeding video to stations around the world. For a few days, state-run television and the DP's *Rilindja Demokratike* were the only news in town.

On March 3, my Human Rights Watch colleague and I went to see the head of the U.S. Information Agency, Charles Walsh, at his office in the pyramid. In contrast to Ambassador Lino, Walsh had a critical bent, making him a favorite of the opposition and an enemy of the government, as well as of Lino. While we talked, automatic gunfire rang out nearby. Walsh got on his radio to inquire what had taken place. The reply was both comforting—no one had been killed—and disturbing: parliament had reelected Berisha to a second presidential term, and his supporters were celebrating with Kalashnikovs.

While half the country roared, parliament had voted 113–1, with four abstentions, to give Berisha another five years. The members of parliament stood, clapped, and chanted his name.

"To be elected president of a country is certainly a landmark in the life of every simple man," Berisha said in his acceptance speech. "To be reelected president of a country is as a whole a sublime privilege."[15]

Instead of offering a hand, he made a fist.

* * *

According to top police, army, and SHIK officials from the time, Berisha's goal was to isolate the south. The military established checkpoints to contain armed groups, including on the Mifol Bridge outside Vlora. SHIK head Gazidede sent army and police forces to Fier and the one southern city the government still controlled, Permet. At the same time, DP militants and SHIK agents scoured the poor neighborhoods of Tirana, offering volunteers a weapon and $50 a day.

In retrospect, Gazidede had no chance. The army and police had largely dissolved. Gazidede was a determined man, doggedly loyal to Berisha, but with no experience in military affairs, let along in subduing a popular revolt.

"Gazidede had good intentions but no organizational skills," said his deputy Bujar Rama, a military officer during communism, who in 1997 commanded the government forces in Permet. At one point, Rama said, SHIK dispatched teams with anti-tank guns that require a team to operate. "No!" Gazidede screamed. "One gun for every man!"

On March 4, the air force deployed fighter planes and the antiquated MiGs dropped bombs in the hills near Vlora to incite fear. Two pilots abandoned the mission and flew to Italy, where they requested asylum. One of them said he had been ordered to bomb civilians, but the Albanian Defense Ministry rejected the claim.[16]

Rather than stop the revolt, the madness spread. Looters seized anti-aircraft guns in Tepelena and tanks in Saranda. They emptied army tunnels in mountainsides that held guns and spare parts. In Vlora, protesters and the political parties formed what they called a Salvation Committee—thirty-five people, including representation from the Democratic Party—to manage the protest-turned-revolt and to administer some sort of local rule. Former military officers, many of them fired after 1992, organized checkpoints.

In Tirana, the BBC and VOA returned to the air but news was fragmented and contradictory. Opposition politicians were largely hiding from SHIK and DP volunteers. Journalists were either in hiding or spending their days in the Rogner. Behind sliding glass doors, the lobby filled with wild tales: the army is marching on the south, Vlora is surrounded, civilians are getting bombed. Foreign journalists could not make it south of the government checkpoint on the Mifol Bridge.

The European Union called for maximum restraint from all sides. The Italians proposed a new government with a broad base. Washington was more direct. "We regret very much that the Albanian authorities are using this state of emergency to intimidate opposition politicians and to shut down the Albanian press and to shut down Voice of America," a State Department spokesman said. He added, "I think our advice would be to restore democracy; restore democratic rights to the opposition; restore rights to the journalists who are now being intimidated."[17]

Berisha felt the pressure, his advisors said. But rather than concede, he pursued two tracks. He began a dialogue with the opposition and continued military action in the south. Gazidede might not win back territory, but it was better to enter talks with sword in hand.

* * *

As then Democratic Alliance leader Neritan Ceka explained to me years later, he had little faith that his efforts would work, but he had to try. The country was slipping out of control and only dialogue could avoid bloodshed and maybe civil war. He had not spoken with Berisha for more than five years, but on the morning of March 5, 1997, the archeologist turned politician left a letter at the president office asking to meet.

That same day, another DP founder, Preç Zogaj, had the same idea. He and a friend approached VOA correspondent and Berisha confidente

Mero Baze in the Rogner Hotel to ask if they could speak in a quiet place. The three men slipped away from the crowd, and Zogaj told Baze that Berisha had refused to answer Ceka's letter. The opposition is isolated and afraid, Zogaj said, and the country needs dialogue.

Baze listened intently, both Zogaj and Baze recalled for me. Berisha is isolated too, Baze said, holed up with a few aides and guards in the presidential office. He agreed that a political solution was needed, but his relationship with Berisha had soured when the VOA broadcast cable was cut. Still, Baze offered to try.

Baze spoke with Berisha by phone and went to the president's office around 1:00 p.m. "Berisha was devastated, without much hope," Baze told me. "He was continuously alone. I think he had only two secretaries." Berisha listened to the proposal for talks but did not commit.

That afternoon, Albania teetered on the edge. The south was heavily armed. Berisha and his supporters were defiant and also armed. The danger of serious violence loomed greater than at any time in 1990 or 1991.

To the opposition's delight, Berisha agreed. He said he would meet the Socialists and Democratic Alliance, but only in secret. The opposition met at the Rogner to plan. Zogaj and Ceka drove to the home of the Socialist Rexhep Meidani, whose phone line had been cut. The three men picked up another SP leader, Namik Dokle, and made it to the back door of the president's office at 9:00 p.m.

The opposition found Berisha alone, the four visitors told me in separate interviews.[18] His face was thin. He looked tired and old. A lot had changed since Berisha, Zogaj, Ceka, and others had founded the DP almost seven years before. The visitors told Berisha that Albania needed a compromise to avoid bloodshed. Berisha resisted. The opposition was organizing communist bands to overthrow the government, he said. Meidani and Dokle rejected the claim. "No, not you," Berisha said. "The others."

After two hours, Berisha gave in. He agreed to meet the ten main political parties the next day to discuss halting military operations and disbanding the Salvation Committees. Berisha agreed only to talk.

The opposition exhaled a collective sigh. Zogaj crossed the boulevard to the Rogner, where Mero Baze was waiting anxiously. "Albania is saved," Zogaj said. He did not know it was about to get worse.

Opposition parties met the next morning at Neritan Ceka's home to prepare for the meeting with Berisha. They agreed to demand a broad-based technical government, new elections, and the inclusion of the Forum for Democracy coalition in the talks.

The meeting at the president's office began with a shock. An aide announced that protesters in Saranda had captured three soldiers and were threatening to execute the men. With that dramatic news setting the tone, the opposition presented the points on which it had agreed: a halt to military operations, a technical government, and new elections. At this point, an aide left the room and quickly returned with an update: the three soldiers were dead. The mood swung abruptly and Berisha went on the attack. He would accept only a forty-eight-hour ceasefire and an amnesty for those who surrendered their arms. The opposition consented to Berisha's demand, with an amnesty for those who returned weapons by March 9. In the meantime, dialogue would continue, but without the Forum for Democracy. Frustrated, the opposition crossed the street to the Rogner to announce the deal. A political process had begun.

The reaction in the Rogner was mixed. Everyone agreed that Albania needed a political solution, but some thought the opposition had been too soft. The most vocal critic was Fatos Lubonja from the Forum for Democracy, which Berisha had blocked from the talks. An impassioned and articulate speaker with credibility from seventeen years as a political prisoner, Lubonja fumed that the opposition had negotiated on Berisha's terms. How could there be a deal without the Salvation Committees from the south, I heard him yell. The Socialists and Democratic Alliance countered that starting a political process was the most important step.

The armed protesters of the south reacted to the deal with anger and a laugh. The revolt was leaderless and random—adventurists, opportunists, idealists, smugglers, and thieves—joined by their hatred of one man, and they would not stop until Berisha resigned. The Salvation Committees in Vlora and other towns refused to surrender their arms and accused the opposition of selling them out.

Seeing a bit of daylight, a stream of foreign delegations arrived. The Dutch foreign minister led a group from the European Union, which called for dialogue and, significantly, new elections. Up until then, only the U.S. government had made that demand. The Council of Europe called for the same but Berisha rejected the demands. "The situation is frozen," head of the Council of Europe delegation in Tirana said. "The president does not seem to realize the international pressure that can be brought on Albania."[19]

* * *

Nestled in the low southern mountains lay the quiet city of Permet, the government's last stronghold in the south, where Gazidede had been assembling forces from SHIK, the army, and the police. The plan, SHIK and army officers told me, was to use Permet as a base to retake other towns in the south. To command the forces Gazidede sent his deputy, Bujar Rama, who had served as an army officer in Permet during communism. Rama organized the police and soldiers from the army base near town. With commandos from Tirana and reservists from the north, he said he had two thousand men.

The first target was Gjirokaster, twelve miles to the southwest, beyond a strip of snowy peaks. The venerable city on a mountainside was protesting but had not slipped completely from government hands. In Bujar Rama's words, it was "half fallen," and the local army commander was asking for help. If Gjirokaster could be secured, the thinking went, the government might retake the nearby towns of Delvina and Saranda. Then the government would have a chance. Around 1:00 p.m. on March 8, three helicopters with government forces set out from Permet. They hurdled the Nemërçkë mountains and soon had rocky Gjirokaster in sight, veering for the airstrip outside town.

The people of Gjirokaster saw the helicopters approach. "The Chechen are coming!" people screamed, referring to Berisha supporters from the north. Local men grabbed weapons and headed for the airport. The helicopters unloaded between fifty and eighty special forces, but armed men blocked the road to town. They shot in the air, disabled the helicopters and seized five soldiers. Unwilling to shoot, the special forces fled into the mountains and back to Permet.

A fourth helicopter landed around 6:00 p.m., perhaps to save the forces from the first raid, but a crowd surrounded it too. "The town has fallen to the people," a man calling himself a rebel leader told the press. "Berisha's troops have turned tail and are in hiding."[20] That afternoon, a mob surrounded the local army base. The commander ordered his soldiers to hand over their weapons. The residents of Gjirokaster, children and adults, stormed in like drunken shoppers at a holiday sale, taking weapons of every caliber and type.

Gjirokaster went Kalashnikov crazy. Kids waved pistols and automatic guns in the air. Grenades littered the ground. The barracks had held mortars, artillery, and anti-aircraft guns, plus reams of ammunition. "It looked like the Battle of Stalingrad," then mayor Ylli Asllani recalled. Border guards and soldiers abandoned the nearby Kakavija border crossing with Greece. The first checkpoint, for anyone adventurous enough to enter Albania, was miles up the road near Gjirokaster, where armed young men built a roadblock to collect money.

In Tirana, news of the government's attack caused a stir because it violated the ceasefire. "We categorically dismiss this report," a Ministry of Defense spokesman said. "On the contrary, the rebel forces have attacked a unit near Gjirokaster."[21] The state press agency later reported that army helicopters had been in Gjirokaster on a "routine mission." Rebels in Tepelena, the report said, had spread a rumor that forces were coming to "conquer Gjirokaster."[22]

That night in Permet, commander Bujar Rama tried to contact Tirana. He telephoned President Berisha and SHIK head Gazidede, he said, but the lines were down. He sent a telegram from the police station asking whether he should stay or go. The mission in Gjirokaster had failed and Permet was now under threat.

Two roads led out. One went northwest through rebel-held Tepelena, and that could not be passed. The other ran southeast along a valley and then north to Korça, through a small town called Ersekë. If Ersekë fell, Rama feared, the troops in Permet would be trapped. Around 8:00 p.m. he communicated by telex with a military officer in Tirana. "The way I described the situation, they understood there was no other way," he said. "There had to be a political solution."

* * *

A stocky, handsome man, then fifty-nine years old, Franz Vranitzky was a respected former head of state. As chancellor of Austria from 1986 to early 1997, he had served longer than any leader in Europe after Germany's Helmut Kohl. Recently out of office, he was looking for a new way to spend his time. When the OSCE chairman, Danish foreign minister

Niels Helveg Petersen, asked whether he would go to Albania as OSCE envoy, Vranitzky agreed.

One week later, on March 8, as Albanian government forces were preparing their attack on Gjirokaster, Vranitzky boarded an Austrian Airlines flight in Vienna and flew two hours to Tirana, a place he had never been. With him were eleven OSCE officials and some politicians, including U.S. congressman Elliot Engel, head of the Albanian caucus in Congress, whom Berisha had refused to meet a few months back.

Vranitzky knew Berisha from the early days of DP rule and remembered being impressed. "He was a kind of hope," Vranitzky told me in his elegant Vienna office. "He was relatively young, outspoken, relatively educated, and he spoke foreign languages."

Using the Austrian-owned Rogner as a base, the delegation first met the opposition. At 10:00 a.m., they crossed the boulevard to see Berisha. The meeting room at the president's office had chairs in a wide curve, Vranitsky recalled, reminding him of an Oriental court. Berisha welcomed the group and launched into a criticism of the OSCE's reports on the 1996 elections. Vranitzky urged Berisha to extend the ceasefire, set to expire the next morning, and to declare new elections. Berisha argued that the communists had orchestrated the rebellion in the south, and only they could stop it.

A frustrated but composed Vranitzky held the first of two afternoon press conferences in the hotel. "We would be very glad and it will be very constructive if the ceasefire could be prolonged for forty-eight hours—to give more time to surrender arms," I heard him tell a packed room of local and foreign media. At that very moment, special forces were retreating through the snowy mountains from Gjirokaster back to Permet.

Around 2:00 p.m. that day, Albania's opposition leaders got word that Berisha was again ready to meet. They gathered at the president's office a few hours later for the second round of negotiations that had started two days before. This time Berisha was more open. Bujar Rama had not yet sent his evening report from Permet, but Berisha knew that the Gjirokaster operation had failed.

For the first time, Berisha said he would accept a broad-based, technical government and possibly new elections. But the government could not include the Socialists. And new elections had to take place within forty-five days. The Socialists said forty-five days was too quick. As for the technical government, they said Berisha could proceed without them if he wanted. They knew that no government could function unless the main opposition party took part.

"Then form a government without the Democrats," Berisha replied.

"There is no value without us and without you," the usually restrained Rexhep Meidani snapped.[23]

During the debate, Berisha stepped out to meet Vranitzky for a second time. Again the Austrian urged Berisha to extend the ceasefire and to establish a caretaker government until elections. This time, with the defeat in Gjirokaster clear, Berisha promised the dialogue would continue. "The government's idea was to crush the rebellion," Berisha's then advisor Genc Pollo told me in 2004. "That failed, so we had to negotiate."

Back at the Rogner, Vranitzky happily announced the news. "This afternoon President Berisha showed a more flexible approach regarding the date of the elections," he told the media.[24] Although much work remained, he reported, Berisha had started talks on a caretaker government linked to general elections that year.

The next morning, police and army units in Permet prepared to withdraw. Their mission had failed. Around 9:00 a.m., representatives of the political parties and local government met at the district office to discuss the city's plan. As a man from the Democratic Party spoke, a bullet from outside struck him in the face, knocking him to the floor. The others dove under tables in panic. Some broke windows in the back and jumped to escape.

Who shot and why remains unclear. Some DP supporters claim it was murder. Bujar Rama said it was an accidental ricochet from a random shot. Stunned by the death, an angry crowd gathered in the center and marched to the police station, where they overwhelmed the few remaining officers. Bullets flew from armed citizens, DP militants, and government troops.

The police and army tried to leave. As their trucks drove through town, the crowd attacked. Six people died, including the parents of the district council head, who were shot in their car.

As chaos engulfed Permet, opposition leaders returned to the president's office for another round of talks. They gathered in a room on the first floor and took seats around a large table. In ten minutes, the door opened and Berisha strolled in, standing upright and looking euphoric. He slapped his hand on the table. "From this hall, let us together declare today that which Albania needs more than ever: the platform of national reconciliation!" he proclaimed.[25]

The opposition and DP members present were stunned. Berisha continued: "The alternative of national reconciliation is the best alternative, the noblest one, therefore I invite you, representatives of the country's main political parties, I invite Albanians wherever they are, to hail this alternative with an open heart at a moment when the country needs this support more than ever."

Television cameras recorded the scene. Cameras had been in the two previous meetings, but the opposition had been told it was for the archives. This meeting was broadcast live across the country.

Sitting at the head of the table, Berisha read from his proposal, prepared in his own hand: a general amnesty, a national reconciliation government, and elections within two months. The opposition and DP officials took notes frantically, trying to catch the points. As Ramiz Alia had done seven years before, Berisha had preempted the opposition.

Surprised by the sudden turn, the opposition still welcomed the deal. With minor changes, around 4:00 p.m. they signed the nine-point agreement. The party members crossed the boulevard to the Rogner and gave victorious interviews to the press.

Again the most critical was Fatos Lubonja, whom I watched berate the opposition for having negotiated without the Salvation Committees. He believed the agreement gave the embattled Berisha an escape. Moderate DP leaders had abandoned the party, he said, and Berisha had only his most loyal crew of Genc Pollo, Tritan Shehu, Bashkim Gazidede, and Agim Shehu. With more resistance, he would go. Wearing a beige baseball cap that strangely said "Nog," he told a gaggle of journalists that the situation was like in the movies and that Albania would be saved only "when the bad guy is dead." After a brief pause, he added: "Metaphorically speaking."

The opposition argued the deal was needed to avert civil war. "At that time, it was necessary to avoid conflict," reflected Rexhep Meidani, the SP leader who would soon assume Berisha's presidential seat. Namik Dokle agreed. "If we had tried to throw Berisha into the abyss, he would have taken Albania with him," he told me in 2002 from his office as speaker of the parliament.

With the path towards a political settlement lit, threatened journalists and opposition politicians cautiously emerged from hiding. On the other side, I saw Ylli Rakipi, the editor of the staunchly pro-Berisha *Albania* newspaper, which had spewed venom for years. "We will now print the truth," he told me.

But across the south, the "rebels" refused to stop. The Salvation Committees agreed that the country needed new elections, but only Berisha's removal would quell their rage. By failing to demand his resignation, they said, the opposition had failed.

At DP headquarters in Tirana I saw a crowd of men waiting to get arms. To them, the rebels were Enver Hoxha agents and irredentist Greeks. "We'll fight if they come to Tirana," one man told me. "Berisha is being too soft," another said.

To calm the south, the international community sent the Italian ambassador to Tirana, Paolo Foresti, a wily politician who had good releations with Berisha. On March 10, he flew to an Italian warship in the Adriatic Sea, while two helicopters picked up eight representatives from Vlora's Salvation Committee at a salt mine outside town, and flew them to the ship. The Italians took the ragged and rugged men to the captain's quarters, where they sat at a cramped table with Foresti and his translator, and were offered prosciutto and spaghetti. "We asked him [Foresti] to intervene and get rid of Berisha," said Luftetar Petoshati, the burly military head of the Salvation Committee, who was on the ship. "We said the weapons were taken because people had been attacked."

Foresti urged the committee to respect the agreement signed in Tirana and to help restore public order. Italy was ready to provide humanitarian aid in return. Before flying back to the salt mine, the committee signed a declaration saying it "undertook to favor the immediate handing back of weapons in the hands of the citizens of Vlora and to ensure public order and progressively restore normal administration."[26]

Even with the best intentions, the committee could not guarantee such calming steps. As the meeting in the Adriatic took place, head of the Salvation Committee Albert Shyti sat on the veranda of a Vlora hotel with his armed guards, laughing as they fired rounds in the air. Across town and throughout the south, heavily armed and trigger-happy citizens roamed. Some of them were defending their families or property, but others had criminal aims.

* * *

The March 9 agreement established the grandly named Government of National Reconciliation. Berisha got to name the prime minister and the opposition named the deputy prime minister and minister of the interior. Among the Socialists, no one wanted the thankless and dangerous job of running the police. With no volunteers, the SP heads chose the youngest person in the party leadership, a twenty-nine-year-old with a boyish face named Pandeli Majko. Rexhep Meidani and Majko met Berisha to discuss the other posts. It was only at that meeting, Meidani and Majko told me separately, that Berisha announced he had changed his mind on the division of seats. The Socialists should nominate the prime minister instead of the Democrats, he declared. Perturbed but eager to keep the process moving, Meidani agreed. Right away he turned to his younger colleague and proposed Majko as prime minister. "I was completely surprised," Majko told me. "But I did not react."

The two men left Berisha's office to consult with the SP leadership about the change. The party agreed that Majko, a communist youth activist and student during the 1990–91 demonstrations, would be their prime minister. But when talks resumed, DP officials said Majko was unacceptable as prime minister because he was "too high in the party." Rather than push back, the Socialists began a desperate search. They needed a person capable of running the government, acceptable to Berisha and, perhaps most difficult, willing to take the job. The young economist Arben Malaj said no. The moderate Agim Fagu could not be found. Berisha rejected the SP chief from Vlora, Eduard Alushi. Exasperated, the party leadership finally came to a name. He was not a popular person in the party but he would probably be acceptable to Berisha, the Socialists thought, and he was unemployed at the time. Rexhep Meidani made the call.

Down in Gjirokaster, thirty-four-year-old Bashkim Fino was at home playing backgammon with a friend when the phone rang. He was short and portly with a round head, large glasses, and thick, black hair. Meidani's voice was hoarse so he passed the phone to Namik Dokle.

"I called you to say one thing," Dokle remembered saying. "And when I complete the sentence you will surely think I'm mad. Are you ready?"

"Go ahead," Fino replied.

"At this moment, you are the prime minister of Albania."

Fino was stunned. He had been following the news on television and listening to the gunshots in town but the former mayor of Gjirokaster was otherwise out of the loop. "Why me?" he asked. Because Berisha has given us the right to name the prime minister, Dokle explained, but he did not accept anyone from the party leadership. You are the right person for the job.

"I hesitated," Fino told me years later. "Everybody would hesitate in that situation."

Meidani got back on the phone. If we do not provide a name within thirty minutes, we will lose the right to name the prime minister, he said in a scratchy voice. Fino warily agreed but with one condition: his old friend from school, the economist Arben Malaj, must join the government too. The Socialists contacted Berisha to say Fino was their final offer.

The Salvation Committee in Gjirokaster was not enthusiastic about the Socialists' choice. Some people wanted the crisis to end and they welcomed the political agreement, but others thought the opposition had sold them out. Berisha was still in power and some of their demands remained unmet.

In addition, they knew Fino as an opportunist who played all sides. As mayor in town from 1992 to 1996, he drank coffee with DP leaders and sent whisky to SP head Fatos Nano in jail. He was a Socialist but had supported Berisha's constitutional referendum in 1994. He also had a business eye, enjoying good relations with local businessman and the DP district head, who reportedly imported oil from Greece. The allegations of corruption were more plentiful than Fino's dense, black hair.

That night, armed men surrounded Fino's home. Some were against the agreement. Some were for the agreement, but against Fino. Some wanted Fino to take the job. Inside, Fino got a phone call from Berisha. "We have a difficult task ahead, but we will work together," Fino remembered the president said. "I'll send a helicopter for you tomorrow, but take care that it's not shot down."

The helicopter arrived and left safely the next morning, taking the new prime minister to Tirana. Fino went straight to the Socialist Party headquarters and then to the president's office with Rexhep Meidani, where Berisha officially named him government head. He crossed the boulevard to his new office to discuss the remaining government posts. According to the agreement, the Socialists got the ministries of finance and defense, while the Democrats kept interior, SHIK, and the state TV. "There were two main points: to avoid civil war and to reach an agreement for the elections," Fino recalled. Both would be Herculean tasks.

12

A Horrible End

The Rogner Hotel was what one journalist called "virtually Albania's only functioning institution," so it was understandable that the new Government of National Reconciliation would work in its restaurant and café.[1] The new minister of justice, Spartak Ngjela, took it a step further by moving in. One of his first acts was to amnesty all prisoners. "Albania is a natural state, if you know your Thomas Hobbes," he explained.[2]

Across town, the director of Prison 313 strolled through his facility to inspect the cells. In one he was shocked to find Ramiz Alia and Socialist head Fatos Nano with six other inmates dutifully awaiting their official release.

"Do you have any alcohol here?" Nano remembered asking. "Just to have some strength after so many hours."

"Only soda," the director replied.

The national prison chief did not answer the phone, so the director got an ambulance and drove the men one by one to their homes, telling them to stay down because of the shooting. "Mr. Nano, I am out of debt with you," Nano said the director told him before speeding off.

In the south, the situation spun further out of control. On March 11, a horde of men stormed the country's largest air force base at Kuçova, formerly Stalin City, seizing weapons and ammunition. A green Mercedes towed a Soviet-made MiG-19 jet down the road. "We are not bandits, we are the people," a man draped in bandoliers told reporters.[3] Amazingly, workers protected the arms factories in Poliçan and Gramsh, where the state produced ammunition, hand grenades, and machine guns. In these remote towns, families relied on the factories for work. In other areas, the Salvation Committees (*Komiteti Shpetimit* in Albanian) lost the little control they had. Albanians referred to them derisively as *Kometeti Shperthimit* (Explosion Committees).

In Vlora, it felt like war. Armed men fought gun battles for control of neighborhoods. In the first week of March, the hospital treated fifty-five

Socialist Party head Fatos Nano (L), just out of prison, and newly appointed prime minister Bashkim Fino at a press conference in Tirana on March 17, 1997. © Reuters

people for gunshot wounds and sixteen people died.[4] Gangs threatened doctors to save certain patients and to let others die. In the mayhem, humor thrived. Driving south to Vlora, four American journalists were passed and then blocked by a Mercedes full of armed men. "Gazetare Amerikane!" the foreigners yelled in Albanian to indicate they were American journalists. "Gazetare Amerikane?" the men with Kalashnikovs replied. "We're mafia Albanese."

In Tirana, DP fanatics threatened to overthrow the reconciliation government. "After March 9, the whole south had weapons," SHIK deputy head Bujar Rama told me. "Northern militants, when they saw such a situation, went out of control. They decided to take weapons as well." Then DP head Tritan Shehu agreed. The arming of DP supporters, he said, "started as an isolated incident but it went out of control."

Rinas Airport cancelled flights and the U.S. government deployed marines to guard the embassy. On March 13, Bashkim Fino and the Reconciliation Government were sworn in as gunfire rippled through Tirana. "God save us," Fino said after taking the oath. "God save Albania."[5]

Franz Vranitzky returned the next day. Rinas Airport was closed so Italian prime minister Romano Prodi offered an Italian Air Force plane from Vienna to Brindisi, where a helicopter took Vranitzky to an Italian warship doing figure eights in the Adriatic Sea. On board, the Austrian met Prime Minister Fino and a delegation from the Reconciliation Government. The Albanians requested an international military force to establish order and prepare for elections. Vranitzky was open to the idea. On the ship's deck, he consulted with U.S. secretary of state Madeleine Albright via satellite phone. Albright was directly involved, Vranitzky said, and "she grew more anti-Berisha" every day.

The call for a stabilization force at first met a tepid response. Albania was dissolving with myriad players: Berisha, the Socialists, Salvation Committees, the new government, and criminal gangs. No government wanted to send soldiers into that morass.

"What you have in Albania is a state of anarchy—a complete breakdown of government," U.S. defense secretary William Cohen said at the time. "This is not principally a military issue right now. It's one of a violent, spasmodic reaction on the part of the people toward their government."[6]

As the country absorbing most of the refugees, Italy had a different view. When no other government volunteered, it assembled a "coalition of the willing" called Operation Alba to pacify its neighbor to the east.

* * *

Prime Minister Fino returned from the warship meeting with Vranitzky and found a chaotic meeting in his office. Ministers were drafting a statement that offered government employees, including soldiers and police, a salary increase of 300 percent if they returned to work.

Across the capital, foreign embassies began evacuating nonessential staff. At the U.S. housing compound, Marines took positions behind sand bags as Americans boarded helicopters, wearing helmets and orange life vests. British special forces rescued two British citizens running an orphanage in Elbasan, along with twenty-two children and a small staff.[7]

At Durres port, smugglers sold places on boats for $250. The Italian coast guard plucked nine hundred people from a sinking gunboat with a broken rudder and no fuel. The U.S. Navy saved a capsized boat.

"I'm not happy thinking about jumping into a boat or swimming for it," a six-month pregnant woman told the press. "But this is what the government has done to me."[8]

Twenty miles away, at the new Coca-Cola plant outside Tirana, the Italian director stood defiantly as armed guards patrolled the grounds. "Why should I leave?" he asked rhetorically. "It's not war at the moment, just a problem with people who don't know the meaning of democracy or law."[9]

* * *

In the south, the local Salvation Committees merged into the National Salvation Committee, with the main aim of removing Berisha. Pro-Berisha groups reacted by forming the All-National Salvation Committee. Announced on the evening news, still controlled by Berisha, the group said it would fight to defend the president.

On March 17, the southern-based National Salvation Committee demanded Berisha's resignation within three days or rebels would march to Tirana. The pro-Berisha committee fired back. Calling itself a military organization of "thousands of armed Albanians," the committee called Berisha "a factor for national, political and social equilibrium."[10]

Two politicians from the Social Democratic Party—Paskal Milo and Skënder Gjinushi—traveled south to help avert a clash. When they arrived in Gjirokaster, they found two members of the Democratic Alliance—Arben Imami and Ridvan Peshkepia—who had come one week before from Corfu. Imami and Peshkepia said they had fled Albania to avoid arrest. The DP said they were orchestrating a Greek-inspired plot.

The four politicians met the National Salvation Committee in the former army officers' club on March 20, and urged restraint. A dozen armed men guarded the building as sheep grazed outside. The committee's thuggish member from Tepelena, thirty-two-year-old Gjolek Malaj, wearing sweatpants, a black leather coat, and fake-fur vest, pressed an aggressive line. "We will send fifty people to Tirana to put Berisha under arrest," he thundered. "If he will not resign we will bombard him."[11]

Other committee members pulled back. "We don't ask for a military solution, just a political means," one said.[12]

In Tirana, Berisha showed no fear. His aide Genc Pollo appeared at the Rogner with Berisha's son, perhaps to dispel rumors that the president's family had fled. "We don't take it very seriously," Pollo told a journalist in the café, in response to the southern committee's threats. "They have no army units."[13]

The next day calmer heads prevailed. The southern committee reiterated its demand that Berisha resign and promised to support the Reconciliation Government. Five days later, Berisha went on the attack. Although most of Tirana believed that SHIK head Bashkim Gazidede had resigned, he appeared in parliament on March 26. In a rambling presentation broadcast on television, he argued that Albania was victim of a plan called "Lotos," devised by Greece to annex southern Albania.[14] Former top communists were involved, Gazidede said, as was a Greek American activist named Nicholas Gage. Gazidede suggested that the U.S. had hastened the crash of the pyramid schemes to overthrow the government and called the head of the Populli pyramid scheme, Bashkim Driza, a former Sigurimi agent who was working for a foreign agency. (On March 17, the state news agency claimed that Driza left Albania on an American helicopter.) Most dramatically, Gazidede implied that the U.S. government was supporting Greece's annexation plan. An unnamed Western diplomat had done this by helping the antigovernment newspaper *Koha Jonë*, Gazidede said.

Political observers knew that Gazidede was referring to the head of the U.S. Information Agency in Tirana, Charles Walsh, who was known for his open criticism of Berisha and his relations with opposition politicians and journalists, in contrast to Ambassador Lino and her staff. The pro-Berisha *Albania* newspaper later made this clear, saying that Gazidede was talking about "the man of the American secret services Charles Walsh."[15]

The DP reaction to Gazidede's speech was mixed. Some members of parliament said Gazidede should not blame others for Albania's woes. Others endorsed his views. The head of the state auditing service, Blerim Çela, added that President Clinton's advisors were Greek, apparently meaning former advisor George Stephanopoulos and CIA chief George Tenet. (Tenet's father had emigrated to the United States from northern Greece near Albania and his mother fled what is now southern Albania—both spoke Albanian.)[16]

The U.S. government never responded publicly to Gazidede's claims. Then ambassador Lino declined to be interviewed for this book, but a cable she sent to Washington at the time partly explains her view. "After the Gazidede show and tell in the parliament tossing out accusations right and left, I did make a very general statement (also read out on VOA Albanian Service) which did not/not directly respond to Gazidede's insinuations but focused on the depth and breadth of U.S.-Albanian relations starting with Woodrow Wilson," she wrote. "In that context I said the U.S. supports the territorial integrity of Albania (Gazidede had implied the U.S. Greek lobby—Greek conspiracy were aiming to split up Albania)."[17]

Gazidede's deputy, Bujar Rama, demurred when I asked about his former boss's claims. "Gazidede had something about an employee of the U.S. who did not work in the embassy," he explained. "But he did not have all those concerns verified." Berisha's then advisor Genc Pollo was equally coy. The government had "heard from various sources" that Walsh was working against Berisha, he said. But it was "not clear if he was acting on his own or on orders."

Interviewed in 2003, Charles Walsh dismissed the allegations. "There was never any set plan to get rid of him," he said of Berisha. "We had to deal with him even though, in our eyes, he had trampled the democratic process to stay in power." Regarding Gazidede's claims, he stated: "Neither I nor anyone else from the USG ever worked for more than the evolution of democratic standards, a transparent economy resilient with free trade, and the development of a civil society."

* * *

Packed to capacity and beyond, the rusting Albanian ship *Kater i Radës* slipped out of Vlora towards Italy on Friday, March 28. More than one hundred men, women, and children were trying to escape. Halfway across the Straits of Otranto, an Italian navy vessel blocked their way. Italy was aggressively patrolling its waters after receiving thirteen thousand refugees.

In the choppy waters, around 6:00 p.m., the two ships collided. Old and overloaded, the Albanian ship succumbed. Fifty-seven people drowned, aged three months to sixty-nine years. Albanians claimed the Italians purposefully rammed the ship. Italians said the Albanian boat made a hazardous and unexpected turn.

March 31 was a day of mourning in Albania. Flags flew at half-mast and parliament held a minute of silence. Wailing relatives in Vlora threw flowers to the sea. The tragedy also put an Italian-led military operation in doubt. As much as the government needed help, Albanians might not accept Italians on their land.

On April 1, Italian prime minister Prodi called Albanian prime minister Fino with an urgent request to meet. Facing resistance at home, the Italian leader wanted Albania's full support for the operation.

"I'm not in Tirana, but in the south," Fino told Prodi.

"No problem," Prodi replied. "I'll come to you."

"I can't guarantee your security," Fino said.

"No problem. I'll take care of it."

Prodi arrived in Gjirokaster the next day with six military helicopters. They landed at the airport as soldiers secured the perimeter and escorted Prodi to the city hall. The two men spoke as Italian soldiers and an Albanian policeman stood guard. Locals joked that the policeman was well equipped: he had pants, a jacket, and cap.

Fino assured Prodi that the Albanian government would welcome the Italian-led force despite the tragedy. In separate meetings, the Salvation Committee promised the Italian ambassador that Italian soldiers could come.

One week later, the Italian parliament approved Operation Alba, with sixty-five hundred soldiers from nine countries.[18] The main purpose, Italy said, was to secure the delivery of humanitarian aid. The unspoken reason was to stem the flow of refugees.

Operation Alba had a difficult task. Albania had no enemy combatants or front lines. The country was lawless and the people were armed, even with tanks. From March to May, the Italians intercepted boat after boat packed with drugs, mostly marijuana grown in the south. "So much marijuana has arrived in Italy in the past few days that the street price has dropped dramatically," an Italian police spokesman said.[19]

In Vlora, the Italians faced three well-armed gangs: Zani, Kakami, and Gaxhaj. The most notorious was the gang of Zani, full name Myrteza Çaushi, who fancied himself an Albanian Robin Hood, stealing trucks of

An armed protester watches a Greek naval vessel with humanitarian aid approach Albania on March 19, 1997. © Reuters

food and distributing the goods in his neighborhood of Çole. Details of Zani's past remain unclear but most agree that he had recently returned to Albania from Greece, where he had reportedly escaped from prison. For DP conspiracy theorists, his prominent role in Vlora's anarchy was confirmation of a Greek plot. Zani's brother was also a neighborhood head of the Socialist Party.

At Vlora's main hospital, dedicated doctors, nurses, and staff battled to keep the wounded alive. Every day criminals brought their comrades with gunshot wounds, followed by threatening gangs with competing demands on the hospital staff.

"If he dies, you die!" one group said.

"If he lives, you die!" said the next.

One day, armed men killed a patient in the operating room, a doctor recalled.

Vlora's cemetery tells the story well. Dead gangsters have gaudy monuments with their faces etched in marble above the dates of their lives and the phrase "Killed by a faithless hand." A large memorial stands for those who drowned in the Otranto boat tragedy. White markers dot the ground for each victim beneath a broad marble slab with a poignant line: "You left a horror without end and were taken to a horrible end."

* * *

With Operation Alba in place, the Reconciliation Government turned its attention to the elections—Albania's fourth since the birth of democracy. The ominous task of supervising the process fell to the OSCE and the irrepressible Franz Vranitzky. The Austrian visited Albania five times over the coming three months to mediate, negotiate, and organize. "Uncle Vrana is coming," Albanians joked, referring to a general of Skanderbeg named Vrana Konti. The delegation stayed at the Rogner Hotel, where the restaurant orchestra played Strauss's Radetzky March whenever Vranitzky left the room, much to the Austrian's dismay.

The experience left Vranitzky tired and frustrated. The Albanian parties fought over every point, first and foremost the election law. Six years into Albania's democratic experiment, the basic rules were not in place. According to Vranitzky, all sides postured but Berisha actively maneuvered to hinder the elections. "We debated and in the end we seemed to reach an agreement," the Austrian told me about the many meetings he had with the president. "But I often found out later that even before the meeting he had drafted a press release with a different view."

Annoyed, Vranitzky called German chancellor Helmut Kohl. "He belongs to the EDU," Vranitzky said about Berisha, referring to Europe's conservative European Democratic Union. "Can you influence him? This is not the correct way to run things."

"I agree," Kohl replied. "But Sali Berisha cannot be influenced."

Other diplomats were equally perplexed. "Whatever he had been, by the first time I saw him, he seemed crazy," said one Western official involved in the process. The person continued: "Was he drunk as some reporters thought? Everyone agreed he did not drink. On drugs? Medication? I came to think this was his problem. He supposedly could hardly sleep. He could not hold to a line of conversation. Any attempts to move forward brought irrelevant outbursts about previous slights and wrongs to him or his family—many dating back a decade. . . . At the same time, his constant maneuvering seemed to show that he was not *that* crazy!"

On May 9, the political parties finally agreed to an election law for a vote to be held before the end of June. But the DP-dominated parliament passed a different law without the opposition's consent. The Socialists threatened to boycott the elections unless the OSCE guaranteed they would be fair. Vranitzky said the Albanian parties were responsible for fairness, but the OSCE would provide technical support and a large observer team. The Socialists agreed.

Later that month, a new newspaper called *Indipendent*, founded by journalists from *Koha Jonë*, sparked a controversy by printing excerpts from a telephone conversation between DP head, Foreign Minister, and Deputy Prime Minister Tritan Shehu and Italian ambassador Paolo Foresti, who was long considered a Berisha fan. The transcript suggested the two men were trying to stymie Vranitzky and manipulate the elections.

"Forestigate" became the hot topic in Tirana. The *Indipendent*'s editor, later a top Socialist, refused to tell me who gave him the tape, but the prevailing view was that it came from the Americans, who wanted to see Berisha gone. United States officials denied this, and a Freedom of Information Act request I submitted shed no light, with seventeen State Department documents on Foresti partly censored or not released. Another theory is that Italian intelligence released the tapes, with backing from Prodi, who wanted to remove the influential ambassador. Interviewed in 2003, after his split with Berisha, Tritan Shehu said the published transcript of his conversation was accurate but the newspaper had taken it out of context. He accused Berisha and Gazidede of releasing the tape to deflect criticism of the president onto Shehu and Foresti. At the same time, Shehu criticized Vranitzky for a lack of objectivity, saying the former Austrian chancellor and banker had "a leftist orientation."

When Vranitzky learned of the taped conversation, he became enraged. He flew to Rome to speak with Prodi and Foreign Minister Lamberto Dini. In addition to the recorded conversation, Vranitzky told me, he had other evidence of Foresti's obstructionism.

"Prodi was open to my complaints but Dini said, 'It's not possible.'" Vranitzky said. Still, Dini recalled Foresti from Tirana, as Prodi had apparently tried to do six weeks before. When Foresti left, Berisha awarded him the Order of Mother Teresa.

* * *

Given the absence of a state, the election campaign seemed smooth. By any normal standards, it was a disaster. The OSCE assisted at every level, importing ballot boxes from Bosnia, ballot papers from Italy, and ultraviolet lamps, batteries, and indelible ink from Vienna. Foreign troops restored some calm, but killings and other crimes took place daily.

In this atmosphere, Democrats could scarcely travel to the south. When one of them did, a crowd beat him badly. In the north, the Socialists faced harassment but were generally able to campaign. At the same time, the state television and radio remained in Berisha's hands. According to one survey, political programs on state TV covered the DP 28.5 percent of the time, compared to 10.7 percent for the SP.[20]

On May 23, special forces arrived in the village of Cerrik in central Albania to secure a visit by President Berisha. The villagers considered it a provocation and opened fire with guns and grenades, leaving six people dead and an armored vehicle smoldering in the square. On June 4, a man threw a grenade at Berisha as he campaigned near Durres. It did not explode and police arrested the man.

On June 10, the top OSCE election official resigned. The OSCE denied that his resignation was due to the inappropriate conditions for elections. "They are absolute and complete lies to say that I resigned for personal reasons," the departing official said from the airport as he prepared to leave. "It is for deeply professional reasons."[21]

Four hundred and seventy-five monitors from thirty-two countries descended on Albania to observe the elections. Vranitzky addressed them the day before the vote. Albanians have lost faith in their democratic institutions, he told them, and elections were the only way to restore trust. He also prepared them for an imperfect process. "Optimism would be a luxury," he said. "Pessimism is not a good tool, so realism is the only option."[22]

Vranitzky and the OSCE knew the elections would be flawed. But they saw them as necessary to rebuild the state. Unless there were egregious violations, the OSCE would give them a passing grade. The U.S. Helsinki Commission, which had been monitoring Albania since 1991, concurred. "In order to hold elections quickly," the commission reported, "the norms for free and fair elections were, in many respects, abandoned."[23]

An unspoken goal of Western governments was also to unseat Berisha, their former darling. The OSCE did not want Berisha gone before elections because it would have "damaged the international community's image of objectivity," Vranitzky told me. It was better, he and others thought, if the Albanians ridded him through their vote.

I arrived in Tirana a few days before the elections to monitor for Human Rights Watch. Although the police and Operation Alba had largely restored order, pockets of lawlessness remained, especially in the north. Again I watched my step. The Democrats still considered me an enemy, having criticized Berisha abroad. Damaged and demoralized, they still thought they could win. I stayed at the Rogner with a small army from the OSCE. They seemed tired and nervous but Vranitzky looked tan and calm.

As if Albania was not chaotic enough, a new character dashed through the hotel one day as I was drinking coffee. He was impossible to ignore. He stood about six feet, six inches tall and was thin, with a long head, gray hair, and large glasses. He had never spent more than a few days in Albania and spoke the language poorly, but claimed to be king.

King Leka, son of King Zog, was two days old when his father fled Albania after the Italian invasion in 1939. He then lived in Britain, Spain, Rhodesia, and South Africa, and reportedly spent time in a Thai jail for an arms deal gone wrong.[24] He first returned to Albania in 1993 and Berisha expelled him after one day. But the madhouse of 1997 offered a chance to return. Disguested by the Democrats and Socialists, Albanians wanted someone to lead them from the abyss.

Leka stood a full head over other politicians, but ideas did not fill that space. Out of Albania for so long, he could not expound on any of the key issues affecting the country. His advisor had spent the Hoxha years as a dentist in the United States. The international community disliked his claim to be "King of the Albanians," meaning those in Macedonia, Montenegro, Kosovo, and Greece—promoting the nationalism that the United States and others had labored to avoid. Berisha, however, saw in him a useful tool because monarchist supporters could dilute the opposition vote. Leka's backers were mostly from the north and fiercely anti-communist. To seduce them, Berisha announced that, on the same day as the elections, Albania would hold a referendum on the monarchy. Albanians would vote for members of parliament and the country's form of government: constitutional monarchy or republic.

On election morning, Vranitzky left the Rogner before breakfast in his TV-blue shirt and cream-colored suit, looking confident and in charge. He inspected a group of monitors and their Alba Force escorts like a general and, with cameras in tow, shook hands down the line. He then returned to the hotel for his notoriously huge breakfast while aides ran outside periodically to make sure the monitors were rolling out.

Before long they did, guarded by Italian soldiers with stylish sunglasses and machine guns mounted on jeeps. They visited polling stations in schools, sports halls and, in one village, the local bar. They encountered no problems directly, but violence did take place. In Fier, gunmen shot and killed a DP election committee chairman. Around the country, men fired automatic guns. Ballot boxes had gaps and broken seals.

Both the DP and SP were sure the other side would steal the vote. "Leftist extreme forces have their armed bands and they will try to influence the elections," a DP candidate in Kavaja told me when I went to inspect a polling station. "But I believe people will vote against the rebellion." A portly policeman outside a polling station near Tirana feared intimidation during the count. "If that happens there will be big problems," he warned, as we watched a Mercedes full of leering men roll by. "Everyone is armed."

The ubiquity of arms actually secured some peace. In the May 1996 elections, only DP bands and SHIK agents had been armed. Now everyone had guns, and gangs from both side watched to ensure the process was correct.

I observed the counting in Tirana's Student City, home of the historic demonstrations in Decmeber 1990. As election commissioners opened ballot boxes, the sound of gunshots reverberated off the dormitory walls and cars screeched their tires on a nearby road. The electricity died and the counting proceeded by candlelight: "Socialists . . . Democrats . . . Democrats . . . ," the commission head announced one by one. At that polling station, voter turnout was 12 percent. The Socialists beat the Democrats by a few votes. The monarchy lost to the republic thirty-six to seventy-three.

That evening, it first looked like the Democrats had prevailed. But official results soon tilted the other way. State television, still in DP hands, filled airtime with the British comedian Benny Hill and Mickey Mouse cartoons. In the end, Albanians had again voted against. The former communists had little support but the public held Bersha and the Democrats responsible for their lost money and the anarchy that ensued. Their dislikes outweighed their likes. After a second round, the Socialists won a convincing 101 of 155 parliamentary seats. The Democrats won twenty-seven. In the referendum, 67 percent of voters favored a republic over a monarchy.

An OSCE statement used a unique phrase that captured the times. The elections, it said, were "adequate and acceptable."[25] A full report later gave qualified approval with a friendly wink, saying the election "can be deemed as acceptable, given the prevailing circumstances in the country."[26]

In Washington, Albania watchers exhaled. Having feared the worst, the acceptable elections set the stage for normalization. The election, one internal State Department analysis said, was "the dog that didn't bite."[27]

In Tirana, foreign journalists and I experienced the anger of DP supporters who blamed us for their loss. An Italian cameraman was beaten outside DP headquarters and a British reporter was shot at by an unknown gunman. As I watched a press conference by DP heads Genc Pollo and Tritan Shehu, a heavy hand slapped the back of my neck. I turned to see a burly man hustling out the door and the chuckles of his friends.

Everyone expected the DP to challenge the results but the gangly King Leka protested first, claiming the monarchy had won the referendum with 54 percent. On July 3, he gathered his supporters in Skanderbeg Square, wearing green camouflage and a beret with a pistol and grenade dangling from his belt, flanked by bodyguards with dark sunglasses and Kalashnikovs. Across the square, children giggled on a bumper-car ride where the Enver Hoxha statue had once stood. Revved up, the monarchists marched down the boulevard to the Palace of Congresses, where the Central Elections Commission was tallying the count. Someone opened fire, forcing commission members to dive for cover. Police responded and, in the melee, one man died and several others were injured.

Albania's self-appointed King Leka (C) in Skanderbeg Square on July 3, 1997. © Reuters

Leka denied that he had sparked the attack. "If we were carrying out an armed action, believe me our people would have been better equipped than just with the pistols," he insisted.[28] The police never arrested Leka, but he left Albania two weeks later to avoid the investigation.

* * *

Journalists and analysts have struggled to characterize Albania's tumultuous year. Some said the north and south fought a civil war: the Ghegs of the northern highlands versus the Tosks of the southern plains. A few called it a religious dispute, although it is not clear between whom. Berisha portrayed it as a communist revolt, with help from Greece and the United States.

The chaos of 1997 was not a civil war along geographic, religious, or tribal lines. Berisha enjoyed support in the north, but many northerners opposed his rule, furious at having lost their cash. Likewise, the DP had supporters in the south.

At its core, the crisis was a revolt by people who felt economically and politically duped. The pyramid schemes provided the spark, but the arrogance of Albania's rulers had primed the country to ignite. For five years, Berisha had monopolized power. When faced with protest, he clamped down, promoted loyalists, and pushed through his reelection. He exploited differences between north and south for political gain, stoking tension and then presenting himself as a guarantor of peace. He built a fire he tried to control.

At the same time, the Socialists took advantage. It was clear by early 1997 that the collapse of the pyramid schemes offered them a chance. They stayed in the background at first as the Salvation Committees formed, and then floated to the fore. They plotted how to return, rather than how to help the state.

Another element was organized crime. Gangs from Albania, Italy, and Greece profited from the chaos. Of the more than sixteen hundred people killed between March and May 1997, most died in shootouts between rival groups. On the road to power, the Socialists also made alliances with local criminals, gangsters, and thieves.

Some former government and DP officials also blame the U.S. government, which, they say, destroyed Albania to get Berisha out. I found no evidence to support this claim, but Washington certainly wanted Berisha gone and likely did expedite the inevitable crash.

Beyond Berisha, the opposition, gangs, and more, the revolt was an expression of despair. Unshaven men firing automatic guns with cigarettes dangling from their mouths was a vulgar show of lost hope. I saw it as a primal scream, a release of energy that shrieked anger, betrayal, and powerlessness. Spraying bullets was a testosterone shot to say: I am!

Above all, I viewed 1997 not as a crisis *in* the country, but a crisis *of* the country. Albania had an entry in the atlas, a national hymn, and a flag. It sat in the United Nations. But the country lacked a collective identity to hold it together. Politicians on all sides were looking to preserve or get power, rather than protect and promote the common good.

The effect of 1997 is still felt today. Looters took more than six hundred thousand weapons of various types and 1.5 billion rounds of ammunition.[29] They destroyed court houses, police stations, and town halls.

Gunman in Vlora, June 1997. © Reuters

More dangerously, Albanians lost faith. They abandoned trust in their leaders and promises of reform.

On July 23, 1997, the new parliament convened and Sali Berisha resigned, as he had promised to do if the DP lost. In a letter to the assembly read on television, he accepted some blame but sniped at the people who had taken his place. "The financial crisis of the pyramid schemes, an undoubtedly negative phenomena of our governing, was exploited as a pretext by the former Albanian communists and their supporters to organize the communist armed rebellion," he said. The result was "the return to power of the last communist nomenclatura in Albania."[30]

Less than six years after losing power, the former communists in Eastern Europe's most Stalinist state were back. The moderate Socialist Rexhep Meidani replaced Berisha as president and party head Fatos Nano became prime minister. OSCE officials told me they felt sorry for Nano when he emerged from prison looking bedraggled. The next time they saw him he had gold cuff links, a tailored suit, large rings, a heavy watch, and a black limousine with bodyguards. It was a sign of things to come.

PART V

Return to Red

Ex-Communists Rule, 1998

13

Democracy 2.0

Rexhep Meidani was eager to work. After parliament elected him president, he drove to his new office with Bashkim Fino and some members of the Republican Guard. They found the office in a disorderly state, with stains and cigarette burns in the carpet from those who had slept there during the crisis. Files were missing, including the 1997 minutes of the Supreme Defense Council.

Meidani stayed calm. The fifty-three-year-old was soft-spoken, tall, and slender with glasses and neat, graying hair. He was orderly and precise, smoking cigarettes in a controlled motion with an even draw like the disciplined physics professor and university dean he had been. He had joined the Socialist Party late, in 1996, and became one of the party's key negotiators in 1997. One year later, he was Albania's second democratically elected president.

The new president met party head Fatos Nano, three months out of prison, to discuss the new government. A few minutes into their talk, television announced Meidani's election and gunfire erupted nearby, startling the men.

Fino lent the new president two members of his staff, a car, a photocopier, and a fax machine. Meidani then resigned from the Socialist Party, even if the law allowed him to stay. "Considering the experience of the former president, who was everything—party, government, parliament, chairman of the Central Elections Commission, director of RTSH [state TV and radio], governor of the national bank, general prosecutor etc.—I chose a direct way: my resignation of Socialist Party membership," he explained.

Across the boulevard, Prime Minister Fatos Nano was settling in. He knew the office from his brief stint as government head in 1991—sweet vindication to return after three years, eight months in jail.

Nano looked different from before his incarceration: heavier and wearing a beard. His close advisors told me that Nano had suffered in prison and emerged a different man, with less self-control. But he remained clever and astute. He had stayed active in the party behind bars, getting a steady supply of news, cigarettes, and drink. Now rehabilitated, with anti-Berisha sentiment running high, he would lead Albania for the next eight years.

Born in 1952 in Tirana, Nano grew up the privileged son of a respected communist who ran the state television and radio for many years. Coming from the post-war generation, Nano held more moderate views, even singing as a young man in a rock band, and he gained prominence in the Party of Labor's reformist wing. In the late 1980s he became an economist at the Institute of Marxism-Leninism. In August 1990 he gave an interview to Voice of America, calling for economic reform. Desperate to show a modern face, in December of that year Ramiz Alia named Nano general secretary of the Council of Ministers and then deputy prime minister. Three months later, when crowds toppled Hoxha's monument in Skanderbeg Square, Nano rose to prime minister, and he kept that post for two months after the first pluralist elections. After the Party of Labor's dramatic tenth congress, when it changed its name and distanced itself from Hoxha, Nano became head of the Albanian Socialist Party.

Nano's ties to the party also set him free. Unlike Berisha, Nano never had to deny his past. Berisha had to justify his switch from ambitious party member and Politburo doctor to leader of the democratic movement. His rabid anti-communism might be traced to that mental leap. Nano was free from such gymnastics. He was more open and without a complex about his past. He was less dogmatic and better able to adapt. Along with this adaptability, however, came a tenuous connection to values and mores. As time showed, Nano would also abandon Albania to save his skin.

In contrast to Berisha, who had full, dark hair, sharp features, and a straight back, Nano slumped. Until laser surgery, his glasses sat on a pudgy face beneath thinning hair; his nickname was Qori—"the blind one." His voice cooed instead of boomed. Berisha was strong headed, disciplined, authoritarian, and tireless. He lived in a Tirana apartment with his family and did not indulge. Nano was wily and unpredictable. He bargained and moved. He liked women and gin. Berisha could be corrupted by power, and Nano by money; or as a friend once put it, "one by the mind, the other by the gut." It was the clever villager versus the city slicker. Patriarchal, determined, and controlled versus freewheeling, loquacious, and loose.

With Nano as prime minister, the new government faced two essential tasks: restore order and rebuild the economy. In large parts of the country the state had weak or no control. The challenge was to strengthen the state without returning to undemocratic ways. As the writer Fatos Lubonja put it at the time, the government's task was to "establish authority without being authoritarian."[1]

"We tried to recreate the state," said Perikli Teta, who had been minister of defense in the Stability Government of 1991 and was appointed the new minister of the interior. Vandals had damaged or destroyed half the police stations and all of the prisons, as well as roughly 130 military posts along the border, he said. Villagers near Kuçova sent the Defense Ministry a telegram that pleaded, "Please take back your tank." In Shkoder, another looted tank had "for sale" painted on the side. "In such conditions we cannot speak about security," Teta said.

Economically, the picture also looked bleak. The lek had fallen against the dollar by 40 percent. Inflation was 28 percent. Millions of dollars invested in the pyramid schemes had disappeared. The World Bank and individual countries gave $6 million for accounting firms to identify and seize the schemes' remaining assets, but the firms had little luck. According to Deloitte & Touche, the five largest pyramid schemes owed depositors more than $370 million but had assets worth $50 million.[2] The police eventually arrested VEFA head Vehbi Alimuçaj and other pyramid bosses.[3] In December 1999, Turkey extradited Shemsie Kadria of the Gjallica scheme. "I did not take money from anybody by force," she pleaded. "I did not know that the things would grow to such an extent."[4]

Parliament formed a commission to investigate the pyramids. The Socialists obstructed the process, the accounting firms said, suggesting that the party had played its part in the schemes' growth. The pyramids were like a village murder; everyone knew the killer, but no one dared speak.

The now opposition Democratic Party took advantage, attacking the government for protecting thieves. "This commission was not for transparency but to block transparency," charged Ridvan Bode, who had been the DP's minister of finance during the pyramids' growth and crash. The DP-run media reminded Nano on a near daily basis of his cavalier promise during the election campaign to return the people's stolen money.

In August 1997, former DP speaker of parliament Pjetër Arbnori began a hunger strike to demand that state television give the opposition equal coverage. "No one supported him but we didn't want the poor guy to die," a Western diplomat following Albania told me at the time. Under international pressure, the parties agreed on a coverage formula and Arbnori ended his strike after twenty days.

The next month the tension turned violent when a Socialist member of parliament and former wrestler from the north, Gafurr Mazreku, argued with the DP's rambunctious Azem Hajdari over speaking time in parliament on the value-added tax. Words turned to fists as deputies pulled the two burly men apart. Two days later, Hajdari was having coffee in the parliament's café when Mazreku approached his table and said some words, witnesses said. A few moments later, as Hajdari was entering the parliament hall, Mazreku opened fire with a pistol a few yards from the door, striking Hajdari four times. A fifth bullet lodged in the wall.

Hajdari survived but the Democratic Party called the attack a communist plot to murder the student leader and DP founder. "This is a political crime," Hajdari decried from a wheelchair, his left arm in a sling, during a press conference at the Military Hospital. He blamed the "authors of the murderous composition, Nano, Gjinushi and Meidani."[5] Berisha led a demonstration in Skanderbeg Square. "Down with the criminals! Down with the government!" the crowd yelled.

The Albanian press reported that the shooting was not about politics but about honor. Members of Mazreku's family had reportedly visited Mazreku in Tirana after the fistfight to urge that he seek revenge. Mazreku allegedly asked Hajdari at the café to reconcile, but Hajdari refused. "Hajdari violated our honor and, after the shooting, this honor has been restored," a Mazreku family member told the press.[6]

The Nano government condemned the attack and had Mazreku arrested. Parliament lifted his immunity and a court sentenced him to eleven years in prison for attempted murder, although he got out early for good behavior. Hajdari recovered but one year later suffered a more serious attack.

* * *

Under outside pressure, the Socialists tried to avoid public scenes of revenge. Still, many DP members on local levels lost their jobs. An official at the U.S. embassy at the time called it "find and replace."

In June, the parliamentary commission investigating the 1997 meltdown had recommended that the prosecutor's office investigate Sali Berisha's role. Five other officials had broken the law, the commission said: SHIK head Bashkim Gazidede, Minister of Defense Safet Zhulali, Chief of the Army's General Staff Adem Çopani, Minister of the Interior Halit Shamata, and State Secretary for Defense Leonard Demi. The police arrested six men on charges of crimes against humanity, only two of whom had been named in the report: Zhulali and Shamata.[7] According to the prosecutor, the two had approved the use of phosgene, a chemical agent used in World War One, against the crowds in Vlora.

Whatever crimes the accused might have committed, the outlandish crimes against humanity charge never stuck. After some time under house arrest and in prison, the state dropped the charges in 2001 due to lack of evidence, although it did not inform the defendants until the next year.

Berisha was never charged. The new government denied it in public, but top officials told me that the international community pressed them to let Berisha off the hook. His arrest, the West feared, would threaten Albania's fragile calm. At the time, the U.S., OSCE, and others could not have imagined that the tireless doctor would one day return.

* * *

Over time and with foreign aid, the economy slowly improved. Order returned, although swaths of the mountainous north remained out of control. As minister of culture Nano appointed the artist Edi Rama, who had been beaten by Berisha thugs in 1997, and the painter-turned-politician tried to revive Albania's cultural life.

A referendum in November 1998 finally approved a new constitution. The DP complained of manipulation, but the OSCE gave its stamp of aproval. Forbidden throughout Berisha's rule, private radio and television stations began to broadcast.

At the same time, Nano and the Socialists kept tight control. They understood that the way to silence the press was not through violence or jail, but with money. Elections would not get rigged on voting day, but manipulated with funds during the campaign. Influence is best exerted not with force, but with cash. Nano and the Socialists were less overt and dogmatic than Berisha and the Democrats, but they knew how to wield power in a sophisticated and effective way.

They also knew how to line their pockets. Their education and knowledge of languages facilitated corruption that quickly became systemic. What had been vulgar theft at border posts and ministries under the DP became the sneaky domain of tenders and licenses. Blue-collar theft turned to white-collar crime. And with this came a palpable arrogance as the former communist elite, stepped on during Berisha's rule, reasserted control. They rightly saw that Berisha was despised at home and abroad, so they strutted with an invulnerable air.

Comparing Berisha and Nano, Fatos Lubonja said that the former had fastened himself to the office gates so that, when he went, Albania went too. Nano lacked this aggression but also did not have the responsibility that leadership demands. "He might let the weight of the power he has taken on fall from his shoulders, saying 'that is all I can stand,'" Lubonja wrote.[8]

A more stinging criticism came from the writer and former Central Committee member Dritëro Agolli who, although close to the SP, had a reputation for speaking his mind. Visiting Nano's office one day, he was shocked by the lack of seriousness in the halls. "Come here, you prick," he heard one minister tell a journalist. Nano was promoting the idea of "meritocracy" at the time, so Agolli created a new word to describe what he saw: *Shkërdhatoracia*, or "Prickocracy." The term resonated loudly in the papers and cafés. "A party without ideals, like an individual without ideas, is easily corrupted and can easily be pulled by its nose for kilometers and years," Agolli wrote.[9]

The year proved both Lubonja and Agolli right. Socialist ministers quickly expanded their businesses and bodyguard teams. Their children studied abroad or got chauffeured in Land Rovers to private schools. The nouveau riche shopped in Italy and drank espressos in Tirana's now-trendy Block, where Enver Hoxha used to live. Corruption had existed under the Democrats, but under the Socialists it spread like mold.

Many Albanians found the arrogance and corruption difficult to digest. During Berisha's rule, the former communists were blamed for all ills. In 1997, Berisha bore the brunt of responsibility. Now Albanians saw all their leaders as opportunistic elites.

14

Illegal but Necessary

The Clinton administration was not thrilled about working with a former communist party, but Berisha's fall left it with no choice. Stability in Albania and the region took precedence over a Cold War grudge.

In October 1998, Nano visited the U.S. to meet Secretary of State Madeleine Albright. Washington's key concern was still Kosovo, where ethnic Albanian guerillas had for one year been attacking Serbian police, prompting a harsh response. The U.S. needed Albania more than before to support a political deal. But by 1998 the U.S. had an additional concern. Militant Islamists were posing a threat to Western interests, and intelligence agencies had tracked some extremists to the tiny Balkan state. Albania was about to become a modest but eager participant in the U.S.-led "war on terror."

At that point, Albania's intelligence service barely functioned. Only the SHIK offices in Tirana, Elbasan, and Fier had escaped undamaged from the 1997 meltdown. Squatters were occupying the building in Peshkopi. Of the ten directorate heads, eight had fled the country, mostly to Turkey, including SHIK head Gazidede. The task of rebuilding fell to a former physics professor with a husky build and large head named Fatos Klosi. Gradually Klosi mended SHIK's international relations and then played an important role in the coming years.

The CIA sent a delegation to Albania at the end of 1997, Klosi told me after he had left the job, but the U.S. was cautious because Klosi was rehiring old members of the Sigurimi—people he said were most capable for the job. When Nano met Albright in October 1998, she urged him to take care because "incriminated elements of the former Sigurimi were returning to work."[1]

That attitude soon changed. "They saw we were not ideological but professional and ready to cooperate," Klosi said. "I opened all doors to prove that we were professional, that we supported the democratic transition, and that we were ready to do something."

* * *

Islamic charities and organizations had started coming from abroad when Albania opened in the early 1990s, running projects to assist orphans, provide humanitarian aid, and construct mosques. Businesses from Kuwait and Saudi Arabia worked in construction. Most companies and organizations provided legal and legitimate services, but some apparently gave cover for individuals with other intents.

The French, British, and U.S. governments began warning Berisha in 1993 about foreigners in Albania connected to terrorist organizations, specifically the Algerian Armed Islamic Group (GIA) and Egyptian Islamic Jihad, run by Ayman al-Zawahiri, today the leader of al-Qaeda. Militants from Jordan, Pakistan, and Sudan, they said, were coming in small groups.

For militant Islamists, Albania of the early 1990s was an attractive base. The dismantling of extreme communism allowed illegal activities to thrive in a maze of porous borders, fragile laws, and corruption. With a weak police and judiciary, and its proximity to Italy, Albania became a convenient hub.

Members of the Albanian SHIK from that time and later told me, and articles in the Albanian and international media corroborate, that Egyptian Islamic Jihad set up small cells for logistics in the mid-1990s, with their members integrating into the community.[2] Albania became a base for money laundering and transit to the West. An office making fake passports opened in Tirana. The U.S. government paid attention, especially after Egyptian Islamic Jihad merged with al-Qaeda in 1998 with a stated intent to target U.S. and Israeli interests.

I never found evidence to suggest that Berisha or Gazidede knowingly assisted these radical organizations, but corrupt officials apparently provided residence permits and sometimes passports to individuals, most likely for the money rather than political or ideological support. Berisha critics allege that Osama bin Laden visited Albania in 1994, but no credible proof has ever emerged of this or other ties, aside from SHIK's laissez-faire attitude towards these groups.

By 1998, Fatos Nano was keen to assist. He declared Albania's participation in the Organization of Islamic Conference (OIC) "not on my government's agenda." The new foreign minister, Paskal Milo, whom police had beaten in Skanderbeg Square after the May 1996 elections, called Albania's OIC membership since 1992 "a constitutional violation" because it had not been ratified by parliament.[3]

With help from the CIA, Fatos Klosi and SHIK bugged telephones and confiscated computers and documents from suspect Islamic organizations, and sent the material to Langley. The Americans never returned the material and the organizations protested, Klosi said. The Saudi and Pakistani ambassadors complained, but there was nothing Klosi could do.

In June and July 1998, SHIK ran its first major operation with the CIA, capturing five suspected members of Egyptian Islamic Jihad led by Ayman al-Zawahiri's brother.[4] A SHIK agent who worked on counterterrorism at the time told me that one of the wanted men was married to an Albanian woman but was having an affair with the woman's mother. When SHIK agents neared the apartment where one of the suspects was living, the man hid in a washing machine, the agent said. As SHIK approached, the man opened fire, killing a member of the team. A senior CIA official corroborated the washing machine attack in his book. The suspect, a "primary al-Qaeda forger," had removed the working elements to create a hiding space, he wrote.[5] The Albanians handed the five captured men over to the CIA, which interrogated them at a remote air base before sending them covertly to Egypt—an early case of illegal rendition by the U.S.[6]

Just after the operation, the Islamic Observation Center in London wrote an open letter to President Meidani warning against the detainees' return to Egypt. "We warn that these suspect practices that contradict the most basic tenets of human rights and the teaching of our true religion will lead only to defeats and the wrath of Allah and Muslims," the letter said.[7] Around the same time, the Albanian embassy in Warsaw reportedly received a call threatening Americans in Tirana. On August 5, a London-based Arabic-language newspaper published a letter from Ayman al-Zawahiri in which he vowed revenge for the arrests in Albania in a "language they will understand."[8] Two days later, bombs exploded at the U.S. embassies in Kenya and Tanzania, killing 224 people.

On August 14, the U.S. embassy in Tirana sent home nonessential staff. The government deployed two hundred Marines and ten Navy SEALS to protect the Rilindja Ridge housing complex that was serv-

ing as a temporary embassy until the proper embassy could be rein-
forced. The State Department urged Americans against travel to Albania
and U.S. officials spoke of a "credible threat from an Islamic terrorist
organization."[9]

That winter, the trial of the men rendered to Egypt began in the Haik-
step military camp outside Cairo, along with more than one hundred
other defendants, sixty-four of them in absentia. Dubbed the "case of
the Albanian returnees," it was Egypt's largest terrorism trial since the
government had tried members of Egyptian Islamic Jihad for the as-
sassination of Anwar Sadat in 1981. In total, eighty-seven people were
convicted, ten of whom were put to death, including two of the men
captured in Albania.[10] The Albanian returnees complained of torture in
Albania and Egypt, including beatings, electric shocks to the genitals,
and being forced to stand for hours in cold water.[11]

"I cannot say they were arrested," then SHIK head Fatos Klosi told
me. "They were caught, put on a plane, and sent to Egypt. This act was
not very legal but necessary. I think we did it well."

15

A Shot, a Coup

Fatos Nano and the Socialist government gradually improved relations with the international community, which was thankful to get Albania off the news. But the domestic political scene stayed fraught. On Saturday night, September 12, 1998, it got markedly worse.

Sali Berisha was working late in the DP office. A party official was briefing him on a recent trip when they heard shots. Both men jumped. It was normal to hear gunfire in Tirana, but rarely so close. Someone opened the door and informed them that a person near the office had been shot.

Party officials ran outside but Berisha stayed upstairs. Less than one hundred meters away, a cluster of people gathered around a husky man. It was Azem Hajdari, aged thirty-five, bleeding heavily and unconscious. Four bullets had ripped through his chest. Next to him lay his two bodyguards, also bleeding. The men were rushed to the Military Hospital but Hajdari and one of his bodyguards died on the way.

Thirty minutes later, Berisha issued a statement accusing the police chief from Tropoja of murder. By 11:00 p.m., he declared that the culprit was Prime Minister Fatos Nano and his bloody communist clique. The government quickly condemned the murder and called for the attacker's arrest.

* * *

President Meidani heard the knock on his hotel door around midnight and knew something was wrong. He was in Greece attending a conference and, by that hour, contently asleep. Azem Hajdari has been shot, his ambassador at the door said. They made immediate plans to fly home.

The president's instinct was right. The next morning, an invigorated DP demanded the dismissal of "Prime Criminal Nano," the creation of a transitional government, and new elections. "If the criminal Fatos Nano does not quit . . . we will use all means to overthrow him," Berisha told supporters.[1] The pro-DP newspaper *Albania* spelled it out in a huge banner headline on the front page: "Nano Killed Azem Hajdari."

A crowd of DP supporters marched to the Interior Ministry, where they fired pistols in the air, threw stones, and set a car on fire. One demonstrator was killed and four policemen were wounded. The protesters continued up the boulevard to Nano's office.

The government sat in emergency session on the second floor when the rowdy gang arrived. Interior Minister Perikli Teta was presenting his report when stones broke the window behind him, shattering glass on his back. "We'll stop the meeting to get the situation in hand," Teta recalled Nano said.

Guards shot in the air as Nano and the other ministers slipped out the back. Some went to the nearby Rogner Hotel and others to their offices. Teta returned to his ministry, where he would spend every night for the next two weeks.

What Fatos Nano did at this point became a matter of dispute. According to some members of the government, he fled to Macedonia, or at least drove near the border. According to then SHIK head Fatos Klosi, Nano sought shelter from a friend and businessman in Durres. Nano addressed the matter twelve years later in a television interview, saying he had spent the night in a state residence near the border with Macedonia. "The decision taken by the escort and the person they were protecting is legitimate in emergency conditions and the nonfunctioning of many support structures," he said.[2]

Meidani arrived in Tirana late that afternoon and quickly consulted with the government and embassies in town. On state television he called for the authorities to catch Hajdari's killers and urged the public to stay calm. "Leave the arms and language of revenge so we can be able to reconstruct our future," he said.[3] The Interior Ministry announced a reward for information leading to an arrest.

Meidani's office reached Genc Pollo, still a close Berisha aide, and expressed the president's desire to attend the Hajdari memorial that the DP had planned the next day in Skanderbeg Square. Pollo said he would check and call back. "I don't recommend it," Meidani remembered Pollo said when he returned the call. "The situation here is not under control."[4]

That night the Democratic Party and its opposition partners sent a delegation to the president. Meidani met them on the first floor and they presented him with an ultimatum that Nano must resign by noon the following day. They also demanded a party roundtable to discuss a new government and the arrest of Hajdari's killers. Meidani said he was ready to talk with the opposition but he rejected government resignations under threat, especially when the identity of Hajdari's killer remained unclear.

When the president went upstairs, he was surprised to find five people waiting in his office. Deputy Prime Minister Skënder Gjinushi was sitting next to U.S. ambassador Marisa Lino, the Italian ambassador, and the head of the OSCE mission in Tirana, which had set up a presence in Albania after the elections. Most surprisingly for Meidani, he saw Prime Minister Nano, who had been missing for almost twenty-four hours.

Meidani told the group about the DP's demands. We cannot make decisions under pressure, he said. Nano cannot resign under threats from the street. Lino had a different view, Meidani and Skënder Gjinushi separately recalled. She suggested that Nano resign, arguing it would calm the scene. Meidani responded that Nano's resignation meant victory for Berisha. Nano was more direct. "Can you guarantee that, if I resign, the situation will calm down?" he said. Ambassador Lino asked to speak with Nano in private. They left the room and returned after five minutes. Neither person has explained what they discussed.

The reunited group formulated some points for the government: (1) distance itself from the murder; (2) call on Democrats to avoid violence; (3) make some government corrections; and (4) fight corruption. Lino then contacted Berisha. I do not control the situation, he told her, according to Meidani and Gjinushi, but if Nano resigns the situation will improve.

Meanwhile, mourners began to fill Skanderbeg Square. The coffins of Hajdari, his bodyguard, and the demonstrator killed near the Interior Ministry lay on the Palace of Culture steps for an all-night vigil. The next morning, thousands packed the square despite a steady drizzle.

"Kill, kill, kill Fatos Nano!" they chanted. "Revenge!"

"You could feel that something would happen," said DP official Ylli Vejsiu, who had been briefing Berisha at the time of Hajdari's murder. Berisha and other DP leaders addressed the crowd. "All the world knows the murderer of Hajdari," Berisha told the excited mob. "This is Fatos Nano."[5]

Around midday, the crowd began to move. Instead of heading to the city cemetery, it turned up the boulevard, carrying the coffins of engraved wood. The crowd split into two, with one group curling behind City Hall. They merged on the boulevard and flowed towards Nano's office. "We will not lay Azem in his grave until the government resigns," they screamed, at which point Berisha left the crowd.

The three coffins landed outside the prime minister's office on the boulevard. The crowd scaled the steps and then retreated. Two men kicked the front doors. The nervous guards inside opened fire as a warning, followed by those on the roof. The mob panicked and stormed the doors.

Three ministers—Thimjo Kondi, Arben Malaj, and Bashkim Fino— were inside at the time. "After the National Guard shot, they got furious," Fino recalled. He and his colleagues scurried out the back. Fino and Malaj crossed the boulevard unnoticed and found refuge in Fino's home.

Throughout the morning, Fatos Nano could not be found. President Meidani called his office repeatedly but got no response. Word spread that he had resigned. "Victory! Victory!" the crowd rejoiced.

Around 1:00 p.m., Nano called Bashkim Fino. The number indicated that Nano was calling from Macedonia, Fino said. "You must return urgently," Fino told me he advised the prime minister.

On the streets, DP militants clashed with police. Cars roared up and down the boulevard carrying men with automatic guns. The DP commandeered two tanks. By afternoon, rioters had broken into the state auditing office, the constitutional court, and the ministries of justice and finance. At the offices of parliament, a crowd used a piece of wood as a battering ram to break the door.

A few blocks away, protesters stormed the state radio and television building, among them Berisha's bodyguard, Izet Haxhia. A captured tank rumbled outside while employees hid in the studios and bathrooms. Guards took off their uniforms and mingled with protesters. A TV manager during Berisha's rule got on the radio and announced that the DP had liberated the station from Nano's clique. The head of King Leka's party proclaimed on television that the state's institutions were "in our hands."

Anti-government protesters atop tanks on Tirana's main boulevard after the killing of Azem Hajdari, September 14, 1998. © Reuters

The government got an urgent message to Berisha, asking him to appeal for calm. Berisha said he would if the television cameras came to him. Around 4:00 p.m., state television broadcast an interview with the opposition leader and former president from DP headquarters, in which he condemned Hajdari's "barbaric political murder, planned by Prime Minister Fatos Nano," but called on citizens to exercise restraint. "We cannot move forward through destruction," he declared. "We must inevitably provide a political solution and move towards a political solution, as a settlement that will give hope to Albania and to the Albanians for the future they deserve."[6]

At the president's office, nervous ministers shuttled in and out. Nano remained missing and Meidani debated whether he should convene the government. Throughout the afternoon he got calls from world leaders: Italian prime minister Prodi, Greek prime minister Simitis, Turkish president Demeril, and U.S. secretary of state Albright, all of them concerned about the degenerating state of affairs.

Around 4:00 p.m., a delegation from the DP and other opposition parties came to talk. The president was on the phone with Austrian foreign minister Wolfgang Schüssel when the group arrived.

"I will not negotiate with them while their supporters occupy state institutions," Meidani said he told Schüssel.

"You should declare this on television," Schüssel replied.

"They have the television too!" Meidani bemoaned.

The president's advisors went downstairs to meet the delegation. The visitors said they had nothing to do with the television occupation, even though the king's party had just declared on TV that state institutions were "in our hands."

"The president can give a message too," one of them told Meidani's advisor Preç Zogaj. "He won't until it's free," Zogaj replied.[7]

By the afternoon of September 14, the crowds were losing steam. Special forces in facemasks had established checkpoints in Tirana and began to manage the crowds. Interior Minister Teta decided he could now re-take the state TV. Rather than storm the building, he asked the journalist Aleksandër Frangaj, formerly of *Koha Jonë* newspaper and by then on the state TV's board, to present the occupiers with an ultimatum: leave the building or be attacked. Frangaj reluctantly agreed and entered the TV headquarters around 6:00 p.m., telling the crowd they had one hour to leave. To Frangaj's relief, the crowd obliged and began to file out of the building, leaving behind spent bullet cartridges and a large pot of rice—a traditional dish served after a funeral.

Frangaj and the staff wanted to inform the public that the state had resumed control of the television facility but the few employees left in the building did not know how to operate a camera. They thought of running text on the screen but no one could work the machine. Finally they managed to transmit from a studio but there were no announcers, so Frangaj appeared before the nation, urging radio and TV journalists to return to work because "I can't run this by myself."[8] Minister Teta arrived forty-five minutes later to announce that the "attempted coup" had failed. The DP was still heavily armed and had two tanks, but Teta stood firm. "I have washed myself like a Christian and I am ready to die," he declared.

On the way back to his office, Teta almost did. In front of the National Gallery of Arts, gunmen opened fired on his armored Mitsubishi Jeep, killing a passer-by. "I saw the bullets bounce off the windows like hail," he recalled.

That night, DP militants milled about their party headquarters, wondering if and when the government would attack. Some said they should take the initiative and storm the police. On the other side, the government debated its next move. Nano was still in hiding, but some of his advisors recommended that the government order special forces to crush the armed protests. President Meidani refused and Minister Teta announced on television that government forces would "defend state institutions, even with our blood."[9] In a strange twist, the government ordered Berisha to leave the country by 5:00 a.m. the next day or face arrest. Berisha said he would not leave Albania and announced a demonstration the following day.

In Western capitals rose an anguished moan: not again. Albania had returned as a trouble spot just as Kosovo was getting more intense. "Members of all parties must work together toward a peaceful solution that respects the democratic process," a U.S. government statement said, sounding more like a plea than a position. The statement also said that Washington would "not recognize or work with a government that comes to power through violent means.[10] The head of the OSCE office in Tirana, Daan Everts, said the U.S. and Europe had sent a signal that Berisha and the DP had "gone too far."[11]

Tension eased the following day. Government forces had retaken the main state institutions peacefully during the night. DP militants still had two tanks but masked police patrolled the streets.

The situation more or less under control, Fatos Nano emerged. He met President Meidani without saying a word about his vanishing act. That afternoon on television he declared the violence an attempted coup. The government issued an ultimatum for all demonstrators to surrender their arms and tanks. After a minute of silence to honor Hajdari, parliament declared a state of emergency.

By this point, the remnants of the revolt could do no more than flash their weapons and clench their teeth. The government could have broken the die-hard group, but not without bloodshed. The main ambassadors in town were pressing the government to pursue dialogue and political steps, while making Berisha know that he lacked their support. From the start, the U.S., Italy, and OSCE had told Berisha that they would not recognize any government that seized power by force. "It is the ridiculous situation with the tanks that needs to be resolved," OSCE head Everts said.[12]

After all-day negotiations, Berisha went to his party headquarters, where the two tanks were parked. "I know that you are disappointed, but the tanks shall be taken by the soldiers who did not kill the people yesterday and did not use them against the crowd," Berisha told a dejected group of supporters from the balcony. "The tanks are the property of the National Guard and the state. They were not Nano's tanks."[13]

That night, the chief prosecutor asked parliament to lift Berisha's immunity. The government announced it would prosecute Berisha for an attempted coup. In total, eight people were killed and eighty injured, the Interior Ministry said, including eleven wounded members of the security forces.

Berisha continued unfazed, calling another demonstration on September 16. "Those who have overthrown the dictatorship of Hoxha will overthrow the dictatorship of the terrorists," he told reporters.[14] About three thousand people marched peacefully under the watchful eye of the police, chanting "Death to communism!" and "Death to Fatos Nano!"

At the Council of Ministers, workers replaced the broken windows and stolen computers while papers fluttered in the halls. Nano held a press conference, standing in front of a wall pocked with bullet holes. The DP tried to stage a coup, he repeated, stressing that the government would talk only when protesters surrendered their arms.

Two days later, parliament lifted Berisha's immunity. The move worried most Western governments, who feared that Berisha's arrest would provoke further unrest. In a letter to President Meidani, U.S. president Clinton urged a "genuine and constructive dialogue" for democracy. "It is a difficult job, but it is the key to ending the violence and polarization that has been a destructive force in Albania's development," he wrote.[15]

The Socialist government eventually recovered. It never arrested Berisha and managed to bring security under control. To appease critics, in late September Nano tried to reshuffle the cabinet. He failed to garner support in the party and was forced to resign. Gunfire echoed through Tirana's streets when television announced the news.

In part the resignation stemmed from outside pressure, especially from the U.S., which believed Nano's departure would help bring calm. According to Socialist Party leaders, however, Nano was also betrayed by young party members who saw their chance at the chair, taking advantage of his having fled the country in a time of need. Nano's replacement was the Socialist Pandeli Majko, who at thirty years old became Europe's youngest government head.

The State Department was glad to see Nano go. Majko was more acceptable as a young face and controllable force, even if a CIA analysis from the time described him as a "political neophyte."[16] Washington's strategy was also to move beyond the Nano-Berisha divide, leaving politics to a new and less antagonistic crew. Indeed, Majko obliged. Under U.S. pressure he reached out to Berisha who, eager to show the West his newfound faith in dialogue, shook Majko's hand at a much publicized meeting in the Rogner. But neither Nano nor Berisha would depart. Despite U.S. attempts to promote a new generation of leaders, Berisha remained the undisputed leader of the opposition and Nano kept his grip on the SP, eventually climbing back on top.

As for Hajdari's killers, the state convicted three men from Tropoja in 2002, one of them in absentia. A fourth gang member was killed in 1999. The precise reasons for the attack on Hajdari remain unclear but it most likely came as a consequence of what one journalist called his "violent temperament."[17] For years Hajdari's involvement in crime was widely discussed, including smuggling in the north. By late 1998, that area was extremely hot. Ethnic Albanian rebels from Kosovo were establishing bases, smuggling arms, and fighting Serbian forces. The war the West feared had begun.

PART VI

Red and Black

The Kosovo War, 1998–1999

16

Argument of Force

Xhavit Haliti watched with shock. His Tirana apartment offered a view of Embassy Street, the guarded diplomatic row. It was July 1990, and hundreds of frantic Albanians were trying to flee the crumbling communist state by storming the German, Greek, and French embassies. The Albanian government soon allowed these people to leave, but the serious and determined Haliti felt no joy. He was an Albanian from Kosovo on his first trip to Albania. For him the exodus looked bizarre. His whole life he had dreamed of seeing the motherland. Now most of Albania wanted to flee.

Haliti's view from Kosovo had been different. Growing up in a village near Pec in the 1970s, and later at university in the capital, Prishtina, Haliti had gazed longingly at Albania as the free homeland where Albanians ruled themselves. In Kosovo, the Serbian police harassed and arrested ethnic Albanians for waving their flag and forced them into a second-class life. Haliti had spent time in prison for his pro-Albanian activities and had fled to Switzerland. In early 1990 a bomb exploded outside his apartment in Zurich, and he blamed the Serbian secret police. In Albania, he thought, Enver Hoxha had built a thriving state. Unable to visit Albania during communism, Haliti's generation had absorbed the propaganda: diligent workers building a socialist paradise, intellectuals enriching Albanian culture, and Hoxha ruling with a wise and benevolent hand. They had no idea that behind the TV cameras lay crumbling factories, prison camps and, by 1990, a desperate embassy siege.

Haliti regrouped. The thirty-four-year-old was intelligent and mature. He moved slowly and with purpose. His eyes were dark and narrow, and far apart on his face. As if to compensate, his eyebrows slid together when he listened with focus, which was most of the time. Above all, the man called "Zeka" had a mission, a fact that others could sense and sometimes feared. His main goal, and the reason for his visit to Tirana, was to win Kosovo's independence from Yugolsavia, and he wanted to do it with force. He would soon become one of the key founders of the Kosovo Liberation Army.

* * *

Haliti met President Ramiz Alia in July 1991. The Albanian president was familiar with the various Kosovar groups. Eager to destabilize Yugoslavia, Albania's communist government had provided money and advice to underground organizations like the Popular Movement for the Republic of Kosova (LPRK), of which Haliti was an active part.

"I met Alia to offer our option to begin a military movement for the issue of Kosovo," Haliti explained for me. "I went to Albania to seek help."

The LPRK and other clandestine groups needed arms, supplies, and training to fight the Serbian state, which had revoked Kosovo's status as an autonomous province in 1990 and was imposing emergency measures to crack down on Albanians there. By mid-1991, war had started in Croatia and Bosnia was teetering on the brink. Some Kosovo Albanians had spoken with the Croats about opening a southern front.

Alia considered the idea. According to Haliti, he believed Kosovo could be liberated only by force. But it had to be done with care, the wizened communist and World War Two veteran said. The Kosovars had to organize and unify their many groups. It was crucial to defend against infiltration by UDB, the effective Serbian secret police.

As liaison, Alia appointed his military advisor, Adem Çopani, the man who would stay in his position during Berisha's rule. With close-cropped silver hair, a square chin, and dark eyes, Çopani was an experienced military man, having served Albanian defense ministers back to Mehmet Shehu. He was also committed to the Kosovo cause. He became what Haliti called a "personal advisor," and the two men stayed in contact up to and during the 1999 Kosovo war.

At first Çopani helped build secret arms depots in Kosovo, but distribution proved difficult without an internal structure. The various cells were far apart and, for security reasons, not in contact with one another. The movement was based on family and regional ties—a loose chain of armed groups united by a common goal.

Haliti met Alia again in September 1991. He wished he could give an optimistic report, but the reality looked bleak. The fractured and inexperienced Kosovars lacked the planning and structure to mount an effective resistance. "You guys are not ready, you are not prepared for this job," Haliti remembered Alia said.

Alia provided some training, both Haliti and then Albanian defense minister Perikli Teta told me. The LPRK sent men to Albania, including a burly fighter named Adem Jashari, who later became an iconic hero when Serbian police killed him and forty-two members of his family. Towards the end of 1991, Ibrahim Rugova's Democratic League of Kosovo also sent men to Albania for training, trying to build what they called a "Ministry of Defense."

Teta remembered the difficulty he had dealing with the Kosovar groups because "too many groups came asking for help." Alia's chief foreign policy advisor at the time, Sofokli Lazri, agreed. "We never knew who was who, and UDB was also active," he said. "If two Kosovars entered Albania, one of them was UDB."

Even if Albania had wanted to help, the state had little to offer. Crowds had toppled the Hoxha monument in February 1991 and successive governments after that. The Albanian army's antiquated tanks and artillery offered no match for the powerful Yugoslav force. Under those conditions, Haliti recalled, "no one wanted to take responsibility for providing arms or making plans."

* * *

Most Albanians in Kosovo cheered the establishment of pluralism in Albania and the creation of the Democratic Party with Sali Berisha at its head. They thought a modern Albania, part of the international community, would benefit their cause. Because Berisha hailed from the north, he would naturally give support. His spirited calls for national unity in the early days of the DP gave the Kosovo Albanians hope that Albania would finally come to their aid.

In Albania, the enthusiasm for ethnic solidarity shone less bright. People in Shkoder, Tirana, and Gjirokaster wanted to buy cars and travel abroad rather than wave the flag. To them, national pride meant little because Hoxha had manipulated national spirit for his repressive ends. The cafés in Kosovo bore mythic Albanian names such as Illyria and Dardania that helped Albanians differentiate themselves from Serbs. In Albania, the new cafés were called Europa and Milan.

Sali Berisha and the Democratic Party quickly aligned themselves
with Ibrahim Rugova and the Democratic League of Kosovo. The two
parties shared a pedigree: both emerged from the new conditions of
1990, both enjoyed Western support for regional stability, and both
encompassed a spectrum of views as political fronts. The two parties
and their leaders—Berisha and Rugova—rose in tandem and would fall
hand in hand.

In February 1991, Rugova made his first trip to Tirana. Ramiz Alia's
foreign policy advisor Sofokli Lazri went to the airport to pick him up.
To his surprise, Berisha, Gramoz Pashko, and other DP leaders were
already there, saying Rugova was their guest. At the end of the trip, Rugova told an interviewer that his party would "establish relations with
the Democratic Party first," even if it was still in opposition.[1]

The U.S. approved of the Berisha-Rugova link as a way to help keep
the Kosovo conflict under control. Washington told Rugova to maintain his nonprovocative position—calling for Kosovo's independence
but without concrete steps to achieve it—and instructed Berisha to stay
in the sandbox and not throw sand. Xhavit Haliti and the LPRK kept
their distance from the DP when it was in opposition because, as Haliti
explained, "they had no capacity to help."

When the DP assumed power in 1992, Berisha allowed the continuation of limited LDK military training. That project ended badly the next
year when Serbia infiltrated the group and made arrests. As Alia had
said, the preparations were not complete. After Berisha became president, Haliti wanted to discuss next steps. "We asked him [Berisha] to
allow our activities," Haliti recalled. "We asked him to close his eyes to
what we were doing because, in fact, what we were doing was outside
the law."

Berisha's reaction was cold, Haliti said. He wanted the LPRK to merge
with Rugova's forces, which were close to the DP. Haliti and others approached Berisha repeatedly for cooperation, Haliti said, but he always
answered the same: "I will act only if Rugova tells me."[2]

According to former DP officials and Berisha advisors, Berisha never
trusted Haliti or the LPRK. He considered them Marxist-Leninists because of their ties to Albania's communist regime. Some in Tirana believed Haliti had worked with the Sigurimi—an allegation Haliti denied.
More importantly, Berisha knew that the U.S. and Europe rejected any

notion of armed revolt. After the failure of the LDK's "Ministry of Defense," Berisha blocked all training and cracked down on the militant Kosovar groups. The LPRK continued its activities in Albania nevertheless, eventually dropping the "Republic" from its name and becoming the LPK. In 1992 it formed a military wing with fewer than twenty people and the Kosovo Liberation Army (KLA) was born. Xhavit Haliti became coordinator for Albania and the West, a strategic position he held throughout the coming war.

The KLA tried to unify the various armed groups across Kosovo. It smuggled in arms, dodging both the Albanian and Serbian police. No help came from Albania, except from what Haliti called "friendly families and institutions," who wanted to assist behind Berisha's back.

Under international pressure to crack down, and suspicious of "leftist" groups, Berisha tried to block the KLA. One of the group's early members, Zahir Pajaziti, spent one month in prison during an arms buying trip to Albania, and only got released after a substantial bribe.[3] In early 1997, Albanian police arrested a young militant named Hashim Thaçi after they caught him with a bag of bullets, but Berisha's military advisor Adem Çopani intervened to secure his release, Haliti said. "Either you have strong friends or you have paid a lot," the police chief allegedly whispered in Thaçi's ear.[4] The young Thaçi went on to play a major role in the KLA and Kosovo's post-war politics.

* * *

In November 1995, U.S. secretary of state Warren Christopher and chief Balkan negotiator Richard Holbrooke gathered the presidents of Bosnia, Croatia, and Yugoslavia at a peace conference on an army base in Dayton, Ohio. A key member of the team was Holbrooke's deputy Chris Hill, who had helped open the U.S. embassy in Tirana. The Dayton Accords, as the agreement became known, brought NATO into Bosnia and created a bifurcated Bosnia with one part for the Croats and Muslims and another for the Serbs.

After Dayton, Albanians in Kosovo began to question their nonviolent approach. For five years they had listened to Rugova promise that the West would address their cause. Now a major international peace conference had come and gone. The United States had rewarded the

Bosnian Serbs with a quasi-state after genocide; it had ignored Kosovars' patience and restraint.

The KLA took advantage. Its fighters had staged sporadic attacks in the early 1990s, mostly targeting the Serbian police, but three months after the Dayton Accords, the young rebels launched coordinated strikes.

The attacks caught Washington's eye. "Slovenia and Croatia were the quarterfinals, Bosnia was the semis, and Kosovo the finals," one State Department official told me. With Dayton signed, policymakers understood that Kosovo was next.

* * *

Back in Kosovo, the student Armend Daçi had done well on his dentistry exam. It was also his birthday, number twenty, and he celebrated with friends. Walking home in Prishtina after the party, he stopped by an automobile. Who knows what Zlatibor Jovanović saw when he peered into the dark from his balcony. A thief breaking into his car? Someone watching his home? He took aim and fired, killing Daçi with a bullet to the chest.

Such shootings were not new. It was April 1996, and violence against Albanians occurred daily. Mostly it came from the police, but civilians also had arms, and they used them with little risk of arrest.

Ibrahim Rugova had been discouraging protests, but hundreds of mourners gathered the next morning outside the Jovanović home. Two days later, against Rugova's wishes, several thousand Albanian women marched on the streets. The reaction outside Prishtina was more intense. The day after the killing, unknown gunmen staged coordinated attacks across the province, killing three Serbian policemen and two civilians. The little-known Kosovo Liberation Army faxed a letter to the BBC, claiming credit for the attacks. Prishtina was abuzz. Was this a hoax, a ploy by the Serbian secret police? Were radical Albanians taking a violent path?

Eager to deny the existence of any other Albanian force, Rugova claimed the Serbian state had staged the attacks to provoke. "The killings of Serbian policemen were never explained," he told me when I visited Prishtina in February 1997 for Human Rights Watch. "They want to invent terror to have a pretext for persecution and arrests." I asked what he planned to do. "We have an Albanian saying: Always listen to your big brother," he replied with a wink. Later I learned that Rugova suggested the FBI or Interpol help the Serbs to investigate the attacks.[5]

To boost Rugova, the U.S. and some European governments encouraged him to sign an agreement with Yugoslav president Milošević on Albanian-language education. The September 1996 deal allowed Albanian students to reenter schools that had been closed for six years, but Milošević never followed through. The agreement's failure further undermined Rugova and gave the KLA additional proof that governments valued the force of argument less than the argument of force.

On October 1, 1996, the United Nations lifted sanctions on Yugoslavia because of Milošević's cooperation on the Dayton Accords. The U.S. maintained what it called the "outer wall" of sanctions, which kept Yugoslavia out of international organizations until the Kosovo crisis was resolved. Still, the KLA had another card: look how the world has forgotten our plight.

* * *

The KLA continued its attacks on Serbian police and civilians. The guerilla group smuggled arms through the mountains from Albania and got training from sympathetic officers in the Albanian army. The goal from the beginning was to start a fire so the West would be forced to act, Haliti and other KLA commanders told me. They knew the KLA had no chance to defeat the Serbian state on its own. Fighting in Kosovo, everyone feared, could spill over the border to Macedonia and destabilize Albania, Bulgaria, and Greece. To preserve regional stability, the KLA hoped, the West and above all the United States would intervene on its behalf.

By this time in Albania, Sali Berisha had broken relations with the United States. The West was pressing him to redo the fraudulent May 1996 elections and, by 1997, to shut down the pyramid schemes. In March 1997 the schemes collapsed. Armed protests spread in the south and Berisha opened the arms depots in the north.

The KLA leadership was perturbed. They craved a strong Albanian state to back their cause. They needed the Albanian police, army, and intelligence service to help their fight. At the same time, they quickly realized that Albania's disaster, and specifically the proliferation of weapons, offered a historic chance.

"Nobody would forgive us if we did not make use of the opportunity posed by the weapons in Albania," said the KLA's first chief commander, Azem Syla.[6] "It created favorable conditions," Xhavit Haliti agreed in typically measured words. "The hungry man does not ask where his bread is baked."

As Albania dissolved, the KLA sent people to buy guns—a Kalashnikov went for as low as $10. Berisha's military advisor Adem Çopani helped, especially after Berisha appointed him head of the army's general staff, by directing the KLA to the depots where they could find arms.[7]

The KLA instantly grew. Donkeys trudged across the rocky border laden with guns and ammunition. By summer 1997, parts of Kosovo were no-go areas for the Serbian police, what Albanians called "liberated territory."

On November 28, 1997, KLA fighters clashed with Serbian forces in the village of Lauša (Llausha in Albanian), leaving an ethnic Albanian teacher dead. Twenty thousand mourners came to the funeral, including three men wearing camouflage and masks—the first public appearance of the KLA. "The KLA is the only force which is fighting for the liberation and national unity of Kosovo!" one of them said with his mask off. "We shall continue to fight!"[8] The crowd responded with chants of "KLA, KLA!"

* * *

As the KLA went public, the Socialists held the reins in Tirana, and the Kosovo fighters were thrilled to see Berisha gone. Under the DP, they had struggled to operate in Albania, always dodging the police. Plus, the KLA knew the former communists from years ago, when they had contact with the old regime. Battered Albania was not able to help the KLA, but neither would it block its work.

The new Albanian government of Fatos Nano walked a thin line. On the one hand, it sympathized with the Kosovo guerrillas. On the other, the international community stood firmly against Kosovo's independence and supported Rugova.

"It was a delicate position between the desire to support Albanians in Kosovo for their rights and our international obligations to support a peaceful resolution of the conflict," explained Paskal Milo, Albania's foreign minister at the time. "In particular we were obliged by our friendly relations with the U.S."

In November 1997, under pressure from Washington, Nano agreed to meet Milošević at a gathering of Balkan leaders in Crete, the first meeting of Yugoslav and Albanian leaders in fifty years. The two sides decided beforehand to meet as delegations but, to the Albanians' surprise, Nano agreed to Milošević's request that they meet one on one. The meeting was set for thirty minutes, but the two men talked alone for an hour and a half. "I was outside with [Serbian president Milan] Milutinović waiting for the meeting of our two bosses to end," Paskal Milo recalled.

According to Nano, he followed the U.S. line and asked Milošević to meet Rugova. Milošević refused, saying that Rugova headed a secessionist and irredentist movement. "I could invite you to the square and four thousand Albanians would shout, 'Long live Milošević!'" Nano claimed Milošević said.

Berisha and the Democratic Party used the meeting to attack Nano, calling him a traitor for meeting the "Butcher of the Balkans." The KLA held no such view. "I did not like Nano meeting with him because I knew he would be attacked for it," Xhavit Haliti told me. "But I never thought something bad would happen for Kosovo. Nano was under international community pressure to meet—the government of Albania was obliged to do it. The superpowers sometimes require that such meetings take place."

More irksome for Haliti was Nano's refusal to meet him. "Nano was afraid to meet me because he knew why I wanted to meet," Haliti said. "He was afraid the international community would respond badly. What would the U.S. government say?"

Instead of waiting for Nano to come around, Haliti did what he had been doing since 1990: he went to the Albanian institutions that worked in his field—the police, army, and SHIK. He found sympathetic individuals in each service, especially SHIK, and that relationship proved crucial as the conflict spread.

17

A Formula

President Bill Clinton's special envoy to the Balkans, Bob Gelbard, was known as a table-thumping, cowboy-style diplomat who did not mince words. In February 1998, he lashed out at the KLA. "The UCK is a terrorist group by its actions," Gelbard said in Prishtina, using the Albanian acronym for the KLA. "I used to be responsible for counter-terrorist policy in the American government. I know them when I see them."[1] He repeated the claim the next day in Belgrade, while announcing a series of U.S. concessions to Milošević for his cooperation on Bosnia.

Five days later, the KLA ambushed the Serbian police at a place called Six Oaks in the central region of Drenica, killing at least two. After a firefight, Serbian forces entered the villages of Likošane (Likoshane) and Ćirez (Qirez) as the KLA retreated. They stormed the compound of the Ahmeti family and detained ten men of the house plus one guest. In what would become a disturbing pattern, they shot and killed all eleven men, leaving blood, teeth, and flesh in the front yard. A message painted on the wall read: "This is what will happen next time too."[2]

On March 5, 1998, Serbian forces surrounded the compound of a local KLA fighter in the nearby village of Prekaz. The obstinate Adem Jashari, a husky man with a thick mustache and beard who had trained in Albania, refused to surrender despite a relentless assault. The attack killed Jashari and an estimated forty-two members of his family, save an eleven-year-old girl.

The killings lit a fire. More than fifty people had died in the three attacks, among them at least two dozen women and children. Rugova's peaceful politics were done. For Albanians in Kosovo, it was time to fight. Villagers rushed to join the KLA, ballooning the group's activities into an open revolt. Gruesome photos of the Jashari family spread through the Albanian communities in Europe and the United States. Xhavit Haliti had set up a fund called Homeland Calling, and thousands of Albanians sent their dollars, francs, and marks.

Internationally, the reactions were split. Diplomats from the United States and Europe condemned the violence and called for mutual restraint. They threatened Milošević with tougher sanctions, though the European Union continued to call the KLA a terrorist group.

The Central Intelligence Agency had a different view. Analysts watched as the KLA rapidly grew. The armed group was becoming a factor on the ground while Rugova was losing influence every day. On the other side, Milošević was not serious about negotiations, as the bloody attacks had shown. As such, the CIA apparently reasoned, it was better to get to know the armed Albanian group. This might also prevent the KLA from looking to Islamic states or organizations for help, as the Bosnians had done. The two views in Washington—cynicism about the KLA versus watching and perhaps supporting the group—would develop into what the Albanian government and the KLA considered the "two streams" of U.S. policy. In general, the split was between the State Department and the intelligence community, but different views percolated inside those groups. Some thought the KLA could be crushed and Rugova would survive. Others believed the KLA was for real, Milošević could not be trusted, and only a military solution would bring a suitable result. Both streams opposed Kosovo's independence as a separate state.

* * *

The killings in Drenica sparked a flurry of diplomatic activity. NATO secretary general Javier Solana visited Albania to promise support. Strobe Talbott, U.S. deputy secretary of state, went one week later and praised the government for supporting Kosovo's "forces of moderation and restraint."[3]

Fatos Nano recalled the second visit. "Strobe Talbott was just giving me the political message of the State Department," he told me with a smile. He encouraged Albania to "support the non-military solution." Reliant on U.S. support, Nano could not refuse. "Albania backs the moderating and wise policy of Ibrahim Rugova," Nano told the press after Talbott left.[4]

At the same time, the CIA was trying to learn more. Who was behind the KLA? How were they organized? Could they be trusted? The point man in Tirana was the head of the Albanian intelligence service, Fatos Klosi, the bearlike man known affectionately to the KLA as "the professor." A physicist by training, he shared Xhavit Haliti's pragmatism and calm. More than anyone in Albania, he was in a powerful position and willing to help.

According to Haliti, Klosi, and other senior SHIK officials, Klosi worked hard to foster a relationship between Haliti and the CIA station chief in Tirana. Eventually the two men began to meet every day. "We helped the CIA to understand the Albanian reality," Klosi said.

Haliti agreed. "The SHIK was the center where contacts and information were exchanged," he said. "Especially between the KLA and the international community."

SHIK officials remember the CIA station chief as intelligent, experienced, and policy oriented. He came from a diplomatic family. He soon became convinced that the KLA was for real, and that it would respect U.S. interests. According to Klosi, over time he and Haliti encouraged Washington to "see the KLA as a liberation force and not a terrorist group."

* * *

The tide slowly turning, in March 1998 Fatos Nano agreed to meet Xhavit Haliti and a delegation of the KLA. "They wanted us to put attention, political and nonpolitical" on Kosovo, Nano recalled.

Nano agreed that the Albanian intelligence service could continue its clandestine support of the KLA, both Haliti and Klosi said, but the government could not be publicly involved. If anything appears in the press, Nano told his guests, he would deny the relationship and denounce their work.

"Nano told me from the beginning that we will say we know nothing," Klosi said.

"We reached an agreement that functioned during the entire time with Nano and Klosi," Haliti said. "We devised a formula that worked."

According to the formula, Albanian diplomacy supported mediation efforts with Rugova, while trying to convince Europe and the United States to trust the KLA. Meanwhile, Klosi and SHIK continued to help the KLA organize and arm. The lawlessness in the north provided the government with a handy excuse. Gunrunning and training might be taking place in the mountains, Nano told diplomats, but the police there lacked control.

* * *

By spring 1998, the U.S. government had two contradictory concerns. First, was the KLA a Marxist-Leninist group? Second, was it cooperating with Islamic states or groups? Haliti tried to assuage both fears. The affinity for Enver Hoxha was a relic of the past, he explained, a result of propaganda and Kosovar dreams. Only Kosovo's liberation guided the group. As for Islamic aid, the Iranian government and others had approached the KLA, and some foreign fighters had come to help, he said. But the KLA was determined to cut all ties with enemies of the United States.

To win trust, Haliti said he opened the books. He shared information on KLA bank accounts and promised to buy guns from U.S.-approved sources, even if that cost more. In April 1998, the KLA and CIA, with facilitation by SHIK, reached an agreement on three essential points, Haliti and Klosi separately said. First, the KLA agreed not to use violence outside of Kosovo, including attacks in Serbia proper. Second, it promised not to cooperate with armed Islamist groups. It would refuse fighters, arms, and funds. Third, Haliti promised to block funds from drug trafficking and other illegal sources. Albanians in the Balkans and Europe had a reputation for dealing heroin and prostitution, and none of this should finance the KLA.

The KLA leadership was reluctant to tell me what it got in return. "Absolutely nothing," Haliti snapped when I asked. "We pursued our policy and they pursued theirs." In all likelihood, there was more. To start, the State Department never put the KLA on its list of terrorist groups. This made it easier to raise funds abroad. More concretely, evidence points to training by U.S. and British military experts at KLA camps in northern Albania. Most importantly for the KLA, it was building trust. The three-point agreement was the start of a partnership, a parallel running of interests that culminated in the NATO bombing of Yugoslavia in March 1999.

With CIA consent and SHIK support, money and guns flowed. By the spring of 1998, the had KLA expanded its presence across Kosovo. Serbian civilians in these areas got harassed and expelled, and the KLA sometimes killed those who refused to leave.

In Albania, foreign diplomats continued to peddle the peaceful approach. Talbott and Gelbard returned to Tirana on April 18, 1998, and asked the Albanians of Kosovo to renounce violence. Richard Holbrooke and Gelbard then convinced Milošević to meet Rugova for the first time, and that took place in Belgrade on May 15, 1998. Washington rewarded Rugova with a visit to the White House. "Fundamentally, we want to demonstrate that the path Dr. Rugova pursues, one of non-violence, one of support for democracy, is the right path for Kosovar Albanians to follow," Gelbard explained.[5]

That same month, SHIK head Klosi visited Washington for a meeting with CIA director George Tenet. As Klosi bluntly explained: "The CIA was for war, the State Department for talks."

* * *

Just after Rugova's meeting with Milošević, the Serbian police and Yugoslav army unleashed an offensive along the border with Albania, where the KLA was getting supplies and recruits. Security forces attacked villages thought to harbor the KLA, forcing roughly forty-five thousand people to flee through the mountains to Albania and Macedonia. In Albania, the town of Bajram Curri took most of the displaced. I went there for Human Rights Watch to interview refugees.

The OSCE had an office in town, run by a former British military officer with red hair and a metal hook for a hand. His staff monitored the fighting from the crumbling stone pyramids that marked the border. An occasional boom resounded in the distance, sending birds into the air. Smoke rose from the villages below.

In Bajram Curri, KLA fighters strolled down the main street and drank coffee in the only hotel. One man who called himself a commander showed a list of people from his village who he said had given money to the KLA. "I will bomb their homes myself and tell them I did it," he said, speaking about those who did not support the cause. In the nearby village of Tropoja, a few miles from Sali Berisha's family home, I saw an arms bazaar with people testing their weapons in the air. Automatic machine guns, artillery pieces, and grenade launchers lay on potato sacks in the street. "Even the Chinese are contributing to Kosovo," said an Albanian policeman in another village, waving his hand at two ancient pieces of artillery. Next to him was a truck piled high with burlap sacks full of pungent marijuana, probably bound for Belgrade. When journalists and humanitarian workers arrived, the northern bandits

went to work, stealing cars and satellite phones. Armed men in bala-
clavas ambushed my friends from the Associated Press and took their
cameras and editing gear. The Albanian policeman the group had hired
as a guard demanded more money because, he said, "you put my life
at risk."

The chief gangster of Bajram Curri was Fatmir Haklaj, who had become the area police chief in summer 1997, after Berisha fell, and would
later be named in court as the killer of Azem Hajdari. In January 1998,
gunmen killed Haklaj's brother, and Haklaj killed a border police commander in revenge. He resigned from the police but was taken back
when the case collapsed due to lack of evidence, and he controlled the
border zone until his murder in November 1999.

* * *

Far from the gangsters, guerillas, and Chinese weapons in Bajram
Curri, the debate in Washington was getting intense. Everyone agreed
that Kosovo should only get autonomy within Yugoslavia rather than
full independence. But could that come through negotiations or did it
require the use of force? And what ramifications would the use of force
have?

The Serbian offensive along the border pushed the State Department
closer to support for war. Hawks argued that Milošević responded only
to force. Also, the offensive had devastated civilians but left the KLA
relatively unscathed.

Richard Holbrooke and Chris Hill, who by then was ambassador to
Macedonia and Clinton's envoy to Kosovo, kept pushing for a negotiated
deal. "Most of us were not willing to go that way [of war] because you're
basically shoving the moderates out the window," Hill explained for me
years later. "But you couldn't just deal with Rugova because there was no
heft there." Hill described the two streams as "we must do this together,
all the Albanians" versus "Rugova is over, it's the KLA."

The KLA learned of these differences from U.S. officials who sympathized with the militaristic view. Following their advice, KLA leaders
told me they tried to keep Holbrooke and Hill out of the loop. When
the diplomats requested meetings, they sent low-level commanders. In
June 1998, Holbrooke met two village commanders, a poet and a lawyer, while sitting on a floor cushion in an Albanian home, an AK-47

262 | A FORMULA

propped against the wall. That summer Hill finally met Xhavit Haliti on advice of the CIA. "I met him in Tirana but I realized he was a procurement guy, not really the head," Hill said.

The Albanian SHIK meanwhile was setting up meetings for Bob Gelbard. In May, he secretly met a KLA representative at the U.S. embassy in Geneva. The day after Holbrooke's meeting in the village, Gelbard met the man again. The State Department was getting acquainted with the rebel group, but they stressed in meetings that the Albanians should have one negotiating team under Rugova.

Around the same time, a large CIA team arrived in Tirana. Some of them traveled north to monitor the fighting and perhaps to help with training. The savvy, policy-oriented station chief in Tirana was replaced by a former Marine—"an implementer," as a top SHIK official called him. At that point, Klosi told me, "we understood that America took the situation seriously."

* * *

The KLA tried to fulfill the three promises it had made to the CIA: no actions outside Kosovo, no Islamic help, and no funding from drugs. On the first point, there was debate because some KLA members from Macedonia wanted to start a larger war. They agreed to postpone their operations and, after the Kosovo war, the ethnic Albanian National Liberation Army fought a short-lived insurgency against the Macedonian government.

Regarding mujahadeen and Islamic aid, the KLA leadership issued orders to sever ties, but not everyone respected the decision. Although few KLA members sympathized with Islamists, some said the KLA should learn from Bosnia and accept help from any source. One KLA activist told me he went to Bosnia to recruit mujahadeen who had fought there in the war. According to SHIK head Klosi, by mid-1998 a small number of mujahadeen were already in Kosovo—two groups of sixteen and twenty people—but the KLA ordered them to leave.

"Through the channels under my control, nobody came in," Haliti told me, when asked about Islamist fighters. "I heard that some entered through other channels but they had no contact with the general staff."

On July 18, 1998, twenty-four Islamist fighters set out for Kosovo from northern Albania with a group of about two hundred KLA fighters. Six kilometers into Kosovo, Yugoslav forces ambushed the group, killing eighteen of the foreign fighters and four of the Albanians, according to the Yugoslav government and a KLA member who was present during the attack.[6] It remains unclear whether the group was caught due to Yugoslav vigilance or a leak, perhaps by KLA members eager to keep Islamist fighters out. Survivors told OSCE and European Commission monitors that KLA "guides" had led the group into an ambush and then fled.[7]

As for the promise to reject illegal funds, the KLA claims it tried. But Albanian criminal syndicates in Europe probably supported the KLA. Former KLA members have been accused of extensive criminal links, including Xhavit Haliti and Hashim Thaçi, in reports from the Council of Europe, Germany, and NATO.[8]

* * *

Emboldened by its Western contacts, the KLA continued to expand, assuming loose control of approximately 40 percent of Kosovo. Military police in uniform confidently stopped cars in KLA areas to check documents. KLA spokesmen talked about liberating Prishtina.

In its exuberance, the insurgency forgot that the Serbian police and Yugoslav army were among the best-trained and well-equipped forces in Europe. And they considered Kosovo their holy land. Milošević had sparked his political rise via the Kosovo issue. He and others in Serbia would not cede Kosovo without a fight.

The KLA tried to take its first city, Orahovac, on July 19, 1998. The operation badly failed. Serbian forces retook the city in two days. In a counter-offensive from July to September, government forces swept through the areas of KLA control, sending the rebels to the hills. Shelling and shooting displaced 250,000 people.

I arrived in Kosovo for Human Rights Watch as the counter-offensive was coming to a close. Government forces had routed the KLA from its strongholds in Drenica and the valley south of Pec. On September 26, 1998, a colleague and I visited the hamlet of Gornji Obrinje (Abri e Epërme) in the hardscrabble Drenica hills. Locals warned us of landmines placed by the KLA, so we parked nearby and walked through a field. In a gully we saw the mangled bodies of five children and two

A dead girl from the Deliaj family outside the Kosovo village of Gornji Obrinje on September 29, 1998. © Wade Goddard

adults lying in wet leaves, one of them a baby about one year old. A plastic tarp hung between two trees over a bloody mattress. Relatives of the victims said these people had been sleeping outside due to the fighting nearby. We watched as they carried the bodies on a makeshift wooden stretcher to a field for burial. Twenty-one members of the Deliaj family had been killed.

I later testified about the Gornje Obrinje killings in the war crimes trial against Slobodan Milošević, and the smell of those bodies took years to fade. The massacre also revealed a disturbing side of the KLA. To get attention and Western support, the group needed sympathy, and civilian deaths helped the cause. The KLA frequently attacked Serbian forces and then retreated through a village, exposing civilians to the predictably overaggressive response. The three turning points in the conflict—the Drenica killings, the Gornje Obrinje killings, and a January 1999 massacre in the village of Račak (Raçak)—all came at civilians' expense.

* * *

With his counter-offensive over, Milošević agreed to a ceasefire and the deployment of OSCE monitors. That same month in Tirana, after turmoil following the Azem Hajdari murder had calmed, the young Pandeli Majko replaced Fatos Nano as prime minister of Albania. The KLA did not expect a policy change—"the formula" had been working well—but they were surprised by what came next.

At a government meeting on November 16, 1998, the day after Majko turned thirty-one, the prime minister unexpectedly condemned the arms smuggling through Albania and demanded that Fatos Klosi resign. Two days later, the police blocked the guns and ammunition that had been flowing into Durres port and then to the north, denying the KLA their main source of supplies.

Why Majko blocked the arms remains unclear. One possibility is that he smelled profit, economic or political. Another option is he did it on the State Department's request. American envoy Chris Hill was peddling a draft for Kosovo's autonomy at the time and maybe he or others wanted to squeeze the KLA. According to then foreign minister Paskal Milo, the U.S. and Europe were pressuring Majko to control the KLA and help with negotiations. Nano had felt this pressure too, Milo said, but he resisted "because he was more skillful."

I met Majko in 2004, when he was minister of defense, and asked why he had blocked the arms. He said Albania's biggest image problem at the time was trafficking, and he wanted to change that. "We wanted to help Kosovo within the constitution and the law," he told me from his oversized office. "I did not want to do it in a secret way." There were additional reasons, he added, "which maybe I'll put in my memoir."

The arms stayed blocked for a few months but Fatos Klosi remained SHIK head because President Meidani refused to approve his dismissal. "It would have ruined the game," one senior SHIK officer said.

18

To War

The ceasefire and international monitors helped the KLA. The group welcomed the deal because, in the words of one commander, it was good "for further mobilization, for the training of our soldiers, and for pulling our strength together."[1]

CIA director George Tenet agreed. "The KLA used the ceasefire and the presence of international verifiers to reoccupy all of the territory it lost last year," he told the Senate Armed Services Committee in February 1999. "It has kept up a continuous series of small-scale attacks against Serb security forces."[2]

Milošević also used the time to rearm, apparently thinking he could resist international pressure and repel the KLA challenge with force. He replaced doubters in his inner circle with loyalists, notably the head of the army and secret police. The army conducted "exercises," which often involved attacking the KLA. By this time, the Clinton administration was mostly convinced of the need for force. After genocide in Bosnia and Rwanda, the U.S. public was asking why the government was doing nothing to save lives. NATO's credibility was also at stake. After repeated demands for Milošević to stop had been ignored, the alliance looked weak—not the image Western leaders wanted for NATO's fiftieth birthday celebration in Washington, scheduled for April 1999. The problem was how to sell a military intervention to the American public. Why should one American soldier die?

The turning point came in the village of Račak. KLA ambushes near the village on January 8 and 10 killed four Serbian police. In response, Serbian forces stormed the village where the KLA had been active, killing forty-five people. International monitors found many of the bodies in a gully, where they had apparently been executed. The OSCE mission head, U.S. diplomat William Walker, called it a massacre by government troops.

The evidence suggests that Walker was right, but details of the killings remain a matter of debate. A Human Rights Watch investigation pointed strongly to executions, but someone might have altered the scene for maximum effect.[3] The U.S. government highlighted the killings and President Clinton called Račak a "deliberate and indiscriminate act of murder."[4] Later, when explaining the bombing of Yugoslavia, he evoked the village. "Make no mistake," he said at a press conference. "If we and our allies do not have the will to act, there will be more massacres."[5] With Račak, the "two streams" in the U.S. government merged. Madeleine Albright and the State Department agreed to bomb, as did NATO's top commander, U.S. general Wesley Clark. The time for talks had passed.

Except for the British, European members of NATO wanted to give Milošević one more chance. On February 6, 1999, the French and British co-hosted a conference at a chateau in Rambouillet, France, to reach a political deal. In reality, the U.S. presented Milošević with an ultimatum: accept foreign forces in Kosovo and the province can stay in Yugoslavia—sign or get bombed.

Milošević refused to attend the conference and he rejected the deal. He probably never believed that, after so many empty threats, NATO would really bomb. Even if the U.S. was ready to take military action, he may have reckoned, Serbia's allies of Greece, France, and Russia would prevent an attack. The Serbian delegation drank cognac, played piano, and kept the Albanians in the chateau awake with their late-night songs.

Milošević's intransigence did not surprise the hosts. But from the moment a member of the Albanian delegation set off a chateau metal detector with his pistol, the Albanians frustrated the Americans, British, and French. First, the KLA and LDK representatives barely spoke with one another, and when they did speak it was to fight. At one point the KLA's thirty-year-old political director, Hashim Thaçi, who headed the delegation, threw an ashtray at LDK official Bujar Bukoshi after Bukoshi called him a "kastravec," which literally means "cucumber" but is best translated as "punk." More substantively, Thaçi, Xhavit Haliti, and the KLA delegates rejected the proposal for a U.N.-administered Kosovo inside Yugoslavia. They said the KLA had started the war and sacrificed lives for Kosovo's full independence, and nothing less. Thaçi got threats from field commanders, who warned him not to sell Kosovo out. The Albanians proposed a U.N. presence for three years followed by a referendum on independence. The U.S. and European governments said no.

Allowing Kosovo's independence, they feared, would set a precedent for the Balkans and other areas with irredentist aims.

The conference deadline passed and Madeleine Albright arrived to continue the talks. She and the British told the Albanians it was the best deal they could get, and they would lose support if they failed to sign. Albright's deputy, Jamie Rubin, took Thaçi for man-to-man walks. The Albanian writer Ismail Kadare sent a letter, as did Albanian president Meidani. Important for the Kosovo issue was "international support and the security of the continuation of this support until the final solution of the issue," Meidani wrote.[6] In contrast, Sali Berisha argued against anything less than a referendum on independence. "No Albanian can sign the loss of Kosovo's independence," the DP said on February 20.[7]

Albright was incensed. She had labored to build a coalition for military intervention, and now she was blocked by the people she wanted to help. Thaçi recalled Albright's anger. "If you don't sign the agreement now, you will be responsible for your country and your people," he remembered she said. "There the war will continue. We will go away."[8]

With the clock ticking, the participants found a solution to buy time. The Albanians agreed in principle to the proposed deal but said they must go home to consult with commanders in the field. Satisfied that the Albanians would sign, Washington agreed to reconvene in two weeks.

A French military plane flew the Albanian delegation from Paris to Tirana. The KLA leaders disembarked and the rest flew to Macedonia, where they started the two-hour drive to Kosovo. After a few days in Tirana, Thaçi, a comrade, and some bodyguards slipped through the mountains into Kosovo to get approval for the proposed deal. On the evening of March 11, Thaçi reportedly met the general staff and three members of the Rambouillet team.[9] Not all commanders consented, but a majority agreed. They disliked having to forego immediate independence but they had no desire to cross the United States. The U.S. and other Western governments were also reportedly threatening to squeeze the KLA's funding and source of arms.[10]

The Albanian delegation returned to France and signed the agreement on March 18, 1998. After three years, the agreement said, an international meeting would "determine a mechanism for a final settlement for Kosovo, on the basis of the will of the people, opinions of relevant

Albanian president Rexhep Meidani (C) talks with Kosovo Liberation Army leaders Xhavit Haliti (L) and Hashim Thaçi in Tirana on March 1, 1999. © Reuters

authorities, each Party's efforts regarding the implementation of this Agreement, and the Helsinki Final Act."[11] The Serbs refused to sign.

The next day in Washington, President Clinton, embroiled in the Monica Lewinski sex scandal, held his first solo news conference in over ten months. "Even though they have not obtained all they seek, even as their people remain under attack, they've had the vision to see that a just peace is better than an unwinnable war," he said of the Kosovo Albanians. "Now only President Milosevic stands in the way of peace."[12]

* * *

NATO planes conducted their raids from the safety of fifteen thousand feet. The KLA served as eyes and ears on the ground, helping to identify targets. A former Pentagon official told me that KLA members sometimes pointed targeting lasers at a rival's house. Xhavit Haliti met General Wesley Clark at least three times.[13]

Under cover of NATO bombs, Milošević unleashed a brutal attack. Serbian and Yugoslav forces systematically expelled more than 850,000 ethnic Albanians, mostly to Macedonia and Albania. Police and soldiers rounded up villagers, separated the military-age men, and in some cases killed them on the spot. An estimated ten thousand Kosovo Albanians lost their lives.[14]

Colleagues from Human Rights Watch and I traveled to Albania and Macedonia, sitting at the borders as the flood of refugees arrived. In both countries, sprawling tent camps grew in the dust and mud. In one village, five witnesses said, Serbian police had lined up more than sixty men in a stream and opened fire. "I was shot in the shoulder and flew into the stream, where I pretended to be dead," a survivor told me, showing the bullet wound.

The international media descended on the Albanian town of Kukes, a few miles from the border. At the crossing, traumatized refugees arrived with their quickly assembled possessions in hand. Some had been walking for days. One family pushed a grandmother in a wheel barrow. Many had no news of relatives left behind.

The reception in Albania was generally warm, and many people were housed in private homes. But refugees also complained of crime and abductions, including gangsters luring Kosovar girls for sex work in Italy or Greece. As I learned years later, the KLA also ran detention centers in at least Kukes and Durres, holding Serbs and Albanians suspected of being spies.[15]

The Albanian government assisted NATO and the KLA as best it could, although it publicly denied giving direct support. Some minor Yugoslav incursions into Albania took place, which Tirana downplayed, and Albania succeeded in staying out of the war.

After blocking KLA supplies since November 1998, Prime Minister Majko opened the gates. Albania accepted thousands of young Kosovar men from abroad who wanted to fight. They came by plane and boat, leaving lives as students and workers in Switzerland, Sweden, Germany, and the United States. "I'm here to defend my people," one young man told me as we rode the ferry from Italy to Durres, just before he vomited into the sea.

The KLA used at least two Albanian army bases to train recruits, one in Feken east of Tirana and the other in Burrel. After a few weeks, the KLA shipped the newcomers north for final training and then to the front. In April, a few hundred volunteers arrived from the United States, known as the Atlantic Brigade. Up north before their deployment, a U.S. official paid a visit, one of the volunteers recalled. "We will win this war," the official reportedly said. "You, soldiers of the Atlantic, you also represent America. Kick some Serbian butt guys. Good luck."[16] Albanians in the U.S. were also sending millions of dollars and weapons without resistance from their government.

The NATO campaign lasted for seventy-eight days. Realizing that the coalition would hold, on June 9, 1999, Milošević ordered his generals to stop. They signed an agreement on the withdrawal of Serbian and Yugoslav forces from Kosovo, the entrance of NATO troops, and the province's administration by the United Nations. NATO soldiers, journalists, and refugees poured into Kosovo before the Serbian troops had left. The Serbs of Kosovo fled in droves to avoid revenge.

Albania was like a popped balloon. The aid workers, journalists, and foreign troops left as quickly as they had come. Albania had played a role in world affairs, but it swiftly returned to the grinding scene of poverty and political fights.

In Kosovo, the KLA established a provisional government and tried to assert control. It went after the remaining Roma and Serbs, and Albanians it viewed as political foes. Eager for stability in the region, the international community turned a blind eye.

In 2010, a Council of Europe report accused the KLA's so-called Drenica Group of post-war abductions, killings, and a "handful" of organ theft cases in Albania, plus ties to organized crime.[17] Among others, it named as perpetrators Xhavit Haliti and Hashim Thaçi, who was Kosovo prime minister from 2008 to 2014.The European Union launched a criminal investigation, and in July 2014 the prosecutor announced that he had enough evidence to merit an indictment for crimes against humanity against unnamed ex-KLA leaders.[18] A special court based outside of Kosovo is expected to be established soon.

Thaçi and Haliti, also a senior Kosovo politician, strongly denied the charges. "If I was such a big criminal, then I would have been arrested by NATO a long time ago," Haliti said.[19] Thaçi called the report unsubstantiated slander.

Wherever the case leads, organized crime has thrived in Kosovo since the war. As early as autumn 1999, the U.S. mission in Prishtina was reporting that "organized crime gangs in Kosovo are involved in drugs, prostitution, and smuggling." The actors included "traditional local organized crime (O/C) groups from Serbia, Albania and possibly elsewhere, and the KLA/PGOK [KLA/provisional government of Kosovo]."[20] Leaked documents apparently from NATO called Haliti a "major criminal leader in Kosovo."[21]

Kosovo's new war became the fight against corruption, but Haliti had traded his leather jacket for a cashmere coat.

19

Busts in Our Heads

February 20, 2001, marked ten years since a joyous crowd had toppled the bronze statue of Enver Hoxha in Skanderbeg Square. With the Socialist Party in power, the government avoided a commemoration. Only Democratic Party head Sali Berisha held a demonstration. He seemed to forget that, in February 1991, the then opposition DP had distanced itself from the felling of Hoxha's statue so as not to appear a destructive force.

One former student wrote a reflective piece about the "December movement," as the student activists of December 1990 and February 1991 were called. "Where are all those students today?" he wrote. "Did they keep faith in the ideals of that time or are they resigned to the interests of parties and personal profit?"[1]

The author knew the answer. The former students were in political parties. They were in business. They were businessmen in parties. Or they lived abroad. The ideals of that time—rebirth, reconstruction, and renovation—had been replaced by resignation and revenge.

To understand the mood I traveled north to Shkoder to meet the courageous men who had tried to topple Stalin's bust eleven years before—the first demonstration against the regime. "Ten years ago we knocked down Enver's bust, but we replaced it with another," bemused the dignified Tomë Sheldija in the small foreign-language library that he ran. "We must destroy the busts in our heads."

A few days later I traveled south to Kavaja, where an anti-communist agitator had thrown Hoxha's book onto the soccer field in March 1990. An abandoned carpet plant loomed over the town square with broken windows and a crumbling façade.

"What happened?" I asked an old man walking by.

"Freedom and democracy arrived," he said, without slowing down.

Indeed, in the square stood an arcing, white marble sculpture called "Freedom-Democracy"—a Socialist Realist protrusion built to resemble two fingers in the air. It was smeared and stained, and someone had defecated on the base.

* * *

After the Kosovo war, it looked like Sali Berisha would slip from the scene. Under his leadership, the DP had lost credibility at home and abroad. Inside the party, critics questioned his hardline approach, but Berisha rebuffed all attempts at his removal. "We tried to debate these issues within the party," said Genc Pollo, Berisha's faithful ally for the previous seven years, who was then the deputy DP head. "But there was little room." As he had run the government, Berisha kept the opposition firmly in grip.

In July 1999, twenty DP parliamentarians defied a party boycott of parliament and took their seats. That fall, Pollo announced he would challenge Berisha for party chair. Like all those who had tried before, the urbane Pollo, for years the DP's smooth interlocutor with the outside world, had no chance against his cunning village master. With Pollo's defeat clear before the vote, he withdrew his candidacy, claiming that he and his family had received threats and that Berisha was going to rig the vote. Berisha easily retained the chairmanship and expelled Pollo from the party leadership.

One week later, the Socialists held their party congress, and it was Nano's turn to strike. After resigning as party chair that January, he devised a comeback by mobilizing the grassroots. He criticized Prime Minister Majko for shaking Berisha's hand in the much publicized reconciliation meeting that Western governments had orchestrated. Cocky with support from abroad, Majko promised to resign if he lost the party chair. Nano's cunning paid off. He narrowly defeated Majko at the congress, forcing him to step down.

To replace Majko, the Socialists chose their third most powerful man, Ilir Meta, a young, beefy politician and former weight lifter from central Albania with a round face and short, gray-speckled hair. Born in 1969, Meta was a student with Majko and also attended the historic 1990 meeting with Ramiz Alia without saying a word. Like Majko, he avoided the democratic movement of his fellow students and stayed with the Socialist Party. But Meta was different from Majko—far more conniving and shrewd. He understood patronage and party organization. He lacked Nano's experience, but he was learning fast.

Meta's first test came with local elections in October 2000. The DP participated but boycotted the second round, which allowed the Socialists to win most of the major cities. The artist Edi Rama, who had become minister of culture in 1998, ran as an independent candidate on the Socialist ticket and became mayor of Tirana.

Genc Pollo disagreed with the DP boycott and left Berisha to start the Reformed Democratic Party. But most Albanians saw Pollo as a careerist who had stayed with Berisha through the worst of 1997. He criticized Berisha after leaving him, and did not reflect on the scandals that had taken place while he held power: the May 1996 elections, the pyramid schemes, or the 1998 attempted coup. Another politician who joined Pollo, former DP head Tritan Shehu, had the same baggage, plus the Lushnje beating with leeks.

The next political event was parliamentary elections on June 24, 2001. After five confusing rounds, the Socialists won a majority with seventy-three of 140 seats. The Democrats and their opposition partners took forty-six. Using a relativity reserved for Albania, the OSCE said the elections "marked progress over past elections," despite ballot box stuffing, counting tricks, and political pressure on the election commission.[2] The DP complained but accepted the result.

Ilir Meta remained as prime minister, but Fatos Nano was gaining strength. That fall, he launched an assault on government corruption, complaining of a "moral crisis" in the state. Meta was forced to remove three ministers Nano had criticized, although the prosecutor never filed charges. Nano then made a surprising move. After years of antagonism and vitriol, he publicly shook the hand of his archenemy, Sali Berisha, even if he had criticized Majko for doing the same. Some thought Albania was entering a new phase of dialogue. But Nano and Berisha were calculating every move. Both faced challanges inside their respective parties and pressure from abroad to leave politics, so they benefited from shaking hands.

In January 2002, Nano garnered enough support in the party to force Ilir Meta to resign. But he still lacked strength to take his place, so the affable Pandeli Majko retook the post. This time, however, more than half the ministers came from Nano's camp. Six months later Nano's efforts bore fruit. He forced Majko out and took the throne for himself—his third round as prime minister. Ilir Meta became deputy prime minister and foreign minister. Majko became minister of defense.

278 BUSTS IN OUR HEADS

Atop again, Nano was revived. He had laser surgery on his eyes, sped his black Mercedes around Albania, and graced the social scene. In November 2002, he left his wife of thirty years to marry a woman twenty years his junior.

Nano also pursued his foes. Apparently as part of a deal with Berisha, he fired more than a dozen top officials, including SHIK head Fatos Klosi, who had steered Albania's intelligence service through the Kosovo war. Berisha hailed the move, saying Klosi should be investigated for murders and corruption.

The Socialists, meanwhile, were reaping the benefits of power. Nano's friends allegedly controlled the Durres port. Ilir Meta ran construction. Party leader Gramoz Ruçi was called the "Bey of Saranda" for his business empire in the south. The U.S. embassy later reported that Ruçi had "long-standing ties to narcotics traffickers and organized crime."[3] At the same time, 25 percent of Albanians lived below the poverty line.[4]

More tragically, apathy reigned. As an activist from an energetic youth movement called Mjaft (Enough) wrote: "People are resigned to a reality they think they cannot change, immune to corruption and tolerant of injustices."[5]

* * *

On January 9, 2004, an American movie was playing on Albania's popular private television station Top Channel when a news presenter interrupted the show. Live on the phone, the presenter said, was a man on a boat that was sinking in the Adriatic Sea.

"We're in the open sea," the man on the phone cried. "We're about to sink and we've shot the flares."

"Where are you?" the presenter asked.

"We're near the island of Sazan," the man replied frantically. "We are a lot of people. We're about to sink. . . . We shot flares but no one is coming."

The call was no joke. The man had called the police to no avail, so he phoned the only place he thought might help. Twenty-one people drowned that night, including the man on the phone.

Prime Minister Nano was abroad at the time. He returned two days later and said he had been out of the country for a medical exam. By then it was too late. For many Albanians, not just the opposition, Nano's tardy return and the police's inaction typified the government's indifferent attitude. Not only did the moribund economy drive people to risk the stormy seas, but the state did nothing to save those who failed to reach the other side. Protesters gathered outside Nano's office with candles and signs. Sympathetic Albanians gave money to the victims' families.

The Berisha-led opposition quickly jumped. They initiated a no-confidence vote against the prime minister, which Nano survived. Then they organized a coalition called "Nano Go," which demanded Nano's resignation and new elections.

The movement struck a chord. On the surface, Albania looked better, with new roads, two cell phone companies, and skyscrapers in the Block. But the skyscrapers looked down on large swaths of the capital without light. In summer, the water was frequently cut. Outside of Tirana, the roads crumbled. The schools, the hospitals, and other social services were inefficient and corrupt.

The first demonstration took place on February 7, 2004, when an angry crowd threw stones at the prime minister's office. Guards shot in the air, injuring some protesters. Workers built a metal barrier around Nano's office, with the excuse that the building was under construction. At night someone cleverly spraypainted an ironic sign: "Beware, Above No One Working."

On February 20, the opposition planned a huge demonstration to commemorate the thirteenth anniversary of the toppling of Hoxha's monument. Western governments urged both sides to relax. In what sounded like a mantra, they repeated that political differences must be handled in the proper institutions instead of on the street. Berisha promised the protest would stay peaceful. The government said it would use force if buildings were attacked.

A large crowd gathered in Skanderbeg Square with signs against Nano and his "SP clique." Berisha waved from the edge of the podium as a bodyguard gripped the back of his suit to keep him from falling forward. The theme song from the movie *Fame* ("I'm gonna live forever") blared from loudspeakers. Across the square, where Hoxha once stood, turned a Ferris wheel and other carnival rides for kids, including a mini-train called "American Express."

Opposition leader Sali Berisha during a "Nano Go" anti-government protest in Skanderbeg Square on February 20, 2004. © Fred Abrahams

To my surprise, some of Berisha's former adversaries joined him on stage. I saw Preç Zogaj, co-founder of the DP, who had lambasted Berisha's authoritarianism, and Nikolle Lesi, the publisher of the newspaper *Koha Jonë*, which Berisha thugs had burned in 1997. Another DP founder, Arben Imami, who was beaten in Skanderbeg Square after the 1996 elections, told me he joined the protest because "Nano has gone that far."

After forty-five minutes, the crowd marched up the boulevard to the Council of Ministers with its new metal fence. Opposition leaders wedged themselves between the few aggressive members of the crowd and the riot police surrounding the building, urging people to show restraint.

The United States praised both sides. "This was a significant major improvement over the violent February 7 demonstrations, and a major step forward for Albanian democracy," a U.S. diplomat said.[6] Twelve years into democracy, a nonviolent protest was called a "major step."

20

The Doctor Is Back

In July 2005, Albania was set for its sixth parliamentary elections since 1991. Fatos Nano and the Socialists had amassed enormous wealth, and they wanted more. Sali Berisha and his coalition were feeding on Albanians' frustration. Only eight years after the calamitous pyramid schemes, the doctor was poised to return.

On one level, the campaign had a serious tone. Both sides hired American consultants with ties to the Republican Party. The parties staged elaborate rallies and ran slick ads. On a deeper level, the campaign involved the same dirty tricks as before. Albanians had learned how to buy votes and stuff the ballot boxes. A campaign advisor to the Socialists told me that a candidate could buy one electoral zone for between $100,000 and $300,000. One vote cost between $1.50 and $4, he said, but I heard of one candidate paying up to $300 in a contested race.

Some parts of the country were staunchly Democrat, mostly in the north, and some were strictly Socialist, mostly in the south. In the swing zones, the candidates typically bought off a local businessman, who paid voters. In the past, parties had given voters a premarked ballot. The voter took the ballot into the polling station, dropped it in the box, and brought a clean ballot for the next person. By 2005, voters used cell phone cameras to prove they had voted for the candidate who paid.

A collection of smaller parties also ran. On the right, former Berisha aides Genc Pollo, Tritan Shehu, and others had the Reformed Democratic Party. On the left, Ilir Meta split from the Socialists to form the Socialist Movement for Integration. The smaller Social Democrats, Republicans, Democratic Alliance, the ethnic Greek party, monarchists, and others existed as before, but Meta's new party was the one to play a significant role.

The Socialist Party message was clear: Berisha is dangerous and Albania cannot return to violent times. Using the slogan "Defend the Future," ads showed wild men from 1997 shooting Kalashnikovs. The DP's thrust was corruption. Albania needs a "prime minister" and not a "crime minister," Berisha said. Posters showed the doctor's smiling face above the slogan "With Clean Hands."

Berisha stayed disciplined and calm. He opened the party to a new generation of politicians, many of them educated outside Albania, and he invited back some of the DP founders with whom he had so forcefully clashed. Gramoz Pashko, who had battled Berisha for the party leadership in the early days, ran for the DP. Arben Imami did the same. "It is necessary to have change," Imami explained over coffee at Café Fame, below his spacious apartment in the Block. I asked about the beating he had endured in 1996. "It was something political and not personal," he replied. "And now I need to think about what is best for the country."

In contrast, the Socialists drifted. Nano took little interest in campaign strategy, his aides said, and he continued to gallivant and drink. His new wife ordered party bosses and her business associates around with a foul mouth. The leadership suffered from the same affliction of past governments: arrogance and overconfidence. Nano believed, his aides said, that he would always win so long as Berisha stood on the other side.

On election day I visited Shkoder to see Tomë Sheldije, the venerable owner of the Librari Internationale, who had helped organize the Shkoder demonstration in 1990. "Voting is a responsibility, but I don't want to put a hat on any of those men," he scoffed. Outside of town, I met the Socialist candidate for the Kopliku region, a husky man named Paulin Sterkaj, who proved that Albanians had switched sides in both directions. A former wrestling champion, Sterkaj had been head of the police special forces under Berisha through March 1997.

"After 1997, the institutions were rebuilt, there was higher investment, better infrastructure, and relations with private business and the state became more consolidated and correct," he said to explain his flip. He complained that people had falsely accused him of abuse when he was with the police, including of women. "I never beat my own wife, let alone another's," he said.

By late afternoon, both sides declared victory. In Tirana, Gramoz Pashko pulled up in a black Land Rover as I walked down the street, saying he had probably lost his district. "That's okay, I made my contribution," he said. That was the last time I ever saw Gramoz. He and his son tragically died in a helicopter crash in 2006.

Around 8:00 p.m., I was watching election coverage at a café in the pyramid when the news announced a DP win. I stared in disbelief. After falling from grace eight years before, the doctor was back. A beaming Berisha held a press conference, looking composed and strong.

In the end, the DP won fifty-six seats, and the Socialists forty-two. The police reported seventy-seven incidents, including the death of a Republican Party observer. The OSCE said the elections marked progress, but "complied, only in part, with OSCE commitments and other international standards for democratic elections."[1]

Many of my friends said they had voted for the Democrats out of anger with the SP. "I have to vote against these guys," one journalist said. The next day he called back remorsefully, as if he had slept with an old girlfriend: "I think I made a mistake." As was typical in Albanian elections, the people had voted against.

Two other factors helped Berisha win. First, the DP successfully used Albania's electoral law, which included a complex formula for the proportional list. Second, the new party of Ilir Meta won five seats and split the left. Over the coming years, Meta's power would steadily grow.

* * *

Sali Berisha's return sparked a debate in Albania and abroad: Had the doctor changed? His supporters said he had reflected and learned. His detractors feared a vengeful autocrat. I did not believe a person like Berisha could change, but I was willing to give him a chance. If he had not changed, the conditions around him certainly had. By 2005, Albania had a more credible opposition, a stronger media, and a better informed international community. Governments had not forgotten the kangaroo courts, rigged elections, and pyramid schemes.

The new faces in government did not inspire confidence. Genc Pollo rejoined Berisha as minister of education, and later deputy prime minister. Ridvan Bode, who ran the Finance Ministry during the pyramid schemes, resumed that post. The interior minister in 1996 and 1997, when police beat protesters in Skanderbeg Square, Halit Shamata, became deputy minister of education and science. Arben Sefgjini, former Tirana SHIK chief, became head of the tax office, despite facing charges of having tortured and murdered an ethnic Albanian businessman from Macedonia in 1995. Most striking was the reemergence of ex-SHIK head Bashkim Gazidede, director of Berisha's political police, who appeared without explanation after eight years of hiding abroad. Berisha appointed him head of a government office dealing with property—a slap in the face for SHIK's victims. When Gazidede died from cancer three years later, after receiving state-funded care abroad, Berisha eulogized him as the man who had "stood firm for the defense of the state, the constitution and the national interest."[2]

As before, Berisha worked nonstop. As before, he meddled in every ministry's work. He approved business deals and placed articles in newspapers.

An early target was the intelligence agency, by then renamed SHISH, which Berisha proposed to fold into the Ministry of the Interior. He disliked the agency's Socialist-appointed director, who had built a close relationship with the United States. But Berisha backed down after what the U.S. embassy called "intense international opposition."[3] He pushed again in 2006 by trying to remove the SHISH director, Bahri Shaqiri. Washington pushed back again because it considered Shaqiri a "friend."[4] A cable from the embassy said Shaqiri and the agency had "demonstrated their capabilities and willingness to assist the USG in any way requested."[5]

The next summer parliament elected a new president and Berisha supported a biologist named Bamir Topi, who had become a DP member of parliament in the scandalous 1996 elections and served as minister of agriculture and food in the last year of Berisha's first reign. Topi obliged Berisha by doing what his predecessor Alfred Moisiu had refused to do: discharge the general prosecutor, Theodhori Sollaku, who had been investigating some senior officials for corruption. The judiciary seemed to have taken a hit but, to everyone's surprise, the new prosecutor, a thirty-five-year-old woman named Ina Rama, fought to preserve her independence. Berisha at first praised Rama as a guardian of justice, but soon attacked her as biased and unfit.

At the same time, the government maintained its pro-Western stance as a moderating force in the Balkans and, since 9/11, an enthusiastic contributor to the "war on terror." A few hundred Albanian soldiers were already deployed in Afghanistan and Iraq. In May 2004, before the elections, and again in October 2005, under Berisha, Albania helped the CIA with the agency's network of illegal secret prisons for terrorism suspects—the so-called "black sites."[6] In 2006 Albania began accepting for resettlement some prisoners released from Guantanamo Bay.

In September 2006, Berisha hired former U.S. secretary of homeland security Tom Ridge as a consultant for $480,000 per year. The main goal, Berisha and Ridge announced, was to win Albania full membership in NATO. In violation of U.S. law, Ridge failed to register his contract with the U.S. government for twenty-one months, and he did so only after a Justice Department investigation.[7]

One month after signing up Ridge, Albania sealed a $535 million no-bid contract with the U.S. construction firm Bechtel and its Turkish partner Enka to build a thirty-seven-kilometer highway through the rugged northern mountains as part of an ambitious project to link the port of Durres with Kosovo. The Albanian minister who signed the deal, Lulzim Basha, was later indicted for fraud, but the case was dismissed on technical grounds after what the U.S. embassy called "shaky rulings" by the court.[8]

In mid-2007, the U.S. boosted Berisha by announcing the visit of President George W. Bush—the first U.S. president ever to set foot in Albania. "How do you think they'll receive me over there?" Bush asked an Albanian journalist who interviewed him before the trip.[9] "They'll love you more than you can handle," the journalist said he replied.

Bush landed in Tirana on June 10, 2007, and about his reception the journalist was right. Children in folklore costumes gave the president and first lady flowers and the National Guard fired a twenty-one-gun salute. Cheering supporters lined the road, as they had for James Baker seventeen years before. Large banners adorned the route saying "President Bush in Albania Making History."

On an eight-day tour of Europe towards the end of his second term, Bush had met emotions from dislike to disgust, but mostly Muslim Albania welcomed him with open arms. The post office issued a set of commemorative stamps. Tirana renamed a road in his honor.

Bush met Albanian soldiers serving in Iraq and thanked Albania for its help against terrorism. He stressed U.S. support for Kosovo's independence. In the afternoon, he visited the small town of Fushe Kruje north of Tirana and worked the crowd. His jacket off and sleeves rolled

U.S. president George W. Bush greeting supporters in Fushe Kruje on June 10, 2007. ©
Reuters

up, he hugged raucous well-wishers, while dark-suited Secret Service
agents clutched him from behind. Old women kissed his cheeks and tus-
sled his hair. Before entering a black SUV, he reached onto the roof and
pulled himself high, waving to the cheering crowd: "Bush, Bush, Bush!"

Berisha beamed. "Today is a great day, historic for all Albanians," he
proclaimed at a joint press conference. "Among us is the greatest and
most distinguished guest we have ever had in all times."[10]

The opposition also fawned. "It's not about being blind," said Tirana mayor Edi Rama, who had become head of the Socialist Party in
2005. "The U.S. is something that is really crucial for the destiny of the
world."[11]

The only glitch came later that day, when video spread on the Internet
that showed Bush losing his wristwatch in the Fushe Kruje crowd or,
some claimed, having it stolen. The White House said the president had
discreetly passed the watch to a guard.[12] Bush critics joked that a thief
had saved Albania's dignity.

* * *

The village of Gërdec lies a few kilometers from Tirana's airport, but it was hardly known. That changed abruptly on March 15, 2008, as did perceptions of Albania as a state moving towards the rule of law.

As a condition for joining NATO, Albania had to dismantle the massive stockpiles of antiquated munitions it had amassed during Hoxha's rule. With U.S. aid, the government had hired an American company, which subcontracted an Albanian firm to do some of the job. At a depot in Gërdec, villagers worked in dangerous conditions to extract explosives from bullets and shells. Around noon on the fifteenth, massive explosions ripped through the depot, shattering windows at the airport. Twenty-six people lost their lives and hundreds were wounded by fire, shrapnel, and flying glass.

Defense Minister Fatmir Meidiu resigned and Berisha demanded a full investigation. But when the plucky general prosecutor Ina Rama began to make progress, Berisha accused her of political bias. The pressure increased when allegations emerged that Berisha's son might have been involved. Meidiu was indicted along with more than two dozen others but the Surpeme Court later ruled that, because Meidiu was re-elected to parliament in June 2009, he enjoyed immunity under Albanian law. Berisha promptly appointed him environment minister.

The new U.S. ambassador in Tirana, John Withers, jumped to the general prosecutor's defense. He criticized attacks on the judiciary and stressed the need for independent institutions. "To me that was the turning point, the start of the substantive problems that emerged more and more," he told me in 2013 about Gërdec.

One year later, the New York Times revealed another scandal. This time an American company called AEY was implicated—and the company's twenty-two-year-old president convicted in the U.S.—for illegally selling old Chinese ammunition from Albania to the Afghan army under a Pentagon contract.[13] Berisha's son was reportedly implicated in the deal.[14] In September 2008, an Albanian source for the Times turned up dead on a rural road.[15]

The Gërdec and AEY scandals did not slow NATO. In April 2008, the alliance invited Albania to start accession talks and full membership came one year after that. One condition for membership, John Withers told me, was that the SHISH director Berisha wanted to remove must keep his post for three more years.

The role of Berisha's son and daughter, Shkelzen and Argita, the latter a prominent lawyer, became an open topic of debate. When a Socialist Party member raised it in parliament in July 2008, Berisha fired back, interrupting the deputy's speech with a vulgar insult of his sister.[16] "Although profane outbursts by Berisha in Parliament are nothing new, this latest tirade by the PM has shocked even Albania's hardened political class and media," Ambassador Withers reported to Washington.[17]

To understand the scandals, I sat in September 2008 with Berisha's former advisor Mero Baze, who had served him loyally through 1997 and had attacked me for being "leftist" and "anti-Albanian." He was on a crusade against Berisha, giving details about the prime minister's family and dirty deals. I asked Baze why he was criticizing Berisha now after having served so long as his trusted aide. He answered that Berisha had broken his promise to govern with "clean hands." I strongly doubted Baze's avowed distaste for corruption; indeed, most Tirana observers said his radical switch came after a deal gone bad.

I also met my old acquaintance Arben Imami, who was serving as Berisha's chief of staff. Of course there was still corruption, Imami explained, but it was much better than before. Under Nano, every minister was on the take, he said. After the meeting I realized that, with Socialist governments after 1997, Imami had held three ministerial posts.

Unfortunately the opposition offered little inspiration. Tirana mayor Edi Rama had replaced Nano as Socialist Party head, and many Albanians had hope for the refreshing artist, who had challenged Berisha as president. Rama had impressively cleaned up Tirana, demolishing hundreds of illegal structures and splashing colors on the city's drab apartment blocks—what he called an "intervention."[18] But critics said Rama failed to address the structural faults behind the façades. Others called him "Mr. 10 Percent" or "Berisha in jeans" for the kickbacks they said he received from construction magnates. Members of the Socialist Party complained about Rama's autocratic style.

The cynicism increased in April 2008, as parliamentary elections neared, when Rama and Berisha agreed to change the constitution and, that November, the electoral code. The loudest critic was Ilir Meta, the former prime minister who had split from the Socialists to form his own party. He led a nine-day hunger strike inside parliament against the "consensual crime" of the new code, which he argued would harm smaller parties. Parliament passed the new code regardless 113–1. The acrimony of the adversaries ended where their mutual benefits began.

* * *

Parliamentary elections on June 28, 2009, were close. The Democrats took sixty-eight seats compared to the Socialists' sixty-five. Voter turnout was 50 percent. To reach a majority, the DP formed a coalition with four smaller parties, including the ostensibly leftist party of Ilir Meta. The OSCE found another phrase to express dislike and acceptance: "While meeting most OSCE commitments, these elections did not fully realize Albania's potential to adhere to the highest standards for democratic elections."[19] Ambassador Withers got more to the point. "It has very much come to our attention that there is a strong undercurrent of people tied to organized crime that participated and/or were involved in possibly manipulating the June 28 elections," he told Washington. "The three major parties, the Democratic Party (DP), the Socialist Party (SP) and the Movement for Social Integration (LSI), all have MPs with links to organized crime."[20]

The Socialists said Berisha had rigged the vote and they refused to accept the result. They boycotted parliament and staged demonstrations, including a hunger strike outside Berisha's office. The U.S. and E.U. urged the Socialists to rejoin parliament, but Edi Rama refused.

The shrewd Ilir Meta served as kingmaker in the new government. Despite just four seats in parliament, he became deputy prime minister and minister of foreign affairs, a perch from which he could expand his business. According to a secret U.S. embassy cable from 2009, Meta was already "very wealthy" and widely considered "spectacularly corrupt."[21] The next year, Albania extradited a Meta aide to the U.S., where he was wanted for murder, kidnapping, drug trafficking, extortion, and arson.[22]

By now Ambassador Withers was openly criticizing the government, including its attempts to politicize the intelligence service.[23] The extent of his frustrations became clear in November 2010 when WikiLeaks released the trove of U.S. diplomatic cables it had obtained, including batches from the embassy in Tirana. One cable entitled "Criminals Making the Laws in Albania's New Parliament" listed members of parliament from all major parties with ties to organized crime.[24] Another noted "growing credible evidence that the Prime Minister's immediate family, senior members of the opposition party, and numerous members of the parliament engage in corrupt acts on a large scale."[25]

In January 2011, corruption allegations against Ilir Meta broke into the public when a pro-opposition television station broadcast a secretly filmed video that appeared to show Meta discussing bribes to build a hydroelectric plant.[26] Meta resigned, but the Socialists sent their supporters to the streets, spurred by anti-government demonstrations at the time in Tunisia and Egypt that were sparking the Arab Spring. On January 21, a violent crowd attacked Berisha's office with stones and Molotov cocktails. The Republican Guard opened fire, killing four. Dozens were wounded, including protesters and police. The opposition threatened to protest more and Berisha railed about an attempted coup.

General Prosecutor Ina Rama opened an investigation while Berisha gave bonuses to the Republican Guards on duty that day. He formed a rival parliamentary inquiry and accused Edi Rama, Ina Rama, SHISH, and President Bamir Topi of trying to overthrow the government. The U.S., E.U., and OSCE called for an "independent investigation free from political interference" and gave the general prosecutor their "full support."[27] The U.S. offered the services of the FBI crime lab to analyze ballistics and footage from two video cameras outside the prime minister's office.

A court eventually acquitted Meta of the corruption charges. A few days before the decision, Berisha publicly visited Meta at his home and then again at a hotel. "We meet with Berisha on a continuous basis and we discuss various issues, but not the decisions of courts," Meta explained.[28] Eventually two Republican Guard members were acquitted of opening fire on the crowd. A third person had already been found innocent of deleting video of the clash. The U.S. said it was "dismayed" at the verdict, which "undermined confidence in the ability and willingness of the Albanian judicial system to deliver justice."[29]

* * *

Four months after the violent demonstration, Albania saw its closest-ever election. Initial results showed Socialist Party head Edi Rama winning Tirana city hall for a fourth term by a mere ten votes. Berisha and the DP candidate, Lulzim Basha, demanded a recount, which they argued should include ballots mistakenly placed in the wrong boxes. The

DP-dominated Central Elections Commission agreed to include miscast ballots and Berisha's protégé won by ninety-three votes. The OSCE said the commission's "highly disputed" decision further undermined confidence that it was "acting as an impartial and independent body."[30]

The Socialists eventually ended their boycott of parliament but the tension scarcely ebbed. The United States and European Union repeatedly condemned the confrontational politics that blocked Albania's effort to join the European Union. Albania had won visa-free travel for its citizens to the E.U. in December 2010, but Brussels put the country's request for candidacy status on hold pending corruption reform and the resolution of political disputes. Some E.U. ambassadors in Tirana were forcefully blunt. "Is there any possibility that corrupted politicians, so criminals, can lead this country straight to the EU?" the departing ambassador from Denmark remarked in July 2012.[31]

That summer, President Topi's term ended—his relationship with Berisha had soured and he was not reappointed. As a replacement, Berisha chose his minister of the interior and then justice, Bujar Nishani, whom General Prosecutor Rama had accused of impeding her investigations. Nishani repaid his master by doing what Topi had refused to do: replace the High Council of Justice head and change the director of SHISH. In December 2012, General Prosecutor Rama's term ended and an apparent DP supporter took her place. After seven years in power, Berisha had wrested control of the presidency, the intelligence service, and the prosecutor's office. As Karl Marx famously wrote, history repeats itself, first as tragedy, then as farce.

21

Pendulum Swing

The U.S. and E.U. made it known they were watching. High-level visitors stressed the need for Albanian parties to cooperate and compromise, like a frustrated parent telling siblings to get along. As parliamentary elections in 2013 neared, diplomats and foreign officials called the vote a test: it would show the maturity of Albania's democracy and readiness for the E.U.

The government hired two major U.S. lobbying firms, the Podesta Group and Patton Boggs, with the influential businessman and former diplomat Frank Wisner, whose father had helped found the operations directorate of the CIA and had tried to overthrow Hoxha in the 1950s. Wisner had recently served as U.S. envoy to Kosovo and was personally involved in Patton Boggs's Albania work.

In November 2012, as Albania celebrated one hundred years of independence, Berisha raised eyebrows by talking about "Albanian lands" in neighboring states—a breach of the long-standing deal to avoid nationalism.[1] A few months later, at a conference in Munich with leaders from the Balkans and beyond, Berisha stressed the "national unity of the Albanians" from five different states.[2]

Berisha's nationalist spurt had a domestic aim. Frustration with the government and opposition had spurred a vocal nationalist movement and new political party called the Red and Black Alliance, which Berisha strived to outflank. Still, the international community hit back. In a memo to the Foreign Ministry that leaked to the media, the State Department said the government was playing a "potentially dangerous" game that could "impact our relationship."[3] Germany's foreign minister cautioned that "[n]ationalist emotions and feelings should be treated very carefully."[4] Most Western governments supported independence for Kosovo and decentralization in Macedonia but they rejected a larger Albanian state.

In April 2013, the election campaign took a sudden turn. After four years in the ruling coalition, with high posts until the corruption scandal, the pragmatic Ilir Meta took his Movement for Socialist Integration to the other side. He and Edi Rama portrayed the union as a natural reunification of the left. Meta's video scandal had sparked the January 21 demonstration, in which four people died, and Rama had publicly ridiculed Meta's "instability" and "paranoia," but defeating Berisha became the bigger goal.[5]

All sides tried to manipulate the vote. International observers saw the DP and SP force teachers and pupils to attend rallies.[6] At the Ministry of Justice, the minister ordered managers to mobilize DP voters in their neighborhoods, and threatened them when they refused. Meta's party cajoled and threatened voters with jobs.

The voting on June 23, 2013, began ominously with a shooting death in Lezhë, but for the most part level heads prevailed. The Socialists won sixty-six seats compared to the Democratic Party's forty-nine. The big surprise was Meta's Movement for Socialist Integration, which jumped from four to sixteen seats. The nationalist Red and Black Alliance failed to enter parliament.

For three days, Berisha stayed out of sight. One person told me he had gone to Italy. Another said he had suffered a heart attack. A third had information that he had retreated to Mount Dajti, as if planning a Partisan attack. Berisha broke his silence on June 26 with a dramatic concession speech in front of supporters at Democratic Party headquarters. "We lost this election," he said with a scratchy voice. "And believe me that for this loss all responsibility falls on one person, only on me."[7]

The results for the big parties came as no surprise. The vote was mostly not for Edi Rama or the SP but against the authoritarianism of Berisha and the rampant corruption of the past eight years. Unexpected was Meta's dramatic leap, given his four-year alliance with Berisha and persistent charges of corruption. The common view in Tirana was that Meta's team had perfected the art of buying votes with money and jobs. Perhaps the party's advisors from the U.S. firm Greenberg Quinlan Rosner expressed it best when they said, without irony, that Meta had wooed voters by "focusing intensely on their employment concerns and providing a compelling vision and plan for job creation."[8]

The international community praised the process, with an OSCE official calling the elections free and "quite fair."[9] The E.U. said they had passed in an "overall orderly manner."[10] But the Socialists' wide margin of victory meant the dispute mechanisms never faced a test. Had the results been close, the drama of the preceding Tirana mayoral election would have looked tame.

* * *

Edi Rama has a radically different character than Sali Berisha. The six-foot-six former national basketball player comes from Tirana's elite and has no complexes about his past. The son of a respected sculptor, Rama did not grow up in the Block but he flittered at its edge. He also rejected the ideology of his parents' generation. As a young artist he challenged taboos. As a professor at the Academy of Arts he pushed against dogma. When the democratic movement began, he and a friend formed a group called Reflexione to explore Albania's troubled past. When I first met Rama in 1993, he was walking down the boulevard in shorts and a T-shirt with stick figures in different sexual positions. The shorts alone were radical at the time.

At the same time, Rama craves to keep things under his control. He works hard to manage his image as what one American journalist called a "Balkan original."[11] He decorated the prime minister's office with wallpaper of his own doodles. His friends call him bombastic. U.S. ambassador John Withers took it a step further, saying in a 2009 cable to Washington that both Rama and Sali Berisha have a "distinct authoritarian streak."[12]

More concretely, during his political rise, Rama gained support from a host of powerful tycoons. Critics say he owes these men a lot in return.

Now the artist-politician must lead, and the challenges are immense. Albania survived Europe's financial crisis because its economy is largely detached from the Euro-Atlantic system. Still, remittances from immigrants in Italy and Greece have dropped. Growth in 2013 dipped to a meager 0.4 percent—the lowest it had been in more than fifteen years. Unemployment rose to 15.6 percent.[13] Tranparency International ranked Albania the fourth-most corrupt country in Europe, ahead of Belarus, Russia, and Ukraine.[14]

On the other side, the fate of the Democratic Party remains unclear. Berisha acknowledged defeat and Tirana mayor Lulzim Basha became

Socialist Party head and current Albanian prime minister Edi Rama at an election rally in Tirana on June 26, 2009. © Reuters

the official party head, but the relentless doctor will never stop. And he has apparently amassed great wealth. At seventy years old, he could aim for another return to replace what he calls "the failed painter" and his "neoblockmen."

A key player going forward is the businessman and parliament speaker Ilir Meta, who is influential and rich. And he has Rama in a tight spot. His break with Berisha showed that he will jump from side to side when it suits his needs.

The bigger problem is weak institutions. The judiciary is politicized and corrupt. Criminal groups hold sway over politicians and have little interest in deep reform. It is not that Albanians do not know how to hold fair elections or run independent courts. It is that influential stakeholders have no interest in seeing such change.

After three rejections, in June 2014 the European Union approved Albania's application for candidate status, which means Albania is allowed to knock on the club door. The E.U. called it the "logical consequence" of reform efforts, and at the same time made clear that membership remains many steps away.[15]

The incentive of E.U. membership can pull the country forward. But change will be slow so long as powerful business interests, legal and illegal, hold sway over political life. The new cast of officials, some of them open-minded and well-meaning, must overcome layers of bad practices and policies, and the power brokers that support them.

Epilogue

Albania's modern history can be described with Tirana's cafés, and each phase had a defining locale. When Albania opened in 1990, the Dajti Hotel was a hub of social life. The café with a parquet floor and high windows offered a tranquil place to talk politics, mostly with former communists who felt at ease in the faded room. By my arrival in 1993, Tirana's elite drank coffee in the pyramid, the former Enver Hoxha Museum. Journalists, ministers, and members of parliament sat at low tables with red upholstered seats to gossip and scheme. Over time, cafés grew around the pyramid's edge, down the boulevard, and into Rinia Park, each with a specific clientele: pro-government journalists, opposition journalists, writers, professors, actors, and exiled Kosovars. From 1994 to 1997, the liveliest café was Bar West on Rinia Park's northern side, known as Fidel's after the name of its owner. A prefabricated glass-and-metal hut, it served the politicians, journalists, and intellectuals who opposed Berisha and the spies who monitored their lives. Everyone played it cool, sipping espresso in the morning and raki in the afternoon, watching who talked with whom. To this day, a weekly magazine from Tirana has a political gossip section called "Bar West." In 1995, the Rogner Hotel drew those who could afford the price for coffee with a biscuit on the side. The café and patio became the stage for the drama of 1997 and, as one journalist noted, "virtually Albania's only functioning institution." When I returned in 2001 to research this book, the Rogner was still a café of choice. But most interviews took place in the once-sequestered Block, where the Politburo members had lived. The neighborhood had become the bustling center of business and chic cafés, such as Manhattan, Rio, and Fame. High-rises sprouted around Enver Hoxha's villa, one with a revolving restaurant. Finally, in 2005, came the Sheraton, which bumped the Rogner to a lower class. Behind a wall and long driveway at the end of the boulevard, it symbolized the widening gap between Albanians and their leaders.

Empty pedestal of the Enver Hoxha statue in Skanderbeg Square, March 1991. © Reuters

The café evolution shows how far Albania has come: from a dilapidated, fascist-era hotel to a modern, international chain. No one can deny that Albanians' lives have vastly improved. They travel, they debate, and they change their government. But to me the measure is not how Albania looks at the top but how far it has come as a whole. It is tempting to see the new cafés and restaurants as progress until one steps into Tirana's periphery, or to most other cities, let alone the rural areas, where blackouts and muddy roads prevail. In 2014, the poverty rate— people living on less than about $1.25 per day—was 12.4 percent.[1] Violence remains common on the streets and in homes, with women and children bearing the brunt.

In this context, the argument about independent institutions becomes concrete because these bodies should defend people's rights, and not just those who belong to the ruling party or can fill an envelope with cash. Two and a half decades after communism, Albania still needs media, police, and courts that serve as honest arbiters of disputes.

If a revolution is meant to replace the old power structures with something new, Albania did not have that break. It had protests, some of them authentic, and then a process of choreographed change. Power passed from one sector of the elite to another. At the same time, this transfer instead of rupture probably spared Albania a lot of pain. Given Hoxha's extreme repression, 1990 could have been a very bloody year.

Throughout the transition, Western states that espouse democracy have often fallen short. The U.S. focused on short-term regional stability at the cost of democratic growth. The U.S. rightly cared about regional affairs over local politics, but it could have used its vast power to encourage moderation abroad and at the same time promote the rule of law at home. Instead, in the desert of Albania's early post-communist politics, the U.S. watered one sprig.

The error of die-hard Berisha supporters was not that they backed the man—he was arguably the most capable person to lead Albania in the early years. The error was giving him so much power and uncritical support, which fed into Albania's track record of strong leaders. In a country emerging from four decades of dictatorship, it was critical to foster a separation of powers and checks on the rule of one man. The failure to do so emboldened Berisha and made his authoritarianism worse.

Thankfully that approach has changed. The U.S. and E.U. now protest when politicians squeeze a prosecutor. They complain about corruption. But they have not taken the proactive approach that Albania needs and the leverage they have allows.

In the end, however, Albanians hold the key. After two decades of frenzied individualism, they can step back and examine their common project. What is Albania's long-term economic plan? What type of army serves the country's needs? How can education best train the youth?

Albania's leaders can show the way by thinking more about hospitals and schools than about posts and profit. They can use their positions to serve rather than to hoard. They can govern instead of rule. But citizens need to demand this from their leaders. Their voices can count not just during elections but as a constant refrain for responsibility, transparency, and accountability.

The younger generations give reason for hope. They are not bound by the burdens of fear and servitude. They have matured as Albania rejoined the world, absorbing cultures and engaging in debate. At the same time, they have grown up on a drifting ship, with principles thrown to the wind. They have watched swindlers get promoted, enter parliament, and run the state. They have learned how to pay for exams, and diplomas too. Which spirit dominates—emancipation or deception—will determine Albania's next café.

ACKNOWLEDGMENTS

Many people made this book possible. I am grateful to the Open Society Institute for its early support through a fellowship, which funded the first phase of research, especially Aryeh Neier, Gara LaMarche, and Laura Silber. I thank Peter Osnos and Robert Kimzey for their faith in the idea, which got me going.

In Albania, my indispensable partner was Artan Puto, one of Albania's best historians. I could not have written the book without his help. Many other people in Albania and Kosovo assisted with their expertise and advice, including Elsa Ballauri, Andi Bejtja, Mimoza Dhima, Delina Fico, Kathy Imholz, Benet Koleka, Tina Kraja, Remzi Lani, Fatos Lubonja, Beni Qena, Altin Raxhimi, Engjell Serjani, Edvin Shvarc, and Ylber Hysa. Gazi Haxhia and his family gave warmth from my first days in the country. Agim Buxheli granted access to his video archive. Muharrem Ylmeri safely navigated many potholed roads. Above all, I thank Fron Nahzi, my first boss in Albania, then a mentor, and then a dear friend. More than anyone, he lifted the curtain for me to peek.

Many people read drafts of the book, in whole or in part. I am grateful to Phineas Baxandall, Ros Baxandall, John Feffer, Merita Ilo, Fron Nahzi, Artan Puto, Altin Raxhimi, Chuck Sudetic, and Janet Steen from Editrixie. For the images, I thank Wade Goddard, Lulzim Lika, Veronica Matushaj, Anri Sala, Ivy Shen, Redina Tili, Gani Xhengo, Muharrem Ylmeri, and Fani Zguro.

Thank you to the staff and fellow residents at Blue Mountain Center in New York for one month of peaceful productivity. And thanks to past and present colleagues at Human Rights Watch. Ivana Nizich first let me work on Albania and Holly Cartner guided our efforts through the pyramid scheme crisis and Kosovo war. The staff at NYU Press greatly improved this book in quality and appearance.

Most importantly, I thank my family—my parents, my sister and her family, and my wife and children—for their perpetual support.

NOTES

PROLOGUE

1. "Our Aim" (in Albanian), *Reporteri*, October 20, 1993.
2. "Three Americans in the Faculty (Without Counting the Dog)" (in Albanian), by Aurel Plasari, *Zëri i Rinisë*, November 19, 1993.
3. "Poetic Cycle by Koçi Petriti" (in Albanian), *Aleanca*, November 3, 1993.

CHAPTER 1. HOXHA'S HEART

1. "Albania After Shehu: Foreign Poicy," United States Department of State, Bureau of Intelligence and Research, June 22, 1982.
2. I interviewed three of Hoxha's doctors, Dr. Sabit Brokaj, Dr. Ylli Popa, and Dr. Hektor Peçi. See also "How Enver Died in My Hands—Interview with Dr. Sabit Brokaj" (in Albanian), *Panorama*, December 1, 2003.
3. English-language news of Radio Tirana, April 11, 1985.

CHAPTER 2. FENCES FALL

1. Speech of Ramiz Alia to the Eighth Plenum of the Central Committee (in Albanian), *Zëri i Popullit*, September 29, 1989.
2. "Government of the GDR and Politburo of the Central Committtee of the SED Resign" (in Albanian), *Zëri i Popullit*, November 9, 1989.
3. "On Events in the Czechoslovak Socialist Republic" (in Albanian), *Zëri i Popullit*, November 25, 1990.
4. Speech of Comrade Ramiz Alia to the Professional Union (in Albanian), *Zëri i Popullit*, December 13, 1989.
5. "On the Deepening of the Measures for the Revolutionization of the Life of the Party and the Whole Country, Decision of the 9th Plenum of the Party of Labor Central Committee" (in Albanian), *Zëri i Popullit*, February 4, 1990.
6. Ibid.
7. Secret Report from Minister of Internal Affairs Simon Stefani to Comrades Ramiz Alia and Adil Çarçani, "On Some Activities by a Group of People in the City of Kavaja" (in Albanian), Ministry of Internal Affairs, Directorate I, Tirana, April 9, 1990.
8. Ibid.
9. "Socialism—Guarantee for Freedom, Independence and Progress" (in Albanian), *Zëri i Popullit*, May 1, 1990.
10. Law number 7380, May 8, 1990.

11. "On the Perfection and Democratization of Penal Legislation and Some Organizational Measures" (in Albanian), Report presented on behalf of the Council of Ministers by Comrade Manush Myftiu, Deputy Prime Minister, *Zëri i Popullit*, May 9, 1990.

12. "Literature, Time, Albanian Civilization" (in Albanian), by Ismail Kadare, *Zëri i Rinisë*, March 21, 1990.

13. "In Search of Lost Time" (in Albanian), by Prof. Ylli Popa, *Zëri i Popullit*, April 28 and 29, 1990.

14. "Intellectuals Facing the Duties of the Time" (in Albanian), by Dr. Sali Berisha, *Drita*, May 20, 1990.

15. "Democracy and Humanism—an Inseperable Duo" (in Albanian), by Dr. Sali Berisha, *Bashkimi*, September 17, 1990.

CHAPTER 3. THE SYSTEM SHAKES

1. MPJ, v. 1990, d. 44, p. 5, Ministry of Internal Affairs, Directorate of the People's Police, Nr. 645, Tirana, June 16, 1990, "On the Situation and Problems in Relation to the Physical Safety of the Foreign Embassies" (in Albanian), signed by Minister of Internal Affairs Simon Stefani.

2. MPJ, v. 1990, d. 498, p. 50, June 24, 1990, signed by Reis Malile.

3. MPJ, v. 1990, d.B VII, p. 15, "Subject: On the Events on the Grounds of the Embassies" (in Albanian), Report by Chief of the General Office of Investigation Qemal Lame to Minister of Foreign Affairs Reiz Malile, July 3, 1990.

4. MPJ, V. 1990, d.B VII, p. 14, Protocol Nr. VN NR. 161/90, Tirana, July 2, 1990.

5. Fevziu, Blendi, *Jeta ime . . . Intervistë me Blendi Fevziu* (Tirana: UET Press, 2010), p. 69.

6. MPJ, d. 44, v. 1990, "Information of July 11, 1990."

7. Ibid.

8. "First Albanians Arrive in Czechoslovakia; 5,000 Cram Embassies," Associated Press, July 9, 1990.

9. "Democratization on the Road of the Party" (in Albanian), General Sector of the Staff of the Central Committee of the Albanian Party of Labor, Tirana, 1990. See also "Meeting, Comrade Ramiz Alia with Innovative Intellectuals in the Capital" (in Albanian), *Zëri i Popullit*, August 11, 1990.

10. "Ismail Kadare Deserts" (in Albanian), *Zëri i Popullit*, October 27, 1990.

11. "Albania's Leading Writer Is Granted Asylum," by David Crary, Associated Press, October 25, 1990.

12. "Albanian Leader Says the Country Will Be Democratized but Will Retain Socialism," by David Binder, *New York Times*, May 13, 1990.

13. "Comrade Ramiz Alia Received U.N. Secretary-General Javier Pérez de Cuéllar" (in Albanian), *Zëri i Popullit*, May 13, 1990.

14. Address by Ramiz Alia to the U.N. General Assembly, September 28, 1990.

15. "Speech of Ramiz Alia to the Albanians in Boston" (in Albanian), *Zëri i Popullit*, October 3, 1990.

CHAPTER 4. STUDENT CITY

1. "Students in Albania Clash with Police," *Reuters*, December 10, 1990.
2. Fevziu, Blendi, *Jeta Ime . . . Intervistë me Blendi Fevziu* (Tirana: UET Press, 2010), p. 93.
3. Ibid., p. 94.
4. Berisha interview with Blendi Feviu, Opinion program, TV Klan, December 2010. (See "Full Interview, Sali Berisha: The Year 1990 and Founding of the DP" [in Albanian], *Tema*, December 10, 2010.)
5. Ibid.
6. Mustafaj, Besnik, *Midis Krimeve dhe Mirazheve* (Tirana: Onufri, 1999), p. 57.
7. Ibid., p. 56.
8. Ibid., pp. 56–57.
9. Berisha's December 2010 interview with Blendi Feviu, Opinion program, TV Klan.
10. "Demands of the Students Presented at the Large Meeting Held in Student City on December 10, 1990" (in Albanian).
11. "Mysteries of December 1990" (in Albanian), by Blendi Fevziu, Klan TV, December 16, 2010.
12. The two votes against political pluralism were cast by Spiro Koleka and Rita Marko.
13. "Comrade Alia Meets with Representatives of the Students" (in Albanian), *Zëri i Popullit*, December 12, 1990.

CHAPTER 5. A DEMOCRATIC PARTY

1. "Albania's First Free Party to Be Formed Today," Reuters, December 12, 1990.
2. Part of the speech is available at http://www.youtube.com/watch?v=xBDxzMB38v U&feature=player_embedded#! (accessed September 22, 2014).
3. "Meeting in Student City" (in Albanian), *Zëri i Popullit*, December 13, 1990.
4. "Declaration of the Initiative Commission of the Democratic Party" (in Albanian), *Zëri i Popullit*, December 14, 1990.
5. "Remembering the Demonstration of December 9, 1990, in the Skanderbeg Square," by Shinasi Rama, *Illyria*, December 10–12, 2002, and "The Demonstration of December 9, 1990, in the Skanderbeg Square and the Polarization of the Student Movement," by Shinasi Rama, *Illyria*, December 13–16, 2002.
6. "A Letter of the Students to Adil Çarçani, the Chairman of the Council of Ministers" (in Albanian), *Rilindja Demokratike*, February 7, 1991.
7. "First Meeting of the Democratic Party" (in Albanian), *Rilindja Demokratike*, February 16, 1991.
8. "Statement of the Council of Ministers" (in Albanian), *Zëri i Popullit*, February 19, 1991.
9. "Declaration of the Organizing Commission of the Student Movement" (in Albanian), Tirana, February 18, 1991, http://ow.ly/BLgsG (accessed September 22, 2014).

10. "Political Diary: Three Days to Overthrow Three Statues" (in Albanian), by Mitro Çela, *Rilindja Demokratike*, February 23, 1991.
11. "Who Toppled the Statue in Tirana, Interview with Rajmonda Bulku" (in Albanian), *Albania*, February 21, 2001.
12. Albanian Radio and Television, February 20, 1991.

CHAPTER 6. VOTE FOR THE FUTURE
1. "Statement of the Central Committee of the Albanian Party of Labor" (in Albanian), *Zëri i Popullit*, February 22, 1991.
2. Interview with Ambassador Peter F. Secchia, Foreign Affairs Oral History Project, Georgetown University Library.
3. Cable from U.S. Secretary of State to U.S. Embassy Belgrade, "Briefing Foreign Ambassadors Traveling to Albania," September 18, 1983.
4. "Albania after Shehu: Foreign Poicy," United States Department of State, June 22, 1982.
5. "Draft Statute and Minimal Program of the Democratic Party," *Rilindja Demokratike*, January 5, 1991.
6. "Our North Star—The National Cause, Speech of Dr. Sali Berisha, Member of the DP Initiative Commission, during the Rally in Student City" (in Albanian), *Rilindja Demokratike*, January 5, 1991.
7. Cable from U.S. Embassy in Sofia to Secretary of State, "Conversation with Albanian Opposition Leaders," March 13, 1991.
8. United States Department of State Briefing Memorandum, "Meeting with Dr. Salih [*sic*] Berisha and Gramoz Pashko," March 14, 1991. See also cable from U.S. Secretary of State to U.S. Embassy Belgrade, "Acting Secretary Kimmitt Meets with Albanian Democratic Leaders Berisha and Pashko," March 25, 1991.
9. This and other details of Berisha's life come from his interview with the journalist Blendi Fevziu: Fevziu, Blendi, *Jeta Ime . . . Intervistë me Blendi Fevziu* (Tirana: UET Press, 2010), pp. 73–104.
10. Ibid, p. 84.
11. Ibid, p. 86.
12. Interview with Sali Berisha on *Hardtalk*, April 10, 2008, http://news.bbc.co.uk/2/hi/programmes/hardtalk/7340471.stm (accessed September 22, 2014).
13. Interview with Blendi Feviu, Opinion program, TV Klan, December 2010. See also "Full Interview, Sali Berisha: The Year 1990 and Founding of the DP" (in Albanian), *Tema*, December 10, 2010.
14. "Democracy's Race against Fear," by Kenneth Roth, *Nation*, May 6, 1991.
15. "American Assistance Conditioned on the Victory of Democratic Forces" (in Albanian), *Rilindja Demokratike*, March 23, 1991.
16. "On the Contrary, a Great Victory," by Ismail Kadare, *East European Reporter*, Vol. 4, No. 4, Spring/Summer 1991.
17. "Testimony of Dr. Sali Berisha," Democratic Developments in Albania, Hearing before the Commission on Security and Cooperation in Europe, May 22, 1991.

18. "Testimony of Ismail Kadare," Democratic Developments in Albania, Hearing before the Commission on Security and Cooperation in Europe, May 22, 1991.

19. "We Must Create a Party with a New Physiology; Interview with Secretary of the Central Committee of the Party of Labor of Albania Xhelil Gjoni with Our Editor Petrika Grazhdani" (in Albanian), *Zëri i Rinisë*, June 8, 1991.

20. "Marxist Icon Criticized in Albania; Ruling Party Blames Hoxha for Problems," by Jim Fish, *Washington Post*, June 11, 1991.

21. "Speech of Xhelil Gjoni, First Secretary of the Central Committee of the Party of Labor" (in Albanian), *Zëri i Popullit*, June 11, 1991.

22. Baker, James A., with DeFrank, Thomas M., *The Politics of Diplomacy: Revolution, War and Peace, 1989–1992* (New York: G.P. Putnam's Sons, 1995), p. 485.

23. Ibid., p. 486.

24. "Albanians Mob Baker, Cheer U.S., Europe," by Norman Kempster, *Los Angeles Times*, June 23, 1991.

25. "300,000 Albanians Pour into Streets to Welcome Baker," *New York Times*, June 22, 1991.

26. "Albania: Progress along Freedom's Road (Address by Secretary of State James Baker)," U.S. Department of State Dispatch, Vol. 2, No. 26, July 1, 1991.

27. "Interview with Sali Berisha: Which Forces Are Attacking the DP" (in Albanian), *Rilindja Demokratike*, July 24, 1991.

28. U.S. Central Intelligence Agency, "Albania: Prospects for Reform and the New Government," August 9, 1991.

29. "Culture Agrees Only with Democracy, from the Speech of Mr. Preç Zogaj" (in Albanian), *Rilindja Demokratike*, October 2, 1991.

30. "To the Brink of Disintegration," *East European Reporter*, Vol. 5, No. 1, January/February 1992.

31. See, for example, "Albanian Minister Says Two Killed in Food Riots," by Steve Pagani, Reuters, December 7, 1991.

32. "What Unites Me with Berisha Is Stronger than What Divides Us" (in Albanian), *Rilindja Demokratike*, December 11, 1991.

33. "Criminal Plans—Political Capital at the Expense of the DP and Albania; Statement of the DP Chairmanship, DP Deputies and Ministers" (in Albanian), *Rilindja Demokratike*, December 11, 1991.

34. Pettifer, James, and Vickers, Miranda, *Albania: From Anarchy to a Balkan Identity* (New York: New York University Press, 1997), p. 33.

35. "Albania's Post-Communist Anarchy; Crime, Looting Spread in Balkan Land Once Ruled by Terror," by Mary Battiata, *Washington Post*, March 21, 1992.

36. "U.S. Embassy Boost to Democrats in Albania," by Liam McDowall, Associated Press, February 7, 1992. See also "Chronical" (in Albanian), *Rilindja Demokratike*, February 8, 1992.

37. Cable from U.S. Embassy Tirana, Ambassador William Ryerson, to Secretary of State, "Socialist Press Turns Up the Heat," March 13, 1992.

38. Cable from U.S. Embassy Tirana, Ambassador William Ryerson, to Secretary of State, "The Albanian Elections," March 20, 1992.
39. Ibid.
40. "Democratic Party Declaration" (in Albanian), *Rilindja Demokratike*, August 7, 1991.
41. 1992 Electoral Program of the Democratic Party.
42. "Albania's Second Mult-Party Elections," Commission on Security and Cooperation in Europe, Washington, D.C., April 1992,
43. Democratic Party of Albania brochure, 1992.

CHAPTER 7. REBUILD THE STATE
1. Albanian Telegraphic Agency, April 5, 1992.
2. "Premier Outlines Government Program," Associated Press, April 18, 1992.
3. Cable from U.S. Embassy Tirana, Christopher Hill, to Secretary of State, "U.S. Visit of Albanian MOD Zhulali—His Agenda," June 7, 1993.
4. "Albania Returned to Rapid Growth in 1993—IMF," by Benet Koleka, Reuters, February 21, 1994.
5. Video of the meeting provided by the George Bush Presidential Library and Museum. See also George Bush Presidential Library and Museum, "Remarks Prior to Discussions With President Sali Berisha of Albania," June 15, 1992.
6. Cable from U.S. Secretary of State to U.S. Embassy Tirana, "Secretary's Letter to Albanian President—Supplemental Assistance Package," April 28, 1992.
7. "Bush Warns Serbs Not to Widen War," by David Binder, *New York Times*, December 28, 1992.
8. "Gramoz Pashko: The Loyal Opposition," by Isuf Hajrizi, *Illyria*, September 9–11, 1993.
9. "Cloak and Dagger: A CIA-Backed Team Used Brutal Means to Crack Terror Cell," by Andrew Higgins and Christopher Cooper, *Wall Street Journal*, November 20, 2001.
10. "Democrats Confident in Local Voting," *Illyria*, July 25, 1992.
11. "Democratic Party of Albania," Tirana, 1993, p. 22.
12. "Be Tolerant or Else: Interview with President Sali Berisha," *East European Reporter*, November/December 1992.
13. "Democrats Set Back in Local Voting," *Illyria*, July 29, 1992.
14. "Democrats Suffer Losses in Local Elections," by Liam McDowall, Associated Press, July 30, 1992.
15. "Eight Sacked from Albanian Ruling Party," Agence France-Presse, August 14, 1992.
16. "Be Tolerant or Else."
17. Preç Zogaj, *Koha Jonë*, July 10, 1992 (as published in "Learning From the Past," *East European Reporter*, September–October 1992).
18. "Berisha Critics Form Party," *Illyria*, November 7, 1992.

CHAPTER 8. ONE-PARTY TOWN

1. "Speech of Fatos Nano to the Extraordinary Meeting of the General Steering Committee" (in Albanian), *Zeri i Popullit*, July 28, 1993.
2. Cable from U.S. Embassy Tirana, Ambassador William Ryerson, to Secretary of State, "Former Prime Minister Nano Arrested; Socialists Rally in Tirana," August 2, 1993.
3. "Just for Show," *Economist*, April 9, 1994.
4. Cable from U.S. Embassy Tirana, Ambassador William Ryerson, to Secretary of State, "Socialists Deny Link to Italian Scandals; 'Berisha and Democrats Out to Get Us,'" April 30, 1993.
5. U.S. Central Intelligence Agency, Intelligence Report, Office of European Analysis, "Albania: Fitfull Progress in Judiciary, Media Reform," August 1, 1995.
6. "Past Imperfect that Won't Go Away," by Julie Flint, *Guardian*, February 13, 1993.
7. Statement of the dean's office of the faculty of history philology, Albanian Radio and Television, October 29, 1993.
8. "A Public Letter from a Group of Telegraphic Agency Journalists" (in Albanian), *Rilindja Demokratike*, August 11, 1993.
9. "Truth Does Not Harm Democracy, but Helps It; Interview with *Rilindje Demokratike* Former Editor-in-Chief, Mr. Frrok Çupi" (in Albanian), *Koha Jonë*, August 9, 1991.
10. "Tens of Tanks towards Northeastern Border" (in Albanian), *Koha Jonë*, March 24, 1993.
11. "Albania Plays Down Report on Tank Movements," Agence France-Presse, March 24, 1993.
12. "Explanation Regarding the News 'Tens of Tanks Towards the Northeastern Border'" (in Albanian), *Koha Jonë*, March 27, 1993.
13. "Threats against *Koha Jonë*" (in Albanian), *Koha Jonë*, January 27, 1994.
14. "Embargoed Fuel Sent to Serbs via Albania," by Raymond Bonner, *New York Times*, April 2, 1995.
15. Cable from U.S. Embassy Tirana, Douglas R. Smith, to Secretary of State, "The Failure of the Constitutional Referendum and its Significance," November 18, 1994.
16. Office of the Vice President, Memorandum for Members of the Deputies Committee, Sanctions Enforcement Issues, April 25, 1995, http://ow.ly/BcDob (accessed September 22, 2014).
17. Chris Jarvis, "The Rise and Fall of the Pyramid Schemes in Albania," Working Paper of the International Monetary Fund, July 1999.
18. Naylor, R. T., *Patriots and Profiteers: On Economic Warfare, Embargo Busting and State-Sponsored Crime* (Montreal: McGill-Queens University Press, 2008), p. 435.
19. Office of the Vice President, Memorandum for Members of the Deputies Committee, Sanctions Enforcement Issues, April 25, 1995.
20. "Embargoed Fuel Sent to Serbs via Albania," *New York Times*.

21. Ibid.

22. "Greeks Help Serbs Get Oil, U.S. Asserts," by Raymond Bonner, *New York Times*, April 30, 1995.

23. "Berisha: We Are Ready to Build Nuclear Power Plants for Italy" (in Italian), *Corriere Della Sera*, May 29, 2008.

24. Amnesty International, "Rwanda: Arming the Perpetrators of the Genocide," June 15, 1995.

25. "Turn of the Tide: Rebel Forces Squeeze Rabbani on Three Fronts," by Ahmed Rashid, *Far Eastern Economimc Review*, September 20, 1995.

26. Lane, C. Dennison, *Once upon an Army: The Crisis in the Albanian Army, 1995–1996*, Conflict Studies Research Centre, September 2002, p. 188.

27. Ibid, p. 190.

28. Cable from U.S. Embassy Tirana, Ambassador William Ryerson, to Secretary of State, "Scenesetter for Visit of Secretary of Defense Perry to Albania," July 14, 1994.

29. Memorandum of Understanding on Defense and Military Relations between the Department of Defense of the United States of America and the Ministry of Defense of the Republic of Albania, October 14, 1993.

30. Cable from U.S. Secretary of State to U.S. Embassy Tirana, "Albanian MOD Zhulali's June 10 Meeting with Under Secretary Lynn Davis," June 16, 1993.

CHAPTER 9. THE FALL

1. "Isolated in EU, Greece Wages Diplomatic Battle on Balkan Fronts," by Nikos Konstandaras, Associated Press, September 23, 1994.

2. Baze, Mero, Realitete Shqiptaro Amerikane (Tirana: Koha Publishing House, 1997), p. 32.

3. "George Bush Awarded by Albania for Role in Overthrowing Communism," Agence France-Presse, November 13, 1994.

4. Cable from U.S. Secretary of State to U.S. Embassy Tirana, "Letter from Holbrooke to President Berisha," February 11, 1995.

5. "Albania: The Greek Minority," Human Rights Watch, February 1995.

6. Cable from Secretary of State to U.S. Embassy Tirana, "Official-Informal No. 85," November 10, 1994.

7. Ibid.

8. Cable from U.S. Embassy Tirana, Douglas R. Smith, to Secretary of State, "The Failure of the Constitutional Referendum and its Significance," November 18, 1994.

9. Cable from U.S. Embassy Tirana to Secretary of State, "Referendum—Democracy Gains, with Political Pains," December 1, 1994.

10. "The Vote Against the Draft Constitution Was the Albanians' Verdict against Nostalgia and Fear," by Edi Rama, *Përpjekja*, No. 2, March 1995.

11. Cable from U.S. Embassy Tirana, Ambassador Joeseph Lake, to Secreatary of State, "Selami Removed from PD Chairmanship," March 6, 1995.

12. Letter from President Bill Clinton to Senator Tom Harkin, September 25, 1995.

13. Press Briefing by Mike McCurry and Deputy Press Secretary David Johnson, September 12, 1995.

14. U.S. Department of State, Office of the Spokesman, "Judicial Independence in Albania," October 6, 1995.

15. Council on Foreign Relations, *America and the World*, September 23, 1995.

16. "Human Rights in Post-Communist Albania," Human Rights Watch, March 1996.

17. "Challenges to Democracy in Albania," Hearing before the Commission on Security and Cooperation in Europe, March 14, 1996.

18. "Berisha Defends Genocide Law," *Illyria*, September 19, 1995.

19. Cable from U.S. Embassy Tirana, Ambassador Joseph Lake, to Secretary of State, "Confident Socialists Begin Elections," October 13, 1995.

20. International Republican Institute, "Observation Report on the Albanian Parliamentary Elections of May 26, 1996," 1996.

21. "U.S. Pledges Military Aid to Ex-communist Albania," by Charles Aldinger, Reuters, April 2, 1996.

22. Cable from U.S. Embassy Tirana, Douglas R. Smith, to Secretary of State, "Undersecretary Wirth's Meeting with Judiciary," April 15, 1996.

23. Cable from U.S. Embassy Tirana, Douglas R. Smith, to Secretary of State, "U/S Wirth Meeting with Berisha," April 25, 1996.

24. Cable from U.S. Secretary of State to U.S. Embassy Tirana, "Secretary's Meeting with Albanian FM Serreqi," May 15, 1996.

25. U.S. Department of State Daily Press Briefing, May 9, 1996.

26. International Republican Institute, "Observation Report on the Albanian Parliamentary Elections of May 26, 1996."

27. "The Land of False Labels" (in German), by Norbert Mappes-Niediek, *Die Zeit*, November 1, 1996.

28. OSCE, Office for Democratic Institutions and Human Rights, "Observation of the Parliamentary Elections Held in the Republic of Albania," May 26 and June 2, 1996.

29. OSCE, Parliamentary Assembly, "Report on the Parliamentary Elections in Albania," May 6, 1996.

30. Cable from U.S. Embassy Tirana, Douglas R. Smith, to Secretary of State, "Albanian Elections," May 27, 1996.

31. Statement by OSCE monitors from Norway and the U.K., Tirana, May 28, 1996.

32. "Albania: Democracy Derailed—Violations in the May 26, 1996, Albanian Elections," Human Rights Watch, June 1996.

33. Albanian Telegraphic Agency, May 28, 1996. See also "One Thousand Five Hundred People from All Albania" (in Albanian), *Albania*, May 29, 1996.

34. Ibid.

35. "Over 30 Percent of OSCE Observers in Parliamentary Elections in Albania Were Invited by SP," Albanian Telegraphic Agency, May 29, 1996.

36. "Statement of the President of Albania, Berisha," Albanian Telegraphic Agency, May 29, 1996.
37. International Republican Institute, "Albania Parliamentary Election Observation Mission, Preliminary Statement," May 30, 1996.
38. International Republican Institute, "Albanian Election Day Survey," May 30, 1996.
39. Statement by Nicholas Burns, spokesman, U.S. Department of State, June 1, 1996.
40. "George Bush Makes Snap Visit to Albania," Agence France-Presse, June 14, 1996.
41. Cable from U.S. Embassy Tirana, Douglas R. Smith, to Secretary of State and U.S. Mission Geneva, "Berisha Not to Receive Wirth Delegation," July 17, 1996.
42. Cable from Secretary of State to U.S. Embassy Tirana, "Official Informal No. 93," July 23, 1996.
43. "U.S. Says Albania's Election Dispute Not Over," by Benet Koleka, Reuters, July 2, 1996.
44. Testimony of Rudolf V. Perina, Senior Deputy Assistant Secretary of State, Bureau of European and Canadian Affairs, before the Subcommittee on International Operations and Human Rights of the Committee on International Relations, U.S. House of Representatives, July 25, 1996.
45. The memorandum was written on June 8 and published in *Koha Jonë* on June 15, 1996.
46. "Twenty-Three 'Soldiers' against Albania" (in Albanian), by Sokol Olldashi, *Albania*, June 16, 1996.
47. Cable from Secretary of State, "Albanian Foreign Minister Shehu with Under Secretary Wirth and Under Secretary Tarnoff," October 10, 1996.
48. U.S. Department of State, "Press Statement by Spokesman Nicholas Burns: 'Albania: Local Elections,'" October 31, 1996.
49. Lane, C. Dennison, *Once upon an Army: The Crisis in the Albanian Army, 1995–1996*, Conflict Studies Research Centre, September 2002, p. 122.
50. "Exclusive Interview with Safet Zhulali for Republika" (in Albanian), *Republika*, April 13, 1997.

CHAPTER 10. PROFITEERS' PACT

1. "Albania Gets $21 Million IMF Loan," Reuters, September 23, 1994.
2. "World Bank and Albania: A Solid Partnership," by Kutlay Ebiri, Chief, Resident Mission in Tirana, May 19, 1994. Ebiri was quoting the words of Wilfried Thalwitz, the bank's vice president of Europe and Cental Asia.
3. "Supporting Transition in Central and Eastern Europe an Assessment and Lessons from the IMF's Five Years' Experience," address of Michel Camdessus, Madrid, December 21, 1994.
4. Cable from U.S. Embassy Tirana, Ambassador Marisa Lino, to Secretary of State, "World Bank Concerns Re the Albanian Economy," September 13, 1996.
5. Vaughan-Whitehead, Daniel, *Albania in Crisis—The Predictable Fall of the Shining Star* (Northampton, MA: International Labor Organization/Edward Elgar Publishing, 1999).

6. Cable from U.S. Embassy Tirana, Ambassador Joseph Lake, to Secretary of State, "Albanian Banking System Handicapped by Inefficiency, Corruption, and Inability to Enforce Loans," February 21, 1996.

7. Vaughan-Whitehead, *Albania in Crisis*.

8. "The Banks Are Yet behind the Level of the Reform—Interview with Edvin Libohova, Director of the Savings Bank," *Albanian Economic Tribune*, No. 2 (14), 1993.

9. "Big Pyramid Schemes that Hurt Albanians Now Vex Accountants," by Robert Frank, *Wall Street Journal*, August 6, 1998.

10. "Albania under the Shadow of the Pyramids," by Carlos Elbirt, Transition Newsletter,World Bank Group, Vol. 8, No. 5, October 1997.

11. "Sali Berisha Objects to My Last Column," by John Simpson, *Sunday Telegraph*, March 9, 1997.

12. Letter from Vehbi Alimuçaj to Human Rights Watch, November 2, 1998.

13. Alimuçaj, Vehbi. *The Way to Holding* (Bucharest: Getic Publishing House, 1997).

14. "At Least Four Dead, 20 Injured in Albanian Car Bomb Blast," by Briseida Mema, Agence France-Presse, February 26, 1996.

15. "Berisha Vows Death Penalty for Mysterious Bombers," by Benet Koleka, Reuters, February 27, 1996.

16. "Albanian Police Insist Bombing Was Political," Reuters, March 1, 1996.

17. Alimuçaj, *The Way to Holding*.

18. Jarvis, Chris, "The Rise and Fall of the Pyramid Schemes in Albania," Working Paper of the International Monetary Fund, July 1999.

19. Ibid.

20. Hoxha, Artan, "Why Did It Happen?" Albanian Development Services, April 14, 1997.

21. "How Does Kamberi Function" (in Albanian), *Koha Jonë*, September 18, 1996, and "The Mechanism of Profit at VEFA Holding" (in Albanian), *Koha Jonë*, September 28, 1996.

22. Hoxha, "Why Did It Happen?"

23. Jarvis, "The Rise and Fall of the Pyramid Schemes in Albania."

24. Cable from U.S. Embassy Tirana, Ambassador Marisa Lino, to Secretary of State, "World Bank Concerns Re the Albanian Economy," September 13, 1996.

25. "IMF Warnings of Pyramid Fraud Fall on Poverty Dulled," by Remzi Lani, Inter Press Service, November 26, 1996.

26. "IMF Cannot Commit Suicide," *Albania*, December 10, 1996.

27. Cable from U.S. Embassy Tirana, Ambassador Marisa Lino, to Secretary of State, "GOA Makes First Public Statements on Informal 'Banking' Sector," October 18, 1996.

28. "Notable Days for the History of Albanians" (in Albanian), *Rilindja Demokratike*, December 12, 1996.

29. Press Release of Albania's Permanent Mission to the United Nations, January 30, 1997.

CHAPTER 11. REVOLT

1. "Albanian Foreign Minister Holds Interview with TV," Albanian Telegraphic Agency, January 25, 1997.
2. Press Release of Albania's Permanent Mission to the United Nations, January 30, 1997.
3. "Albanian Police Block Protests, Surround Opposition Leaders," CNN, February 12, 1997.
4. "The Gangster Regime We Fund," by Andrew Gumbel, *Independent*, February 14, 1997.
5. See "My Testimony for the Killing of the SHIK" (in Albanian), *Albania*, March 2, 2004, and "On Febraury 28, 1997, Berisha's SHIK Killed Fatmir Tozaj, Shkelqim Bogdani, Artur Zoto and Seriously Wounded Agim Hazizi" (in Albanian), *Zëri i Popullit*, February 29, 2004.
6. "Former SHIK: I Will Tell You the Horror of February 28" (in Albanian), *Shekulli*, February 29, 2004.
7. Zilje, Gëzim, *1997: Vrases dhe Shpetimitare* (Tirana: Pelioni, 2001), pp. 112–16.
8. "Those World Cup Heroes," by Matthew O'Donnell, *Observer*, February 3, 2002.
9. CNN World News, "Albania's Government Resigns after Clashes Become Deadly," March 1, 1997.
10. "Berisha, Go Away," by Frrok Çupi, *Koha Jonë in English*, March 2, 1997.
11. Decision of the National Assembly of the Republic of Albania Nr. 298, March 2, 1997.
12. "Çopani: Gazidede Commanded Berisha" (in Albanian), *Koha Jonë*, August 14, 1997.
13. Statement of the Spokesman, Albanian Ministry of Defense, March 5, 1997.
14. "Message of President Sali Berisha to the Albanian People," Albanian Telegraphic Agency, March 2, 1997.
15. "Speech of President of Republic Sali Berisha on his Reelection President of the Republic," Albanian Telegraphic Agency, March 3, 1997.
16. Statement of the Spokesman, Ministry of Defense, Republic of Albania, March 5, 1997.
17. Briefing of Spokesman Nicholas Burns, U.S. State Department, Washington D.C., March 4, 1997.
18. See also Zogaj, Preç, *Uncivil War (Luftë Jocivile)* (Tirana: Dita, 1998), p. 240.
19. "Europe's Peace Plans Fall on Deaf Ears in Albania," by Tom Walker, *Times* (London), March 8, 1997.
20. "Rebel Forces Seize Government's Southern Stronghold," *Independent*, March 9, 1997.
21. "Denial of the Defense Ministry," Albanian Telegraphic Agency, March 8, 1997.
22. "Unexpected Aggravation of Situation in Gjirokastra," Albanian Telegraphic Agency, March 8, 1997.
23. Zogaj, *Uncivil War (Luftë Jocivile)*, p. 264.

24. "Vranitzky Is for Continuation of Dialogue among Parties," Albanian Telegraphic Agency, March 8, 1997.

25. "Declaration of Albanian President before Meeting with Representatives of Political Forces," Albanian Telegraphic Agency, March 9, 1997.

26. "Albanians in Talks as Insurgency Spreads," by Joanna Robertson and Helena Smith, *Guardian*, March 11, 1997.

CHAPTER 12. A HORRIBLE END

1. "Hobbesian Albania," by Sylvia Poggioli, *New Leader*, April 7, 1997.

2. Ibid.

3. "Berisha Loyalists Raise Spectre of North-South War," by Tom Walker, *Times* (London), March 12, 1997.

4. "Report on the Situation in the Vlora Hospital from March 1, 1997, to March 6, 1997," Ministry of Health, Republic of Albania, March 6, 1997.

5. "'God Save Us. God Save Albania,'" by Andrew Gumbel, *Independent*, March 14, 1997.

6. News briefing of U.S. Secretary of Defense William S. Cohen, Washington, D.C., March 19, 1997.

7. "Secret Operation by Special Forces Rescues Orphans," by Anthony Loyd, *Times* (London), March 21, 1997.

8. "Child Vandals Join the Destruction at King Zog's Palace," by Tom Walker, *Times* (London), March 17, 1997.

9. "Coca-Cola Defenders Give Tirana Gunmen a Taste of the Real Thing," by Anthony Loyd, *Times* (London), March 17, 1997.

10. "Press Release of the All-National Salvation Committee," Albanian Telegraphic Agency, March 18, 1997.

11. "Albanian Premier's Hometown Reflects National Unrest," by Tracy Wilkinson, *Los Angeles Times*, March 21, 1997.

12. "Albanian Rebel Leaders Huddle On Next Move," by Elizabeth Neuffer, *Boston Globe*, March 21, 1997.

13. "A Rudderless Ship of State," by Josh Friedman, *Newsday*, March 20, 1997.

14. Gazidede's presentation, taken from the parliament's archive, was published by the newspaper *Reportazh* on October 2, 9, and 16, 2001.

15. "Koha Jonë the Soup of Charles Walsh" (in Albanian), *Albania*, April 27, 1997.

16. Tenet, George, *At the Center of the Storm: My Years at the CIA* (New York: HarperCollins, 2007), pp 10–11.

17. Cable from U.S. Embassy Tirana, Ambassador Marisa Lino, to Secretary of State, "Official Informal No. 24," April 21, 1997.

18. The nine countries were Austria, Denmark, France, Greece, Italy, Romania, Slovenia, Spain, and Turkey.

19. "Nuclear Material 'Smuggled to Italy in Refugee Exodus,'" by Richard Own, *Times* (London), March 21, 1997.

20. "Albanian Human Rights Group Finds Bias in Media Coverage of Elections," Albanian Human Rights Group, July 8, 1997.

21. "Bad Week for Britain as Chief Election Organiser Storms Out," by Tom Walker, *Times* (London), June 14, 1997.

22. "Albania Simmers on Brink of Poll Violence," by Andrew Gumbel, *Independent*, June 28, 1997.

23. "Albania's Parliamentary Elections of 1997," Commission on Security and Cooperation in Europe, July 1997.

24. "Queen Geraldine of Albania—Central European Consort at the Mercy of the Tides of History," by Miranda Vickers, *Guardian*, October 30, 2002, and "Arrested Albanian King to Stay in Hospital, South African Court Rules," Agence France-Presse, February 10, 1999.

25. Preliminary Statement of the Organization for Security and Co-operation in Europe, June 30, 1997.

26. Albania Parliamentary Elections, June 29, 1997, OSCE Office of Democratic Institutions and Human Rights, July 1997.

27. Analysis for Secretary of State's morning summary, "Albania: The Dog that Didn't Bite," June 30, 1997.

28. "Arms and the 'Monarch,'" by Guy Dinmore, *Financial Times*, July 5, 1997.

29. United Nations Development Programme, Albanian Human Development Report 1998.

30. Albanian Television, July 23, 1997.

CHAPTER 13. DEMOCRACY 2.0

1. "Building Albania's New Democracy," by Fatos Lubonja, *War Report*, August 1997.

2. "Albania's Pyramid Schemes Look Sick," by Robert Frank, *Wall Street Journal*, March 4, 1998.

3. In 2002 a court convicted Alimuçaj of having defrauded 57,923 people and sentenced him to twenty years in prison. He got out in 2010 after a general amnesty, work in prison, and a presidential pardon.

4. "Turkey Extradites Albanian Woman Involved in 1997 Bank Schemes," Agence France-Presse, December 6, 1999.

5. "Hajdari: Blood Should Be Taken from Nano and Co." (in Albanian), *Koha Jonë*, September 27, 1997. See also "Letter of Azem Hajdari" (in Albanian), *Albania*, September 28, 1997.

6. "Motive Remains Unclear in Albanian Parliament Shooting," Deutsche Presse Agentur, September 20, 1997.

7. The four others were Blerim Çela (former head of the state auditing service), Bujar Rama (former deputy head of SHIK), Sokol Mulosmani (former Vlora police chief), and Kreshnik Lusha (fomer commander of police special forces).

8. "The Berisha Phenomenon and the Nano Phenomenon" (in Albanian), by Fatos Lubonja, *Koha Jonë*, January 25, 1998.

9. "Here Are the Sins of the Current Government" (in Albanian), by Dritëro Agolli, *Gazeta Shqitare*, March 29, 1998.

CHAPTER 14. ILLEGAL BUT NECESSARY

1. Nesho, Agim, *Në Mirëbesim: Shënime të një Abasadori* (Tirana: Korbi, 2006), p. 35.
2. See "Former Security Head Says Albania Worked with Western Services against Terrorism," *Albania*, September 21, 2001; "US Embassy Threatened in Albania," by R. Jeffrey Smith, *Washington Post*, August 15, 1998; "CIA-Backed Team Used Brutal Means to Crack Terror Cell," by Christopher Cooper and Andrew Higgins, *Wall Street Journal*, November 22, 2001; "Computer Yields al Qaeda Memos," by Alan Cullison and Andrew Higgins, *Wall Street Journal Europe*, January 2, 2002; "Confessions of Executed Militant in 1998 Trial Provide Insight into Terrorist Groups," by Hamza Hendawi, Associated Press, October 30, 2001; and "An Investigation in Egypt Illustrates Al Qaeda's Web," by Susan Sachs, *New York Times*, November 21, 2001.
3. "Albania to Downgrade Relations with Islamic Countries," Deutsche Presse Agentur, December 5, 1997.
4. See Mayer, Jane, *The Dark Side* (New York: Anchor Books, 2009), p. 114.
5. See Wallace, Robert, and Melton, H. Keith, with Schlesinger, Henry Robert, *Spycraft: The Secret History of the CIA's Spytechs from Communism to Al-Qaeda* (New York: Plume, 2009), p. 343.
6. "An Investigation in Egypt Illustrates Al Qaeda's Web," *New York Times*; "Military Trial for Militant Suspects," by Khaled Dawoud, *Al-Ahram Weekly*, February 4–10, 1999; "CIA-Backed Team Used Brutal Means to Crack Terror Cell," *Wall Street Journal*.
7. "US Embassy Threatened in Albania," *Washington Post*.
8. "CIA-Backed Team Used Brutal Means to Crack Terror Cell," *Wall Street Journal*.
9. "US Embassy Threatened in Albania," *Washington Post*.
10. "'Albanian Returnees' Executed," by Jailan Halawi, *Al-Ahram Weekly*, March 2–8, 2000.
11. "An Investigation in Egypt Illustrates Al Qaeda's Web," *New York Times*; "Military Trial for Militant Suspects," *Al-Ahram Weekly*; "CIA-Backed Team Used Brutal Means to Crack Terror Cell," *Wall Street Journal*.

CHAPTER 15. A SHOT, A COUP

1. "Four Hurt in Shooting as Protestors Try to Attack Albanian Government," Agence France-Presse, September 14, 1998.
2. Fevziu, Blendi, *Jeta ime . . . Intervistë me Blendi Fevziu* (Tirana: UET Press, 2010), p. 148.
3. "Four Hurt in Shooting as Protestors Try to Attack Albanian Government," Agence France-Presse.
4. Zogaj, Preç, *Paradhoma e Nje Presidenti* (Tirana: Ora, 2001), p. 189.

5. "Four Hurt in Shooting as Protestors Try to Attack Albanian Government," Agence France-Presse.

6. "Opposition Leader Appeals for Restraint, Political Solution in TV Interview," Albanian Television, BBC World Monitoring, September 14, 1998.

7. Zogaj, *Paradhoma e Nje Presidenti*, p. 189.

8. "Government Strikes Back after Opposition Siezes Buildings," by Mirita Dhimgjoka, Associated Press, September 14, 1998.

9. "Three Killed, 14 Wounded in Tirana Police Clashes," Agence France-Presse, September 14, 1998.

10. "United States Condemns Violence in Albania," U.S. Department of State, Press Statement by James P. Rubin, September 14, 1998.

11. "Government Strikes Back after Opposition Siezes Buildings," Associated Press.

12. "Albanian Opposition Gives Up Tanks," by Mirita Dhimgjoka, Associated Press, September 15, 1998.

13. Ibid.

14. "Thousands Demonstrate in Albania in Support of Former President," by Briseida Mema, Agence France-Presse, September 16, 1998.

15. "Clinton Urges Albanian Government, Opposition to Negotiate," Agence France-Presse, September 24, 1998.

16. U.S. Central Intelligence Agency, Senior Executive Intelligence Brief, September 30, 1998.

17. Dervishi, Ferdinand, *Pse e Vranë Azem Hajdarin?* (Tirana: Ilar, 2001), p. 104.

CHAPTER 16. ARGUMENT OF FORCE

1. "We Are a People, We Have the Same Traditions: An Interview with Ibrahim Rugova, Chairman of the Democratic League, Given to Frano Caka" (in Albanian), *Zëri i Popullit*, February 26, 1991.

2. "UCK Cofounder Haliti Interviewed" (in Albanian), *Zëri*, November 6, 13, 20, and 27, 1999.

3. "We Paid Money for Zahir Pajaziti's Release from Prison in Albania: Interview with Rrustem Mustafa—Remi" (in Albanian), *Zëri*, April 22, 2000.

4. "Zeka, Kosovari Misterioz" (in Albanian), by Blendi Fevziu, *Klan*, March 5, 2000.

5. Cable from U.S. Embassy Belgrade, Nicholas Hill, to Secretary of State, "Kosovo Terrorism: Do the Locals See an Opportunity or a Problem?" March 11, 1997.

6. "Kosovo's Syla Details Expansion, Success, Interview with Azem Syla" (in Albanian), *Zëri*, October 2, 1999.

7. "UCK Cofounder Haliti Interviewed," *Zëri*.

8. Judah, Tim, *Kosovo: War and Revenge* (New Haven, Conn., and London: Yale University Press, 2000), pp. 136–37.

CHAPTER 17. A FORMULA

1. Press conference by U.S. Special Representative Robert S. Gelbard, Belgrade, Prishtina, February 22, 1998.

2. "Kosovo: Human Rights in Times of Armed Conflict," Humanitarian Law Center, Spotlight Report No. 26, May 1998.

3. "U.S. Official Asks Restraint by Albanians," by Jane Perlez, *New York Times*, March 17, 1998.

4. "Albanian Premier Discusses Kosovo with U.S. Envoy," Albanian Telegraphic Agency, March 19, 1998.

5. "Gelbard Says U.S. Wants to Use Rugova Visit to Promote Non-Violence," by Robert H. Reid, Associated Press, May 27, 1998.

6. "Terrorism in Kosovo and Metohija—White Book," Yugoslav Ministry of Foreign Affairs, Belgrade, September 1998. See also "Strong Ties with the Mujahadeen" (in Serbian), *Vecernje Novosti*, October 22, 2001, and "Bin Laden's Camp in Kosovo" (in Serbian), by D. Vujicic, *Vecernje Novosti*, September 26, 2001. The chief of the general staff of the Yugoslav army told the U.S. chief of mission in Belgrade on July 20 that twelve Saudi citizens had tried to enter Yugoslavia from Albania (cable from Secretary of State to U.S. Embassy The Hague, July 21, 1998).

7. Cable from U.S. Embassy Tirana, Ambassador Marisa Lino, to Secretary of State, July 21, 1998.

8. Council of Europe, Parliamentary Assembly, Committee on Legal Affairs and Human Rights, Inhuman Treatment of People and Illicit Trafficking in Human Organs in Kosovo, December 12, 2010, Bundesnachrichtendienst analysis or organized crime in Kosovo (in German), February 22, 2005, file.wikileaks.org/file/bnd-kosovo-feb-2005.pdf (accessed September 22, 2014), and NATO KFOR report on Xhavit Haliti, March 10, 2004, http://ow.ly/BLh3f (accessed September 22, 2014).

CHAPTER 18. TO WAR

1. "Most of the Arms in the Llap Zone Were Bought in the Domestic Market: Interview with Rrustem Mustafa—Remi" (in Albanian), *Zëri*, April 27, 2000.

2. "U.S. Senate Committee on Armed Services Holds Hearing on National Security Threats," Political Transcripts by Federal Document Clearing House, February 2, 1999.

3. Human Rights Watch, "Yugoslav Government War Crimes in Racak," July 15, 1999.

4. "Statement on the Situation in Kosovo," President William J. Clinton, January 25, 1999.

5. "President Clinton News Conference," Political Transcripts by Federal Document Clearing House, March 19, 1999.

6. Zogaj, Preç, *Paradhoma e Nje Presidenti* (Tirana: Ora, 2001), pp. 255–56.

7. "No Albanian Can Sign the Loss of Kosovo's Independence" (in Albanian), *Rilindja Demokratike*, February 20, 1999.

8. Fevziu, Blendi, *Jeta ime . . . Intervistë me Blendi Fevziu* (Tirana: UET Press, 2010), p. 381.

9. "Thaçi in 'Secret Signing,'" by Fron Nazi, Institute for War and Peace Reporting, March 12, 1999.

10. Sullivan, Stacy, *Be Not Afraid, for You Have Sons in America: How a Brooklyn Roofer Helped Lure the U.S. into the Kosovo War* (New York: St. Martins Press, 2004), p. 225.

11. Interim Agreement for Peace and Self-Government in Kosovo, February 23, 1998. The Helsinki Final Act enshrines the inviolability of international borders.

12. "President Clinton News Conference," Federal Document Clearing House, March 19, 1999.

13. "The War in the Balkans: KLA Tells Nato: 'Arm Us or Invade,'" by Steve Boggan and Fron Nazi, *Independent*, April 21, 1999.

14. American Bar Association/Central and East European Law Initiative and American Academy fo the Advancement of Science, *Political Killings in Kosovo, March–June 1999*, 2000.

15. "Uncovering Albania's Role in the Kosovo War," BBC, May 17, 2010.

16. Lushi, Uk, *Batalioni Atlantiku* (Prishtina: Zëri, 2001), p. 157.

17. Council of Europe, Parliamentary Assembly, Committee on Legal Affairs and Human Rights, Inhuman Treatment of People and Illicit Trafficking in Human Organs in Kosovo, December 12, 2010.

18. Special Investigative Task Force press release, "Statement by the Chief Prosecutor of Special Investigative Task Force (SITF) on Investigative Findings," July 29, 2014, http://ow.ly/BLhdz (accessed September 22, 2014).

19. "Man Will Mich als Dämon Darstellen" (in German), by Dario Venutti, *Tages Anzeiger*, January 27, 2011.

20. Cable from U.S. Office Prishtina, Lawrence G. Rossin, to Secretary of State, "Organized Crime in Kosovo—A First Shot at Analysis," October 24, 1999.

21. Apparent KFOR document on Xhavit Haliti, March 10, 2004, http://ow.ly/BLh3f (accessed September 22, 2014). See also "Report Identifies Hashim Thaci as 'Big Fish' in Organised Crime," by Paul Lews, *Guardian*, January 24, 2011.

CHAPTER 19. BUSTS IN OUR HEADS

1. "Irreplaceable People," by Edvin Shvarc, *Albania*, February 20, 2001.

2. OSCE, Office for Democratic Institutions and Human Rights, "Republic of Albania, Parliamentary Elections 24 June–19 August 2001," October 11, 2001.

3. Cable from U.S. Embassy Tirana, Ambassador John L. Withers, to Secretary of State, "Criminals Making the Laws in Albania's Parliament," August 13, 2009, http://wikileaks.org/cable/2009/08/09TIRANA552.html (accessed September 22, 2014).

4. United Nations, Millennium Development Goals Indicators, 2002.

5. MJAFT! Newsletter, No. 1, April 7, 2003.

6. "U.S. Commends Albania for Implementing Critical Reforms," Statement of Deputy U.S. Representative to the OSCE Douglas Davidson, February 26, 2004.

CHAPTER 20. THE DOCTOR IS BACK

1. OSCE, Office for Democratic Institutions and Human Rights, "Republic of Albania Parliamentary Elections 3 January 2005, OSCE/ODIHR Election Observation Mission Report," November 7, 2005.

2. "Prime Minister Honors Gazidede: He Was a Servant for His Nation" (in Albanian), *Shqip*, October 27, 2008.

3. Cable from U.S. Embassy Tirana, Ambassador John L. Withers, to Secretary of State, "Berisha Seeks New Secret Police," January 27, 2010, http://wikileaks.org/cable/2010/01/10TIRANA58.html (accessed September 22, 2014).

4. Ibid.

5. Cable from U.S. Embassy Tirana, Stephen A. Cristina, to Secretary of State, "Overview of the Albanian Intelligence Services," December 31, 2007, http://wikileaks.org/cable/2007/12/07TIRANA1090.html (accessed September 22, 2014).

6. On May 28, 2004, the CIA flew a German citizen of Lebanese decent named Khaled El-Masri, whom it had mistakenly detained, from Kabul to the military base in Kuçova, Albania. El-Masri was released near the Albanian border with Macedonia and allowed to leave for Germany the next day. (See American Civil Liberties Union, "Statement of Khaled El-Masri," December 6, 2005, and Senate Select Committee on Intelligence, Committee Study of the Central Intelligence Agency's Detention and Interrogation Program, released December 9, 2014.) On October 5, 2005, the CIA reportedly flew a chartered Gulfstream IV with tailnumber N308AB from Romania to Tirana with instructions to unload all passengers. Another CIA-chartered aircraft, a Boeing 737 with tailnumber N787WH, left Tirana shortly thereafter bound for Lithuania. (See Reprieve, "CSC's Romania Missions Unveiled," July 4, 2012, and Rendition Project, "Aircraft Profile: N787WH," http://ow.ly/BLgHG [accessed September 22, 2014]).

7. "Ridge Files Very Late for Albania," by Anna Palmer, *Roll Call*, June 24, 2008.

8. Cable from U.S. Embassy Tirana, Ambassador John L. Withers, to Secretary of State, "Embassy Concerns over Albania's Consideration for MCC Compact Status," November 13, 2009, http://www.wikileaks.org/plusd/cables/09TIRANA730_a.html (accessed September 22, 2014).

9. A video of the Bush interview is available at http://www.youtube.com/watch?v=I_qOpTnz3Dk (accessed September 22, 2014).

10. "President Bush Participates in Joint Press Availability with Prime Minister of Albania, Dr. Sali Berisha," June 10, 2007.

11. "For One Visit, Bush Will Feel Pro-U.S. Glow," by Craig Smith, *New York Times*, June 8, 2008.

12. "Bush's Watch Theft: Debunked," by Mike Nizza, *New York Times*, June 12, 2007.

13. "Supplier under Scrutiny on Arms for Afghans," by C. J. Chivers, *New York Times*, March 27, 2008.

14. "The Stoner Arms Dealers: How Two American Kids Became Big-Time Weapons Dealers," by Guy Lawson, *Rolling Stone*, March 16, 2011.

15. "Speculation Surrounds Case of Albanian Whistle-Blower's Death," by Nicholas Kulish, *New York Times*, October 7, 2008.

16. See http://www.youtube.com/watch?v=620mGpwAlNA (accessed September 22, 2014).

17. Cable from U.S. Embassy Tirana, Ambassador John L. Withers II, to Secretary of State, "Berisha's Outburst Still the Talk of Tirana," August 1, 2008, http://wikileaks.org/cable/2008/08/08TIRANA585.html (accessed September 22, 2014).
18. "Painting the Town," by Jane Kramer, *New Yorker*, June 27, 2005.
19. OSCE, Office of Democratic Institutions and Human Rights, "Republic of Albania Parliamentary Elections 28 June, 2009," September 14, 2009.
20. Cable from U.S. Embassy Tirana, August 13, 2009.
21. Cable from U.S. Embassy Tirana, Ambassador John L. Withers, to Secretary of State, "Albania's New Foreign Minister," September 24, 2009, http://wikileaks.org/cable/2009/09/09TIRANA637.html (accessed September 22, 2014).
22. "Manhattan U.S. Attorney Announces Extradition of Senior Aide to Albanian Foreign Minister Charged with Murder, Kidnapping, and Other Racketeering Offenses," Federal Bureau of Investigation press release, November 24, 2010.
23. Statement to the Press by U.S. Ambassador John L. Withers, March 12, 2010.
24. Cable from U.S. Embassy Tirana, August 13, 2009.
25. Cable from U.S. Embassy Tirana to Secretary of State, November 13, 2009.
26. See http://www.youtube.com/watch?v=iAPAAuT1EXM&feature=player_embedded (accessed September 22, 2014).
27. Joint Statement Issued by the U.S. Ambassador in Tirana, the Head of Delegation of the European Union in Tirana, and the Head of the OSCE Presence in Albania, January 18, 2012.
28. "Ilir Meta: My Trial Was Transparent," *Southeast European Times*, March 6, 2012.
29. U.S. Embassy statement on January 21st Verdicts, February 6, 2013.
30. OSCE/ODIHR Election Observation Mission Final Report, Republic of Albania Local Government Elections, 8 May 2011, August 15, 2011.
31. "Interview with Ambassador Karsten Ankjaer Jensen" (in Albanian), by Skender Minxhozi, *Java*, July 7, 2012.

CHAPTER 21. PENDULUM SWING

1. "Albanian Leaders Fan Flames of Nationalism, Unnerving West," by Benet Koleka, Reuters, April 16, 2013.
2. Speech of Prime Minister Sali Berisha to the 49th Munich Security Conference, February 3, 2013.
3. "U.S. Warns Albania against Stoking Nationalism," by Benet Koleka, Reuters, February 15, 2013.
4. "Germany Tells Albania to Stop Fanning Nationalist Fires," by Benet Koleka, Reuters, February 22, 2013.
5. Rama, Edi, *Kurban* (Tirana: Dudaj, 2011), p. 304.
6. OSCE International Election Observer Mission, Statement of Preliminary Findings and Conclusions, June 23, 2013.
7. Speech of Prime Minister and Chairman of the Democratic Party Mr. Sali Berisha, June 26, 2013.
8. "GQR Congratulates Albania's LSI," Greenberg Quinlan Rosner, June 25, 2013.

9. "New Albanian Government Unlikely to Lead to Much Change," by Pandeli Pani, Deutsche Welle, June 25, 2013.

10. Statement by the High Representative, Catherine Ashton, and Commissioner Štefan Füle on the parliamentary elections in Albania, June 26, 2013.

11. "Painting the Town," by Jane Kramer, *New Yorker*, June 27, 2005.

12. Cable from U.S. Embassy Tirana, Ambassador John L. Withers, to Secretary of State, "The Center of Power on the Left and the Right," July 8, 2009, http://wikileaks.org/cable/2009/07/09TIRANA453.html (accessed September 22, 2014).

13. International Monetary Fund, Albania: First Review under the Extended Arrangement and Request for Modification of Performance Criteria, July 13, 2014.

14. Transparency International, Corruption Perceptions Index 2013.

15. European Commission, E.U. Candidate Status for Albania, June 24, 2014.

EPILOGUE

1. INSTAT, Albania: Poverty Trends: 2002–2005–2008–2012 (in Albanian), September 2013.

SOURCES

This book is drawn primarily from interviews with more than 200 individuals who participated in Albania's recent political events, Albanians and others, as well as personal observations. Unless cited in an endnote, quotations come from these interviews, conducted between 2000 and 2014. The vast majority of people spoke on the record. Four people refused to speak. The most important of these was Sali Berisha, who ignored three requests and once directly declined. The second was Albania's last communist-era minister of the interior, Hekuran Isai. The third was Enver Hoxha's widow, Nexhmije. The fourth was Marisa Lino, U.S. ambassador to Albania from 1996 to 1999.

The book also uses Albanian government documents from the communist era and more than 150 previously classified U.S. government records from the State Department and Central Intelligence Agency obtained via the Freedom of Information Act, as well as U.S. diplomatic cables released by WikiLeaks. Articles from the Albanian and international media are also used, as are reports from relevant organizations.

To view the government records and other source material, visit www.modern_albania.com.

* * *

Barka, Panajot. 1998. *Kryengritje e Tradhtuar*. Tirana: Mesonjetorja.

Baze, Mero. 2010. *Viti '97*. Tirana: Toena.

———. 1997. *Albanian-American Realities*. Tirana: Koha.

Bethell, Nicholas. 1984. *The Great Betrayal: The Untold Story of Kim Philby's Biggest Coup*. London: Hodder and Stoughton.

Biberaj, Elez. 1999. *Albania in Transition: The Rocky Road to Democracy*. Boulder, Colo.: Westview Press.

Carter, Robert. 1998. *The Accursed Mountains*. London: Flamingo.

Çupi, Frrok. 1998. *Vlora '97*. Tirana: Fan Noli.

Dervishi, Ferdinand. 2001. *Pse e Vranë Azem Hajdarin?* Tirana: Ilar.

Durham, Edith. 2000. *High Albania*. London: Phoenix Press.

Fevziu, Blendi. 2010. *Jeta ime . . . Intervistë me Blendi Fevziu*. Tirana: UET Press.

———. 1999. *Para dhe Pas Kamerave*. Tirana: Onufri.

———. 1996. *Histori e Shtypit Shqiptar 1848–1996*. Tirana: Marin Barleti.

———. 1993. *Piedestale Pa Statuja*. Tirana: Albinform

Fischer, Bernd J. 2009. "The Second World War in Albania: History and Historical Agendas." *Albanische Geschichte: Stand und Perspektiven der Forschung*. Munich: R. Oldenbourg Verlag.

———. 1999. *Albania at War, 1939–1945*. West Lafayette, Ind.: Purdue University Press.

Gardin, Giacomo. 1988. *Banishing God in Albania: The Prison Memoirs of Giacomo Gardin, S.J.* San Francisco: Ignatius Press.

Gjidede, Pavllo. 2000. *Nga Gorbaçovi te Ramiz Alia*. Tirana: Erik.

Halliday, Jon, ed. 1986. *The Artful Albanian: The Memoirs of Enver Hoxha*. London: Chatto & Windus.

Hamzaj, Bardh. 2000. *A Narrative about War and Freedom; Dialogue with the Commander Ramush Haradinaj*. Pristina: Zeri.

Hockenos, Paul. 2003. *Homeland Calling*. Ithaca, N.Y., and London: Cornell University Press.

Hoxha, Enver. 1982. *The Titoites*. Tirana: Naim Frasheri.

———. 1979. *With Stalin*. Tirana: 8 Nëntori.

Hoxha, Nexhmije. 2001. *Jeta Ime me Enverin, be II*. Tirana: Neraida.

———. 1998. *Jeta Ime me Enverin, Kujtime I*. Tirana: Lira.

Human Rights Watch. 2001. *Under Orders: War Crimes in Kosovo*. New York: Human Rights Watch.

———. 1996. *Human Rights in Post-Communist Albania*. New York: Human Rights Watch.

Judah, Tim. 2000. *Kosovo: War and Revenge*. New Haven, Conn., and London: Yale University Press.

Klosi, Ardian. 2010. *The Gërdec Disaster: Its Causes, Culprits, and Victims*. Tirana: K & B.

Kote, Odise. 1998. *1997 Tregime, Poezi, Ese, Etj*. Tirana: Albin.

Lubonja, Fatos. 2014. *False Apocalypse: From Stalinism to Capitalism*. London: Istros Books.

———. 2009. *Second Sentence: Inside the Albanian Gulag*. London: I.B. Tauris.

Lubonja, Fatos, and Shkreli, Artan. 2000. *Albania's Heritage in Danger*. Geneva: Editions du Tricorne.

Lucas, Peter. 2002. *Rumpalla: Rummaging through Albania*. Tirana: Dritan Editions.

Lushi, Uk. 2001. *Batalioni Atlantiku*. Prishtinë: Zëri.

Mustafaj, Besnik. 1999. *Midis Krimeve Dhe Mirazheve*. Tirana: Onufri.

Nahzi, Fron. 2010. *Between the Bronx and the Balkans*. New York: Lulu.

Nesho, Agim. 2006. *Në Mirëbesim, Shënime të Një Ambassadori*. Tirana: Korbi.

Oakley-Hill, D. R. 2002. *An Englishman in Albania*. London: Centre for Albanian Studies.

Pettifer, James, and Vickers, Miranda. 2006. *The Albanian Question: Reshaping the Balkans*. London: I.B. Tauris.

———. 1997. *Albania: From Anarchy to a Balkan Identity*. New York: New York University Press.

Rama, Edi. 2011. *Kurban*. Tirana: Dudaj.

Sarner, Harvey. 1997. *Rescue in Albania*. Cathedral City, Calif.: Brunswick Press.

Schwandner-Sievers, Stephanie, and Fischer, Bernd J., eds. 2002. *Albanian Identities, Myth and History*. London: Hurst and Company.

Shala, Blerim. 2000. *Vitet e Kosovës 1998–1999*. Prishtina: Zëri.

Vaughan-Whitehead, Daniel. 1999. *Albania in Crisis—The Predictable Fall of the Shining Star*. Northampton, Mass.: International Labor Organization/Edward Elgar Publishing.

Young, Antonia. 2000. *Women Who Become Men: Albanian Sworn Virgins*. Oxford: Berg.

Zickel, Raymond, and Iwaskiw, Walter R., eds. 1994. *Albania: A Country Study*. Washington, D.C.: Library of Congress.

Zilja, Gëzim. 2001. *1997: Vrases dhe Shpetimitare*. Tirana: Pelioni.

Zogaj, Preç. 2014. *Fillimet*. Tirana: UET Press.

———. 2010. *Të Gjithë Nëpër Vendet e Tyre*. Tirana: Dita 2000.

———. 2003. *Nga Hiri*. Tirana: Dita 2000.

———. 2001. *Paradhoma e Nje Presidenti*. Tirana: Ora.

———. 1998. *Uncivil War (Luftë Jocivile)*. Tirana: Dita.

INDEX

AEY scandal, 287

Agolli, Dritëro, 23, 61, 230

Albania: China and, 4, 20, 22; European Union and, 291, 292, 294–96; geography, 1; German occupation of, 16; Greece and, 43, 86, 93, 94, 140, 141, 144, 145–48; Italian occupation, 16; Italy and, 29, 43, 86, 201, 206, 209–10, 213; Kosovo and, 119, 120, 136, 139, 152, 166, 232, 244, 247; Kosovo war and, 21, 248–52, 253–65, 267–71; Macedonia and, 10, 119, 144, 152, 237, 239, 292; NATO and, 143, 285, 287; Ottoman Empire and, 4; religion in, 10, 21, 38; Soviet Union and, 18, 20, 30; United Kingdom and, 17, 116, 117, 118; United Nations and, 37, 39, 44, 139, 176, 253; World War II and, 16–17; Yugoslavia and, 16, 17–18, 248, 259, 263, 269–71

Albania government: provisional (1944–1945), 16–17; reconciliation (1997), 200, 202–3; stability (1991), 98, 103–7. *See also* Albanian parliament; DP rule; Government of National Reconciliation; SP rule; Stability Government

Albanian Americans, 1, 48, 88, 90; anticommunism of, 88; DP and, 90

Albanian constitution: change to, 288–89; defeated referendum, 149–51; new, 229–30

Albanian culture, 10; liberalization in 1970s, 21–22; Palace of Culture, 11

Albanian economy, 10; under Alia, 28–29, 34, 97; under DP rule, 115–16, 123, 124, 139–41, 143, 169–79; under Hoxha,

17, 22; IMF and, 169, 170, 174, 176–78; pyramid schemes and, 171–84, 208, 219, 221, 227; under SP rule, 227, 229, 230, 279, 294; weak banks, 170–71, 174; World Bank and, 169, 170, 174, 177, 178; Yugoslavia and, 116, 139–41, 176

Albanian elections: Berisha and, 93, 94, 123–24, 153–66, 157, 212–16, 281–84, 288–91, 293, 294–95; Central Elections Commission, 161, 163, 165, 217, 291; during communism, 17, 113; corruption in, 281, 293; Council of Europe and, 158, 165; Democratic Alliance and, 157, 160, 281; DP and, 71, 73, 76, 88–90, 93–95, 98, 108–10, 213–17, 277, 279, 281–83; DP rule and, 113, 123–24, 149–51, 153–66, 192, 213–17, 284–85, 288–94; first pluralistic (1991), 88–90, 93–94; foreign advisors and, 281, 292; law, 155–57, 288; Leka, King, and, 215–18; local (1992 and 1996), 123–24, 165–66; LSI and, 289, 293; OSCE and, 212–15, 217, 277, 283, 289, 293; Party of Labor and, 93–95, 98, 108; Ryerson and, 109, 110; second pluralistic (1992), 2, 98, 108–10; SP and, 108–10, 123–24, 156–58, 161, 213, 214, 216–17, 221, 289–91, 293–94; SP rule and, 221, 225, 230, 277, 279, 281–83; Tirana mayor and, 290–91; U.S. and, 88–90, 95, 104, 108–10, 155–57, 159, 160, 162–66, 213–15, 217, 281, 289; Western Europe and, 108

Albania newspaper, 161, 201, 208, 237

Albanian Helsinki Committee, 128

ABOUT THE AUTHOR

Fred C. Abrahams is a human rights investigator and writer who has worked for twenty years in areas marred by political crises and armed conflict, including the Balkans and Middle East. He speaks German and Albanian.